FLAPJA

FEUDALISM

FLAPJACKS AND FEUDALISM

Social Mobility and Class
in *The Archers*

EDITED BY

NICOLA HEADLAM

AND

CARA COURAGE

United Kingdom – North America – Japan – India
Malaysia – China

Emerald Publishing Limited
Howard House, Wagon Lane, Bingley BD16 1WA, UK

First edition 2021

Reprints and permissions service
Contact: permissions@emeraldinsight.com

British Library Cataloguing in Publication Data
A catalogue record for this book is available from the British Library

ISBN: 978-1-80071-389-5 (Print)
ISBN: 978-1-80071-386-4 (Online)
ISBN: 978-1-80071-388-8 (Epub)

ISOQAR certified
Management System,
awarded to Emerald
for adherence to
Environmental
standard
ISO 14001:2004.

Certificate Number 1985
ISO 14001

INVESTOR IN PEOPLE

For John Popham A Class Act

With thanks to all of our contributors, our community of Academic Archers Research Fellows (aka our Facebook group and conference attendees, and you, dear reader), the team at Emerald, and to all the people of Ambridge who prove, year in, year out, to be such a fascinating and infuriating subject of study.

CONTENTS

Section 4: Housing and the Ambridge Fairy

Section 5: It Takes a Village…

LIST OF FIGURES

LIST OF TABLES

LIST OF ABBREVIATIONS

ACEs	Adverse Childhood Experiences
ACRE	Action with Communities in Rural England
Ambridge BC	Ambridge Before COVID-19
BL	Borchester Land
C of E	Church of England
CEO	Chief Executive Officer
CIOB	Chartered Institute of Builders
CPEC	Care Policy and Evaluation Centre
CPS	Crown Prosecution Service
CSA	Child Sexual Abuse
DEFRA	Department for Environment, Food and Rural Affairs
EA	Environmental Agency
ENHR	European Network for Housing Research
FBI	Farm Business Income
GLA	Gangmasters and Labour Abuse Authority
ILO	International Labour Organisation

IoE	Institute of Education
NGO(s)	Non-Governmental Organisation(s)
NPCC	National Police Chiefs' Council
NRCN	National Rural Crime Network
NS-SEC	National Statistics Socio-Economic Classification
NYE	New Year's Eve
OCG(s)	Organised Crime Groups
ONS	Office for National Statistics
PACE	Police and Criminal Evidence Act
PCC(s)	Police and Crime Commissioner(s)
PESGB	Philosophy of Education Society of Great Britain
PFCC	Police, Fire and Rescue and Crime
PPE	Personal Protective Equipment
SLT	Social Learning Theory
SME(s)	Small and Medium Enterprise(s)
UCL	University College London
UNCRC	United Nations Convention of the Rights of Children
WHO	The World Health Organisation

ABOUT THE EDITORS

Dr Cara Courage is a placemaking, arts, activism and museums academic and practitioner, and Head of Tate Exchange, Tate's platform dedicated to socially engaged art. Cara speaks internationally on topics covering the C21st museum, the civic and activist museum, socially engaged art in community and museum settings and arts and urban design, placemaking and planning and has published widely on these topics. Cara is author of *Arts in Place: The Arts, the Urban and Social Practice* (Routledge, 2017), and the co-editor of *Creative Placemaking and Beyond* (Routledge, 2018), and editor of *Routledge Handbook of Placemaking* (Routledge, 2021). More importantly, Cara is also co-founder/organiser, with Dr Nicola Headlam, of *Academic Archers*, and has co-edited three books on the programme, *The Archers in Fact and Fiction: Academic Analyses of Life in Rural Borsetshire* (Peter Lang, 2016), *Custard, Culverts and Cake: Academics on life in* The Archers (Emerald, 2017), and *Gender, Sex and Gossip in Ambridge: Women in* The Archers (Emerald, 2019). Brought up in a farming family, *The Archers* was a constant refrain in her grandmother's kitchen, much to Cara's chagrin at the time. Many years of working from home with BBC Radio 4 on in the background brought about a process of *Archers*-osmosis that eventually wore Cara down to become a fan, though her joy is found more in chastising those in Ambridge than celebrating them.

Dr Nicola Headlam is a founder of *Academic Archers* and an expert on economic development policy. Currently free-lancing, Nicola has worked in local and central government, as Head of the Northern Powerhouse and in parliament, as a regional and local specialist in the Parliament Library. She has conducted extensive international post-doctoral research and policy development work at the Universities of Oxford and Liverpool, always focussed on how to use evidence for policy development. Prior to that her doctoral thesis looked at the interface between the governance of economic development and infrastructure in Greater Manchester. Nicola has influenced policy at all levels and is a regular media commentator.

ABOUT THE AUTHORS

Claire Astbury, 25 years working in housing and 18 years listening to *The Archers* inspired Claire Astbury to present her first *Academic Archers* paper in 2018. She is especially interested in how housing needs are met in the village. Claire's housing background spans local government, housing association and lobbying organisations as well as board membership. Starting on the front line allocating affordable homes sparked a long-term interest in housing policy. Claire's current role is interim director of housing at Luton Council. She holds a postgraduate diploma in housing policy and practice from Sheffield Hallam University and is a Corporate member of the Chartered Institute of Housing. A keen contributor to the *DumTeeDum* podcast as 'Claire from Clapham', her *Archers* vintage is Ruari Donovan. Claire followed her 2018 *Academic Archers* paper with a presentation about online fan cultures to the 2020 conference as part of the fandom panel.

Maggie Bartlett has been a General Practitioner since 1989, working in a variety of rural and urban settings in Derbyshire, Shropshire, Staffordshire and Dundee, Scotland. Alongside this, she is a clinical academic involved in teaching and research in medical education. Maggie worked at Keele University until 2017 where she was the academic lead for

GP-based student teaching in Shropshire and a rural campus for undergraduate medical students in Ludlow. She moved to Dundee in 2017 as Professor of Education in General Practice and in 2019 became the Head of the Undergraduate Division of the School of Medicine. Maggie's research is in undergraduate medical education, focusing on students' learning in general practice, teaching and learning clinical reasoning, ways of measuring the quality of teaching in community settings and setting up new programmes of learning which are designed to improve recruitment to general practice especially in rural areas. Maggie has listened to *The Archers* consistently since she went to university in 1980; she can truly say it is a very important part of her life and that the characters are very dear to her. She attended the *Academic Archers* conference for the first time in 2020 and was proud to present her work there.

Charlotte Bilby had a 20-year career in higher education as a criminologist. Her research interests were in arts and creativity in prisons and probation, fictional images of offenders, and evidence-based criminal justice policy making. While working in universities, Charlotte carried out research for the Home Office, Ministry of Justice and the National Criminal Justice Arts Alliance. Charlotte tried, on numerous occasions, to bring *The Archers* into her teaching: Ed's probation, Helen's time on remand and Freddie's sentence all allowed students to roll their eyes and question what relevance it had to 'real life.' Since leaving academia, Charlotte has worked in criminal justice organisations in the public and third sectors on topics including knife crime, rural policing, sexual exploitation, and trafficking. Charlotte's career helped her question many of *The Archers'* crime-related storylines and discussed these at length with colleagues. She once tweet-heckled the two presenters of a paper on *The Archers* at the British Society of

Criminology annual conference. Not her finest professional moment. It was this experience that instigated Charlotte's papers at the 2018 and 2019 *Academic Archers* conferences, where she unexpectedly found herself defending Borsetshire Constabulary's rural policing plan.

Helen M Burrows, is a Registered Social Worker and experienced Senior Lecturer in social work who worked in the East Midlands both as an independent practice educator and as an Outreach domestic abuse support worker until retirement in 2018. Her professional practice background is in Child Protection and working with adults with complex needs. Helen's research interests include social work education, gender and sexuality in social care, digital engagement, and more recently the role of popular and social media in informal and public education. This has led her to look at fandom, and how fan forums can support learning in a variety of disciplines. Helen has been listening to *The Archers* since around 1964, is the same age as Shula, and shares her birthday with Tracy Horrobin. A long-term member of the *Archers Anarchists* ('The Archers is real, there is no cast'), Helen has been involved with *Academic Archers* since the first conference in 2016. Since then she has presented papers at four of the five conferences to date: on using *The Archers* in social work education, mapping family dysfunction, Morris Dancing, and transformative fandom. Her chapter in this book brings her social work education paper up to date.

Lalage Cambell, now retired, was a Principal Lecturer, Reader and Head of the Department of Applied Psychology at Cardiff Metropolitan University. Lalage's research was based in health psychology initially, then recovery from centrally acting drugs, but latterly its focus was on student experience and wellbeing. Under the name Lalage Sanders, she is the author of over 40 peer-reviewed research papers and two textbooks: *Ambulatory Anaesthesia and Sedation* (1991, Blackwell) and *Discovering Research Methods in Psychology: A student's guide* (2010, Blackwell Wiley, a BPS Publication). Born in 1951, giving her an affinity with *The Archers*, Lalage has been nursing an addiction to events in Ambridge since 1971 when she discovered it almost by accident. She had experienced a very deprived childhood as her mother would switch off the radio (the Light Programme) the moment she heard the first dum-dee-dum. The first episode Lalage heard included a scandalous scene between Nelson Gabriel and Lillian Bellamy and she has been rivetted ever since, apart from a brief sulk after they killed Nigel Pargetter. Lalage has had only a 50% success rate with her offspring as sadly only two of the four are *Archers* fans despite rigorous and sustained indoctrination throughout their childhood.

Rob Drummond is a Reader in Linguistics at Manchester Metropolitan University. Rob researches, teaches and writes about anything to do with spoken language (especially accents), and its relationship to identity. He is particularly interested in the role of language in the 'performance' of our individual identities in any given context, and the perception of that performance by others. Rob is currently working on a big research project with his colleague, Dr Erin Carrie, called *Manchester Voices*. The project aims to explore the accents, dialects and identities of people living in Greater Manchester. Part of this involves driving around the ten boroughs of the region in their 'Accent Van', inviting people aboard to talk about the way they speak. Rob and Erin also work together on the *Accentism Project*, uncovering and examining language-based prejudice in everyday life. Rob only learned about *Academic Archers* at the time of the 2017 conference, by which time it was too late to be involved. An avid listener since Ruth nearly ran off with Sam, he made sure he was involved in 2018 and 2019. Rob had to miss 2020 due to work commitments, much to the dismay of his conference companion, his 20-year-old daughter Maya.

Keith Flett has been an *Archers* listener since around 1960 – his parents listened – but his conscious memories of Ambridge really stretch back to the mid-1960s. Keith is a research historian, organising the socialist history seminar at the Institute of Historical Research, and also works as a national trade union officer for Prospect in the telecoms sector. This combination of working-class history and day-to-day union work has given Keith a particular take on *The Archers* and he has edited the *Ambridge Socialist*, a weekly bulletin, now published online for more than ten years. The *Ambridge Socialist* reports, usually in a fairly light-hearted way, on the class struggle in Borsetshire. That means we back the Grundys and criticise the Archers. The combination of an academic background and an active pursuit of the class struggle means that Keith keeps in touch with a range of *Archers* related groups, including of course the *Academic Archers* and the rather differently focused *Archers Anarchists*. Keith is 63 and lives with his partner Megan (also an *Archers* fan) in central Cardiff and Tottenham. He also runs the Beard Liberation Front which occasionally passes comment on events in Ambridge too.

Paula Fomby is Research Associate Professor at the Survey Research Centre and Population Studies Centre at the Institute for Social Research, University of Michigan. She earned her PhD in Sociology with an emphasis in Social Demography at University of Wisconsin in 2001. As a family demographer, Paula studies the social, economic, and interpersonal factors that lead to family formation and dissolution and investigates the influence of family composition change on children's wellbeing across the early life course. She learned to love *The Archers* in a Sussex country kitchen in 1992, but only became a regular listener via the podcast in 2009. Paula's perfect weekend includes serving as a judge in a baking tent at the Flower and Produce Show, trespassing across Brookfield to climb to the top of Lakey Hill, and indulging in a pint of Shires at The Bull, especially if Jazzer McCreary is buying. An earlier version of the chapter in this volume was presented at the 2018 *Academic Archers* conference in London. Many thanks to Cara Courage and Nicola Headlam for bringing this unlikely and phenomenal community together.

Ruth Heilbronn lectures and researches at the University College London (UCL) Institute of Education (IoE), specialising in teacher education, linguistics and philosophy of education. She taught in London schools for many years and has held Local Education Authority advisory posts before joining the IoE where she led the Modern Foreign Languages Postgraduate Certificate in Education. Ruth has published texts in the areas of the epistemology of practice, mentoring, practical judgement and ethical teacher education. John Dewey has figured largely in her work, as an editor of several collections and organiser of conferences. Ruth is an executive member of the Philosophy of Education Society of Great Britain (PESGB). Contributing to the *Academic Archers* with her co-writer and presenter Rosalind Janssen has afforded a very welcome extension to her academic community of fellow researchers.

Rosalind Janssen is Honorary Lecturer in Education at UCL's Institute of Education. This is where she first met her co-author Ruth Heilbronn and discovered their mutual love of *The Archers*. Rosalind has been an avid listener since the 1960s. An Egyptologist by profession, she was previously a Curator at UCL's Petrie Museum, and then a Lecturer in

Egyptology at UCL's Institute of Archaeology. Rosalind currently teaches Egyptology classes at the University of Oxford and at London's City Lit. She even has a course – *The Archers of Antiquity* – revolving around daily life goings on at Deir el-Medina, a unique New Kingdom village. Rosalind and Ruth have previously presented papers at the *Academic Archers* conferences at the University of Lincoln and the British Library. Rosalind's MSc in Gerontology explains what prompted them to focus on care provision in Ambridge in 2041 for their latest contribution at the Academic Archers 2020 conference at University of Reading. What they could not have foreseen was that, just three weeks later, COVID-19 and lockdown would bring the topic of death in care homes, care in the community, and the contribution of the nation's carers, to the centre of the stage. They accordingly updated their presentation for the *Academic Archers Saturday Omnibus*.

Nicola Maxfield, after completing a history degree, found her academic career forestalled at the first hurdle when instead of going to study for a Masters, she had a baby. Nicola now has two adult sons and has worked as a teacher in Further Education for over 15 years and specialises in subjects relating to health and social care, including psychology, but most recently has been teaching Nineteenth Century History at an Further Education college in North Hampshire. The long postponed Masters will hopefully start at the end of 2020. Listening to *The Archers* since university, Nicola has eavesdropped on Ambridge since Mark Hebdon died.

Christine Narramore started her study of soil at a young age making mud pies, mainly in her aunt's garden. This was followed by enforced gardening at Girl Guides which has led Christine to believe gardening is hard work, which is why when working for Cambridge University she seemed to be the only non-gardener in the department. Christine has a BSc in

Chemistry from Birmingham, an MSc in Soil Science (Soil
Chemistry, Fertility and Management) from Aberdeen University, and a DPhil in Physical Chemistry from Oxford, on
The Calcite/Water Interface. She taught for a semester at the
University of Illinois at Chicago in the Earth Sciences
Department and has worked for environmental consultancies.
However, Christine is now an armchair Soil Scientist, who
mainly bores her children. She has a strong respect for
farmers, farming also being hard work. As a result, Christine
is now taking the much easier route of being a part time civil
servant, whilst being a regular attendee at *Academic Archers*
since the inaugural meeting in London, and more recently
attending the *Academic Archers Saturday Omnibus* talks.

Amy Sanders is a PhD researcher at Cardiff University,
researching the relationship between the third sector and
government with a focus on Welsh equalities organisations.
Born to an *Archers*-addicted mother, Amy's childhood was
enriched with Ambridge-life, listening to village affairs from
before she could speak. This has given her 45 years visiting her
much-loved Ambridge community. Prior to her PhD, Amy
spent over 16 years working on projects that brought the third
sector and public sector together. She was a director of a
Welsh workers' cooperative which promoted equality and
rights. As Projects Coordinator, Amy delivered social change
projects using creative, participatory methods for Welsh
Government, local and public authorities. Her projects ranged
from participation and empowerment work particularly with
groups labelled as 'harder to reach', to equality, rights and
tackling disadvantage, anti-poverty and community development. Amy has also been an Anti-Poverty Officer and a
Community Development Officer. She has educated adults
and children in Wales and internationally (Poland, USA,
Palestine, Indonesia, Portugal.) Amy has a Diploma in Social

Work, a Masters in Social Science, majoring in Community Development, and a first class Honours Degree in Social Philosophy. Active in community performing arts, she models herself on Lynda Snell <sniff>.

Olivia Vandyk was born in Wales to a military family and had a nomadic childhood. Educated in Oxford, she graduated with BA Hons in Classical Studies from King's College, London in 1999. Since then, she has amassed over two decades of experience spanning a variety of industries ranging from business and PR consultancy for FTSE 100 companies, including 16 years working at the highest national levels in both consumer magazines and online. Olivia founded Gingham Cloud, a communications agency in 2015. Her specialisms include creative advisory, copywriting and social media marketing for SMEs. From a research perspective, Olivia's interests particularly lie in the importance of both honesty and tone in how a business communicates. She is also fascinated by the connections that can be made through communities, both on and offline – personal, professional and commercial. Olivia has been an avid *Archers* listener since 2006 when she first started working from home and kept BBC Radio 4 on after the *Today* programme for company. She now makes her home in a Hertfordshire village (which has many similarities to Ambridge), with her husband and four children.

Timothy Vercellotti is a Professor of political science at Western New England University in Springfield, MA, and director of the university's London summer program. He teaches courses on political behaviour, media and politics, and public opinion polling. Tim's current research projects focus on the role that social class plays in mediating the effects of political discussions in the UK, and how trust shaped the choices that voters made when seeking information prior to the Brexit referendum. He holds a PhD in political science from the University of North Carolina at Chapel Hill. Tim became curious about radio drama while taking his students on tours of BBC Broadcasting House during summers in London, and he began listening to *The Archers* in 2014. The patterns of political behaviour that he observed on the program led to his first *Academic Archers* paper, on voting in Ambridge, in 2018. Tim's chapter is based on a second paper that he gave at the *Academic Archers* conference in 2020. He is grateful to have found a welcoming and enthusiastic interdisciplinary community in which to deepen his understanding of and appreciation for *The Archers*.

PREFACE – THE HAVE'S AND HAVE NOT'S: WEALTH AND VALUE IN AMBRIDGE

Cara Courage and Nicola Headlam

This, the fourth book from Academic Archers, *Flapjacks and Feudalism: Class Politics in* The Archers, turns its attention to matters of kinship and wealth in BBC Radio 4's *The Archers*, with sections attending to housing, intergenerational wealth, skills and access to employment and how all of these, and more, shape the life of those in Ambridge. Who has what, or not, who knows who, where people live and work, and who they work with, and the parenting they have, determine how our beloved Ambridgians fare in life. And this is what keeps us tuning in.

Think of the repeat broadcast during COVID-19 lockdown of the 1999 Ambridge New Year's Eve, at the Millennium Ball at Lower Loxley. A black-tie event, the Borsetshire county set drank and danced the night away. With both Archer and Aldridge clans in attendance, we are privy to an extra-marital liaison, with the Brian Aldridge and Siobhan affair reaching its acute phase. This scene was interspersed by a far earthier party held at village pub, The Bull, with more ribald and rowdy fun for Eddie Grundy and his crew, the assembled proletariats led in a conga line to welcome the new millennium. Interposing the two parties, we have the hard boundary between 'the have's and have not's' which is blurred in the normal run of Ambridge events where the propinquity of village life throws the classes together in their day-to-day settings of the shop and village hall.

There is a vexed question hanging over our village: is social mobility possible in Ambridge? This book covers the myriad of ways on which all forms of capital are unequally shared in the village and introduces the snakes and ladders associated with social mobility and class in Ambridge. 'The Fall of the House of Aldridge' could first appear as downward social mobility. Having lost their synecdochal Home Farm the Aldridges are currently squeezed (with only the one best tagine, the ignominy …) into Willow Cottage, far more humble housing than they have been used at Home Farm. Through this storyline, we see that one of the more 'prominent' county families is suffering a reversal of fortune based on historic nefarious business practices of the formerly 'squireish' Brian – but, the family have still maintained a level of social status in the village (if not with the county set) based on their class identity and historical status as landowners. It is at 'the opposite end of the village' that the life chances of characters in the village of Ambridge are more defined – and fixed – by status at birth. The Grundys are perpetually disadvantaged and we see in their life's travails that intergenerational forms of capital – very much the lack of for the Grundys – are the clearest markers for class position in the village of Ambridge and that life chances and social mobility are circumscribed by accidents of birth.

Whereas the Aldridges have the economic capital that the Grundys lack, what both clans have in common though are cultural and social capital, albeit differing. In his defining text *Distinction* (1979) Bourdieu differentiates between: economic capital (wealth and income); cultural capital (the ability to appreciate and engage with cultural goods, and credentials institutionalised through educational success); and social capital (contacts and connections which allow people to draw on their social networks.) Bourdieu's point is that although these three capitals may overlap, they are also subtly different, and that it is possible to draw fine-grained distinctions between people with different stocks of each of the three capitals, to provide a much more complex model of social class than is currently used. This multi-facetted model plays out through the machinations of the Aldridges and Grundys, metaphorically, from the Millennium Ball to the conga line.

The subtle complexities of class and social mobility in Ambridge was something that Charlotte Connor (aka, Susan Carter) foregrounded in her highly sympathetic reading of her character (Connor, 2019). Connor asked us to imagine the cauldron of resentment stirred in the young Susan Horrobin as she saw, through the window of her council house, the indulged Archers girls growing up in privilege. This fostered resilience in Susan as well as a heightened sense of the place of the villagers relative to one another. This sensitivity to the boundaries and codes of social hierarchy are core to the golden age of English sit com whereby the fine gradations of lower middle to upper middle class aesthetics and sensibilities have fuelled classics from Basil Fawlty's manic snobbishness in *Fawlty Towers* (BBC a), to the absurdities of Hyacinth Bucket in *Keeping Up Appearances* (BBC b), and the dialectic between Tom and Barbara Good and Margot and Jerry Leadbetter in *The Good Life* (BBC c).

Susan's sister, Tracey Horrobin, is refreshing in that she is untrammelled by the inverted snobbery that so torments Susan in her routine interactions. By storming the bastions of privilege – the reception desk of Grey Gables and the captaincy of the cricket team – Tracey acts as a robust decongestant to social anxiety and social climbing. Listeners were delighted as she 'levelled with' Helen Archer for advice about the intricacies of dating as a single mother, to Helen's obvious discomfort. Helen has the privacy mores of the petit bourgeoise and was toe-curlingly mortified to talk frankly about blended family dynamics. It was clear in this scene that Helen is 'good' single mother, with the attendant anxieties and angst, and that this gender and class distinction marks her out from 'bad' single mother Tracey, despite the fact that the mechanics of their situations are identical.

Flapjacks and Feudalism: Class Politics in The Archers is presented in five sections, across 17 chapters, and we begin with *It's who you know, and what you know about them*, continuing the focused topic of this preface. In *The Class politics of Ambridge*, Keith Flett applies an x-ray vision the village from a life devoted to teasing out the mobilisation of the class war in *The Archers*. Nicola Headlam, in *One in, One out: Networks in Ambridge*, explores the effects of the death of Joe Grundy and the birth of Rosie Archer on the kinship networks of the village.

The second section, *The Fall of The House of Aldridge, the Rise of the Oppressed Grundys?*, begins with a study of the melancholia at the heart of the Emma and Ed storyline, from Lalage Cambell in *'If you have security, Ed, that is everything': Deconstructing 'security' as a buffer against life's challenges*. The disturbing storyline of modern slavery is then given due focus and political context by Nicola Headlam in *Feeding the Horses: shining a light on exploitation hidden in plain sight in Ambridge*. The following two chapters put Brian under the spotlight: *Borsetshire businessman or feckless farmer?*, by Christine Narramore, who lays the blame for the fall squarely at the door of Brian Aldridge; and then *What to do when you're no longer Borsetshire's Businessperson of the Year, or how to handle a scandal*, by Olivia Vandyk who counters that with some decent reputation management and public relations the family could have recovered their reputation far more quickly.

Examining an ever-popular topic for *Archers* listeners, the third section is all about *Family Function and Dysfunction*. Helen M Burrows opens with a presentation of the use of *The*

Archers in social work teaching, in *Contemporary social problems in a rural setting: using* The Archers *in social work education.* Cara Courage then, in *Academic Archers assembly: putting the parents on trial*, presents the sometimes acerbic, sometimes touching deliberations from the *Academic Archers* cohort on sets of Ambridge parents. The accents of Ambridgians is an ever-popular topic, and next, *Academic Archers* house linguist Rob Drummond looks at the demarcations of language and dialect by an in-depth linguistic family case study of the male Grundys, in *Accent and identity in Abridge: the link between how we speak and who we are.* We then turn to crime in and what impact being one of Ambridge's have's or have not's may have on one, firstly in *'We Should have called him Damien': A discussion of the impact of Henry Archer's early years on potential crimes of the future*, from Nicola Maxfield, who discusses the impact of Henry's early years on potential crimes of the future. Then, the Archers Exceptionalism deployed in the face of transgressions in *Fear, fecklessness and flapjacks: imagining Ambridge's offenders* from Charlotte Bilby.

The fourth section, *Housing and the Ambridge Fairy*, talks of the import of where one lives, and with whom, on life experience in the village. Turning first to that bountiful imp, Claire Astbury presents *Rich relatives or Ambridge fairy? Patronage and expectation in Ambridge housing pathways*, taking a deep dive into the housing history of Emma Grundy set in the context of the rural housing crisis. Paula Fomby looks at how the blended households of Ambridge function to protect young single people who are priced out of the village in *Staying in the spare room: social connectedness and household co-residence in The Archers*. Ruth Heilbronn and Rosalind Janssen, in *Can't afford The Laurels?: Care provision in Ambridge in 2045*, offer us a vision of the future of three Ambridge residents and how their current financial status plays out for them in their later years.

The fifth and final section, *It Takes a Village… The Structure of Ambridge Civil Society* begins with *Parents, siblings, and the pursuit of power: Predicting the future leaders of Ambridge*, from Timothy Vercellotti, positing on who might be the movers and shakers in Ambridge hence. Intergenerational differences and changing social etiquette are discussed in '*From the moment those two joined the committee it's been grunge bands, sumo wrestlers and soufflé competitions': What Ambridge's civil society says about UK politics in 2019*, from Amy Sanders. Our final chapter benefits from interview research from those silent in Ambridge, examining their discombobulated psycho-emotional experience of living in the village, in *A divided village: a narrative study using a theoretical lens of speculative ontology*, from Maggie Bartlett.

REFERENCES

BBC a. Fawlty Towers. Retrieved from http://www.bbc.co.uk/comedy/fawltytowers/

BBC b. Keeping Up Appearances. Retrieved from http://www.bbc.co.uk/comedy/keepingupappearances/

BBC c. The Good Life. Retrieved from http://www.bbc.co.uk/comedy/goodlife/

Bourdieu, P. (1979[2010]). *Distinction*. Abingdon: Routledge.

Connor, C. (2019). I'm not one to Gossip: Roots, rumour and mental well-being in Ambridge. In C. Courage & N. Headlam (Eds.), *Gender, sex and gossip in Ambridge: Women in the Archers*. Bingley: Emerald.

Section 1

IT'S WHO YOU KNOW, AND WHAT YOU KNOW ABOUT THEM

1

THE GRUNDYS AND THEIR OPPRESSORS

Keith Flett

ABSTRACT

The Grundys are the alternative world of Ambridge. Invariably down on their luck, often portrayed as lazy if not feckless and usually incompetent. This chapter speaks up for the downtrodden of Borsetshire and in particular the Grundys. It looks at the development of the Grundy family in The Archers *over almost 50 years now. It relates key elements in their lives, looking not just at the class struggle in the village but also the importance of gender in this. It draws on key players in the Grundy story from the 1970s including the late radio DJ John Peel who was for a time an enthusiast for* The Archers *and who played Eddie Grundy's records on his BBC Radio One show. It also looks at the views of key* Archers *figures such as Vanessa Whitburn and Keri Davies and how they have approached the Grundys. It uses the work of Marx and Engels to try to explain how it is that the Grundys moved from being small farmers to landless labourers. What the chapter doesn't do is to map out a strategy for the liberation of the Grundys from their oppression. It does however look forward to a world turned upside down when at 19.02 hours on a weekday evening on BBC Radio 4 we hear a programme called not* The Archers, *but* The Grundys.

Appearing on the Dumteedum podcast on 29 May 2020 (Dumteedum, 2020), *The Archers* chief scriptwriter, Keri Davies, noted that the first voice we had heard on *The Archers* when it resumed after a COVID-19 break was that of David Archer because after all it is *The Archers*, about the dynasty of the same name. Indeed, it is which is why the *Ambridge Socialist* backs the alternative proletarian dynasty of the Grundys. After 70 years, their time has come. The phrase 'Grundys and their Oppressors' is attributed to former Labour leader Neil Kinnock in Headlam, *Custard, Culverts and Cake* (Headlam, 2017, Chapter 12) and reflects a wider truth about *The Archers* also articulated by Keri Davies. It may be that readers of *The Daily Telegraph* think that *The Archers* should centrally be about the Archer family who are rightfully the ruling clique. Others may have rather different ideas about what *The Archers* is and should be about.

While the Archer family has been with us since 1951, the Grundys certainly have not. They were introduced to the programme by William Smethurst who was producer from 1974 to 1986. Ratings were falling, and there was concern that what was the flagship programme from BBC Midlands in Birmingham would be ditched unless it was livened up somewhat. Even so, that gives us 40-plus years history of the Grundys in Ambridge, and it's fair to say that a good deal of that has become hidden from history, at least until now that is. If the official view was, and to an extent remains, that *The Archers* is centrally about the Archer family, which after all does have a role in most areas of village life, then what exactly is the purpose and role of the Grundys?

The Grundys were not the first plebeian characters in *The Archers*, and there have tended to be two types. The first is the enforcer of the rules and practices of the Ambridge ruling class. This role requires someone with a detailed understanding of the ways of the countryside but also someone who is always prepared to touch the forelock to their 'betters.' Tom Forrest was perhaps the best known character in this mould and his modern-day successor as gamekeeper is Will Grundy. Tom and Will are what the *Ambridge Socialist* would call 'class collaborators', acting against the real interests of their class. On the other side of the equation, we have exponents of rural tradition, folklore, song and so on. Probably, the best known was Walter Gabriel, with his catchphrase 'me old pal, me old beauty.' Played by Chris Gittins there seems to be some doubt as to whether he was ever actually a professional actor, but his role was to provide rural colour. There were others including Ned Larkin and Jethro Larkin, and in the present day Ambridge's poet laureate Bert Fry who in recent times, the poems aside, has been a more complex figure, in part as an agricultural worker whose experience frequently gets the better of David Archer. The role of characters like Walter Gabriel was to provide light relief, colour and basically, laughs. What a strange and often incomprehensible lot these peasant types were.

The Grundys' arrival in Ambridge was not so far removed from all that but this was after all the late 1970s and not the 1950s. There is social progress even in Ambridge. These were times of social conflict from the Winter of Discontent to the rise of Mrs Thatcher. Over time, the Grundys developed as the alternative Archers and characters who a newer, younger audience could identify with. Eddie Grundy (Trevor Harrison) was a country singer sometimes duetting with Jolene (now)

Archer. Harrison actually made records that warranted the occasional play on John Peel's BBC Radio One show. Peel and his producer John Walters formed an Eddie Grundy fan club in the early 1980s, and Peel made occasional Ambridge appearances. Peel aired Eddie's *Clarrie's Song* on his programme in December 1982. Peel wrote in *the Guardian* in 1994 (Peel Wiki, n.d.) about his relationship both with the Archers and the Grundys:

> *Actually, I have featured in* The Archers *on two distinct occasions. On the first I was heard on the radio 'on the radio,' as it were. Eddie Grundy and the hapless Clarrie* [Grundy] *were listening to Radio 1 in the kitchen at Grange Farm when I played one of Eddie's records. On the second, my work was spread over several episodes and I even got to sing* Yellow Submarine *in a van with Eddie and that nice Mrs Antrobus. I've never got into television soap operas at all. I used to be into* The Archers *at one time until it became too kind of issue-driven. I just felt uncomfortable with that... I don't want that in* The Archers. *I used to like it back in the days when they did, "Well, looks like it's going to be dark soon"... I used to like that because I could cope with the pace of it.*

(Peel Wiki, n.d.)

While presenting from Glastonbury Festival for the BBC in 2003, Peel interviewed several Ambridge residents including Ed Grundy (Barry Farrimond). The Grundys at this time represented part of *The Archers* changing with the times and surviving. Phil Archer may have played the organ at St Stephens, but he wasn't the person to launch a pop music career.

Characters in *The Archers* go on for many decades quite often, but writers and producers change as does the emphasis in storylines and listeners' expectations. If the Grundys, and Eddie in particular, first appeared as a move away from the rather staid mainstays of *The Archers* in the 1960s, by the 1990s the emphasis was changing to the Grundys as tenant farmers at Grange Farm. Small farmers in a world of giant firms and a worldwide agribusiness were and are in a tough place, and the Grundys were no different. They were however styled now as not particularly good farmers, inefficient, lacking diligence and so on. This was in comparison with the apparently excellent farming of the Archers and the Aldridges (see Chapter 5). It was a class divide in Ambridge and one that has been maintained to the present day. The view of *Archers* Ambridge is that the Grundys tend to be feckless even if on occasion they might be lovable rogues.

The Grundys were evicted from Grange Farm by the owners, Borchester Land, and the BBC broadcast the news on 26 April 2000. They had been unable to pay the rent. The then editor Vanessa Whitburn said at the time that,

> *It's only realistic for a drama set in the countryside to reflect what's going on there properly. Even six months ago it was obvious that farming was going through its worst crisis since the 1930s. And the most vulnerable, apart from hill farmers, are small-scale tenant farmers like the Grundys. This is what can happen to people like them.*

(BBC Radio 4, 2000)

The comment 'people like them' reflects the view one suspects of some in the BBC about the Grundys and their like. It also reflected the rise of Borchester Land as the aggressive agri-capitalist presence in the area that continues to this day. If the Archers dynasty has effective political control of Ambridge, Borchester Land is running the economy.

Keri Davies, effectively the historian of Ambridge, has written a good summary of the chequered history of Borchester Land. Formed in 1997 as New Labour came to power, it brought the Berrow Estate from Simon Pemberton. The leading figures initially were Brian Aldridge and Matt Crawford. By 2020, Aldridge had been purged, and Crawford was believed to be in South America. As ever there has been no room for sentiment in business in Ambridge. It was Crawford who booted the Grundys out of Grange Farm. He had no interest in or sympathy with such rural plebeians. Instead, wealthy ex-army type Oliver Sterling and his partner, the late Caroline Bone, bought the farm. Initially, Oliver had a herd of beef cattle and then switched to a dairy production including the appearance of a local cheese – a favourite *Archers* foodstuff – called *Sterling Gold*. There was however a twist, perhaps a surprising one. If Borchester Land represented the unacceptable face of modern capitalism sweeping people aside in favour of profit at all costs, Sterling was much more of a patrician, a sort of 'we're all in it together' type, grasping that the better off had some social and moral obligations to the less well off. When Sterling acquired Grey Gables with partner Caroline, he decided to outsource the running of Grange Farm to Ed Grundy.

The Grundy family however were split up after their eviction from Grange Farm, with Eddie, Clarrie and Joe Grundy living in a cramped council flat, Meadowrise. It was this enforced change that made Joe to decide to kill off his ferrets. The class divide in Ambridge had rarely been sharper. In due course, the Grundys were able to afford to rent Keeper's Cottage which they did until they were flooded out in the Great Flood of Ambridge in 2015. During this period, the Grundy culture and personas that many current *Archers* listeners will be familiar with have developed. Gone are the days of Eddie making records and indeed of the Grundys as any sort of tenant farmer. Rather, a windfall allowed the purchase of what is known as Grundy's Field, and this has been used for all manner of sometimes doubtful activities. Probably best known is *The Grundy World of Christmas* which didn't take place in 2019 due to the demise of Joe. Grundy's Field has however played host to two things that have become Ambridge institutions. The first is the sale of turkeys at Christmas, on a sort of no questions asked basis. The second is the Grundy's *Cider Club*, complete in recent times with a portable toilet, which is even, occasionally, emptied.

The BBC once suggested that the two rules of the *Grundy's Cider Club* are firstly that you don't talk about or admit to its existence and secondly, that if you are the last one to leave that you padlock the door. It is of course, like anything to do with the Grundys, rather more complex than that. It is in effect a community cider club, the definition of the 'community' although never formally defined seems to include few, if any, women, and absolutely definitely no one at all with the word Archer in their name. It is a place where the oppressed and friends of the oppressed can gather (provided they are men) and where the oppressor is not welcome or possibly even allowed.

The cider club works on subscriptions with no money exchanging hands in the barn. It's fair to say that the Grundys were old-style craft cider makers to the extent that when a vital part broke in 2019 the only replacement they could find was in a museum piece held at Lower Loxley. The most well-known Grundy's cider is *Tumble Tussocks*, said to be made from a rare Borsetshire apple. Like so much to do with the Grundys, it's more myth than reality as the variety of apple doesn't really exist. However, in 2017, pre-Christmas in Ambridge with Grundy turkey season under-way, the Grundys offered a bottle of cider made from the rare *Tumble Tussocks* apple as an incentive. At a tasting, Professor Jim Lloyd described the cider from the second barrel of three as excellent. The other two, as Joe Grundy freely admitted, were disgusting. The big question was, did Grundy's *Tumble Tussocks* qualify as craft cider or not? An *Ambridge Socialist* poll found 85% of those participating believed it did, as it was made by master cider makers, the Grundys. After Joe died in 2019, Eddie and his brother, Alf Grundy, found mention in his will of a hangover 'cure.' This was apparently to be found with veteran cider drinker, Carmen. The BBC claimed that it contained cough mixture and cod liver oil. In reality of course it was a concoction based on *Tumble Tussocks* cider. The cider barn, unlicensed and unregulated, is perhaps the definitive symbol of an alternative culture in Ambridge that eschews St Stephens and The Bull.

The Grundys got by from 2000–2015, no thanks to the Archer dynasty or Borchester Land. The Great Flood of Ambridge saw Keeper's Cottage flooded. Unfortunately, Eddie hadn't kept up the insurance payments. This was taken to be yet another example of how feckless the Grundys are. Alternatively, we might think that if you don't have a regular guaranteed income keeping up such a payment, compared to paying the gas and electricity, insurance may not be quite a top priority. Fortunately, Micawber-like, something did turn up for the Grundys. Oliver Sterling and Caroline Bone decided to leave for Tuscany for a period and rented out the Grundys' former residence, Grange Farm, to them. They didn't maintain the property properly – again, this costs money – but after some tut-tutting, Oliver left them *in situ* and resides at Grey Gables when in Ambridge.

There is a lot more to the Grundys than Eddie and Joe. It is noticeable if predictable that the rock of the Grundys, Clarrie, someone who both works full-time and keeps the household going, is never venerated in a way that women of ruling class Ambridge like Ruth Archer, Lillian Bellamy, Jennifer Archer, and particularly Peggy Archer, are. Clarrie appeared not that long after Eddie himself had first been sighted in Ambridge, in 1981. Clarrie has been the one who has, as it were, kept the Grundy show on the road. She was responsible for paying off Eddie's debts when they married and had already had to buy her own engagement ring. Clarrie was a Larkin, one of the other historic proletarian families of Ambridge, and has had two children with Eddie – William and Edward. She has worked full-time throughout her marriage, first at The Bull and in more recent times at Helen Archer's diary. Clarrie has been the one above all to be concerned about the love triangle between Will and Ed over Emma (then) Carter. Emma married Will, but it appears found him rather boring. They had one child, George Grundy, before Emma decided that she preferred the arguably less boring Grundy brother, Ed, and married him instead.

The Will, Ed and Emma saga has been a recurring theme in *The Archers* pointing to the fact that the working classes can't really be expected to properly sort out their personal lives which are of course chaotic. Compare this to the treatment of Brian Aldridge's various dalliances and affairs which are treated, in the main, as just one of those things. Several points flow from this. Neither Will nor Ed could be said to follow in any serious sense any of the various traditions which *Archers* writers over the decades have placed Joe and Eddie in. Neither represents the modern face of old traditions struggling on in the face of the Borsetshire Land monolith. A liking for cider for example is not something either is noted for, surely a key point. They don't represent either the sort of lovable rogue characters who get by as they straddle a fine line between legality and illegality with their various activities.

In fact, Will is entirely outside of the Grundy tradition, rather like one of David and Ruth's children turning out to be the Borsetshire organiser of the Socialist Workers Party. That kind of thing does happen, occasionally, in real life, but not in Ambridge. Will, until recently the gamekeeper who presided over the Ambridge shoot, was the key lieutenant of capital in the area. The enforcer of the law that says that the wealthy own the land and everything on it and the poor better keep off or else. The *Ambridge Socialist* has frequently described Will as a forelock tugger, something he did regularly to the likes of Matt Crawford and Brian Aldridge. He had less success with Martyn Gibson of Borsetshire Land, his last boss before he resigned. Gibson saw the kind of forelock tugging peasant as a tradition upon which time had been served. He just wanted Will to do his job and if he couldn't to clear 'orf.' Will never quite managed to finger Eddie for poaching on other people's land, but he came close on several occasions. For Eddie, though family ties were more important than the reality that one of his sons was a class traitor, not something a mistake that the ruling dynasties of Ambridge have ever made or are ever likely to make.

Finally, there is Alf Grundy, an occasional visitor to Ambridge. If the Grundys are portrayed as inhabiting a sort of rural twilight zone between legality and illegality and generally not being very effective at it, Alf provides a wider framework. Alf has proved to be a petty thief, and instances of taking small sums from other Grundys occur from time to time. Alf has made court appearances and according to the BBC served time in prison. He is perhaps the epitome of the undeserving poor as genuine as opposed to a lovable rogue. Of course, ruling class Ambridge has members from Matt Crawford to Brian Aldridge who have committed and been found guilty of much greater crimes, but these are mostly seen as aberrations rather than something fundamental to their character (see Chapters 10 and 11).

Looking at the Grundys in the round, it is however the late Joe who has come to symbolise their place in Ambridge. On the death of the actor who played him, Ted Kelsey, Nancy Banks Smith wrote in *the Guardian* on 25 April 2019:

> *People like Joe Grundy make the countryside look untidy. People like Joe Grundy are Compo in* The Last of the Summer Wine, *Adam Lambsbreath in* Cold Comfort Farm, *Baldrick in* Blackadder *and, of course, Joe's immediate predecessor in* The Archers, *Walter ("Me ol' pal! Me ol' beauty!") Gabriel. When nice people settle in the smiling countryside they find it is already infested with Grundys. Prospero had this problem.*

> (Banks-Smith, 2019)

It is here that reality and fiction meld in a way that perhaps explains a good deal about *The Archers*. It's not really real yet somehow it seems like perhaps it almost could be. The tributes in 2019 were as much for Ted Kelsey as Joe Grundy. The *Archers Anarchists*, a group that continues to claim that *The Archers* is real and that there is no cast – frankly one does wonder on this sometimes – was originally formed around fandom for Joe Grundy it seems. Ted Kelsey was a long-term trade union activist and served as a lay officer for the actors union Equity for many years. If the Grundys were the downtrodden and oppressed of Ambridge, the patriarch of the family, was in real life someone who fought for better conditions for working people. But of course, he was also larger than life, a kind of class caricature. As Nancy Banks Smith noted:

*He was free of all the fashionable problems that
nice people suffer in Ambridge: depression and
coercive control and donor insemination. Regular
spats with Bert Fry (The Bard of Borchester) kept
Joe on his toes.*

(Banks-Smith, 2019)

If we take a view of the Grundys over more than 40 years,
now we can see that as editors and scriptwriters have come and
gone, their role and impact in Ambridge has varied somewhat.
In the early years, they were light relief, slightly quaint rural
characters perhaps. In the middle years, they came to represent
hard-pressed small farmers. In the later period, it has been
something of a mixture of the two. One thing however
remained completely clear and that is whatever the Grundys
represented in Ambridge from time to time they could never
ever be mistaken for Archers or Aldridges or any part of the
ruling dynasties of the village and the wider Borsetshire.

Yet class does not exist in isolation to be studied like a
museum exhibit. It is about an interaction with other classes.
E P Thompson (1963) notes in the preface to the *Making of
the English Working Class* that class is a relationship and not
a thing. The Grundys don't exist in Ambridge in isolation but
in relation to the ruling class of Ambridge. If they have had a
salvation, it is probably this because the Archers, Aldridges,
and Borchester Land spend at least as much if not more time
fighting each other as they do trying to grind the Grundys
down. Brian has his differences with Adam Macy and neither
are fans of Borchester Land; while David Archer has issues
with just about everyone. Marx (1867b) covered the general
point in *Capital Volume 3 part 3*, noting that:

*So long as things go well, competition effects an
operating fraternity of the capitalist class, as we have*

> *seen in the case of the equalisation of the general rate*
> *of profit, so that each shares in the common loot in*
> *proportion to the size of his respective investment.*
> *But as soon as it no longer is a question of sharing*
> *profits, but of sharing losses, everyone tries to reduce*
> *his own share to a minimum and to shove it off upon*
> *another. The class, as such, must inevitably lose.*
> *How much the individual capitalist must bear of the*
> *loss, i.e., to what extent he must share in it at all, is*
> *decided by strength and cunning, and competition*
> *then becomes a fight among hostile brothers. The*
> *antagonism between each individual capitalist's*
> *interests and those of the capitalist class as a whole,*
> *then comes to the surface, just as previously the*
> *identity of these interests operated in practice*
> *through competition. (p.317)*

In short, the ruling class of Ambridge are a band of warring brothers and sisters in which, fortunately for them, the Grundys have at best a walk-on part. But if Marx offers an explanation for how the ruling classes of Ambridge behave, both Engels and himself also looked at the Grundys of this world. As early as 1845 Engels wrote in *The Condition of the Working Class in England* that small farmers were being crowded out by the large farm system which 'reduced them to the rank of proletarians.' 150 years on it was still an accurate description of what happened when Borchester Land determined the future of Grange Farm and its occupants, the Grundys. Marx (1867a) echoed Engels 20 years later when he wrote in *Capital Volume One* (Chapter 25):

> *Nowhere does the antagonistic character of*
> *capitalistic production and accumulation assert itself*
> *more brutally than in the progress of English*

agriculture (including cattle-breeding) and the
retrogression of the English agricultural labourer.
(p.828)

Marx wrote, also in *Capital Volume One* (Chapter 15), of
the revolutionary effect of modern industry on agriculture.
Namely 'that it annihilates the peasant, that bulwark of the
old society, and replaces him by the wage-labourer' (1867a,
p. 590).

It is not known if the Grundys have ever chanced upon or
read any of the works of Marx and Engels, but it is unlikely to
be of great consolation to them that their journey from small
farmers to wage labourers was accurately analysed many
years before they ventured into Ambridge. Perhaps though
there remains a wider sense in which the Grundys oppressed
by the Archers and Borchester Land as they have been, not
always quite 'on the level', do represent a relationship with the
world that is more about people, community, and solidarity
than the 'warring brothers' who dominate Ambridge. When
during its lockdown monologue period the cast gathered
virtually to sing a version of *Barwick Green* the final word
went to Eddie Grundy standing along in a field who said
simply 'take care'.

I've tried here to reflect and un-pick the class struggle in
Ambridge as reflected through the prism of the Grundys
primarily and their various ruling class oppressors. There are
lacunae. It is a long while since there has been mention of
trade union organisation in Ambridge. Mike Tucker was the
union representative, the union Unite being the modern face of
the National Union of Agricultural Workers. While Eddie
possibly wouldn't be a member, Ed very likely would be.
Likewise, it's possible, although not that likely unfortunately,
that Grey Gables would be unionised, also by Unite. It's
absent here though because it's absent from *The Archers*.

Furthermore, any class analysis two decades into the twenty-first century would like at the relationship between gender, race and class. I have written about that proletarian tower of strength Clarrie Grundy above, but again the matter is either understated or absent in *The Archers*. Perhaps, the class struggle in Borsetshire will do something to address these absences in the times ahead, and the Archers dynasty will at last crack.

REFERENCES

Banks-Smith, N. (2019). Nancy Banks-Smith on the Archers' Joe Grundy: Farewell from me and the ferrets. *The Guardian*, 25th April 2019 [online]. Retrieved from https://www.theguardian.com/tv-and-radio/2019/apr/25/nancy-banks-smith-on-the-archers-joe-grundy-farewell-from-me-and-the-ferrets. Accessed on August 28, 2020.

BBC Radio 4. (2000). The Grundys' eviction from Grange farm [online]. Retrieved from https://www.bbc.co.uk/programmes/m000j3ry. Acessed on August 28, 2020.

Dumteedum. (2020). Dumteedum does Keri Davies. [online] 29 May 2020. Retrieved from https://dumteedum.com/dumteedum-does-keri-davies/. Accessed on August 28, 2020.

Engels, F. (1845/1987). *The condition of the working class in England in 1844*. London: Penguin.

Headlam, N. (2017). Kinship networks in Ambridge. In C. Courage & N. Headlam (Eds.), *Custard, culverts and cake: Academics on life in the Archers*. Bingley: Emerald Publishing Limited.

Marx, K. (1867/1991a). *Capital volume one*. London: Penguin.

Marx, K. (1867/1991b). *Capital volume 3, part 3*. London: Penguin.

Peel Wiki. (n.d). *Archers*. [online]. Retrieved from https://peel.fandom.com/wiki/Archers. Accessed on August 28, 2020.

Thompson, E. P. (1963). *The making of the English working class*. London: Victor Gollancz Ltd.

2

TWO-IN/ONE-OUT: NETWORK POWER, KIN-KEEPING AND 'AIRTIGHT' DISTINCTION

Nicola Headlam

ABSTRACT

As a network analyst, I am fascinated by social inter-actions. The ways in which people connect with one another and exercise power and authority by deploying different forms of capital. This piece returns to the underlying and changing kinship network structure of the village of Ambridge over time, explores the role of 'kin-keeping' as deployed by the matriarchs Peggy and Jill. I am most interested in the ways in which gender as performed by the women of the village intersects with abundance or lack of other forms of capital, and how far inequalities persist and why. It is clear that there is an intergenerational power dynamic at play in the spreading or hoarding of the various dimensions of power layered together and how forms of capital inter-sect for protection or precarity. Social and cultural capital at birth in the village is defining in terms of both 'serious' life outcomes as well as how more minor infractions and foibles are viewed. Further, I return to discuss how my various network-based predictions have fared over time. The Headlam Hypothesis and the fate of Ed Grundy – King of Ambridge are revisited and their durability explored.

> *Rich people plan for three generations, poor people plan for Saturday night. However sugarcoated and ambiguous, every form of authoritarianism must start with a belief in some group's greater right to power, whether that right is justified by sex, race, class, religion or all four. However far it may expand, the progression inevitably rests on unequal power and airtight roles within the family.*
>
>   (Steinem, 2019, p. 137)

INTRODUCTION

Time takes on a special quantity in relation to class positioning. Investments and assets degrade slowly, as long as there is a measure of financial competence and prudence deployed. 'One day, son,' promises the bourgeois gentleman, 'all this will be yours...' Meanwhile, there are a range of strategies for framing the norms and practices which are appropriate to any given social group, their elite privileges or the innovations of precarity in work and housing (necessity being the mother, and indeed the grandmother, of invention.) Time is also of particular importance within the annals and canon of continuing drama. That Ambridgians share their whole life course with us means that we are acutely aware of their trajectories, both emotional and financial. Time, then, is a novel dimension to bring to my longitudinal network study on the social and power networks of Ambridge. Maybe writing from the strictures of lockdown in 2020 has sharpened my antennae for the embedded assumptions and lock-ins of class structure in *The Archers* since COVID-19 has shone light into the intersectional inequalities that frame health and social inequality. My title refers of course to the arrivals of Rosie Ruth Grace Archer in 2018, as well as her second cousin Alexander (Xander) Macy-Craig and the death of Joe Grundy in 2019. These are hugely significant moments in Ambridge.

The elision between a niche method for the quantitative analysis of social interactions and a lifelong listening history to *The Archers* has been an interesting and rich vein of form ever since we established our new kind of academic community, *Academic Archers* in 2016. I have returned to the role of kinship in the village a number of times, in the chapter in *Custard, Culverts and Cake: Academics on Life in The Archers* (Courage & Headlam, 2017) and in a series of blog posts (Headlam, 2018a, 2018b). In addition to refreshing; the 'Small Worlds' of the village, first aired at the *Academic Archers* Lincoln conference (Headlam, 2019b), this piece has been an opportunity to review the things I have written on these interlinked subjects and to look again at the underlying and changing kinship network structure of the village of Ambridge over time. In some ways, this is a matter of normative or conventional concern – the ways in which the characters 'hatch, match and despatch' serves to underscore family norms, particularly as regards gendered identities. Following on from my look at informal civic work in *Gender, Sex and Gossip: Women in The Archers* (Headlam, 2019a), I am most interested in the ways in which gender as performed

by the women of the village intersects with abundance or lack
of other forms of capital, and how far inequalities persist and
why.

NETWORK EFFECTS AND SOCIAL MOBILITY

The villagers of Ambridge are a dream population for a
network analyst due to the clear outer edge of their worlds,
and *The Archers* canon as broadcast offers us a 75-year
unbroken longitudinal data set. These temporal and spatial
boundaries are so much neater and more satisfying than the
unruliness of family life in real life. In addition to thinking
through the 'one-in one-out' nature of the recent past the new
contribution of this paper is an extended discussion of the
ways in which families 'rise and fall' in Ambridge. As Haw-
thorne put it, families are always falling and rising in America,
though it is usually assumed that the rigidity of the British
class system works against social mobility between generations. In their powerful book *The Class Ceiling*, Friedman and
Laurison conclude that 'In contemporary Britain it quite
literally pays to be privileged. Even when individuals from
working-class backgrounds are successful in entering the
country's elite occupations they go on to earn, on average,
16% less than colleagues from more privileged backgrounds'
(Friedman & Laurison, 2019, p. 209). It is clear that within
Ambridge there is a long-running link between the spreading
or hoarding of the various dimensions of power layered
together and how forms of capital intersect for protection or
precarity.

It is necessary to take into account the multi-dimensional
ways in which polarisation of social inequality (in the form of
an elite and a precariat), Ambridge shows a stretched social
hierarchy with 'Sticky Ends' – a small elite (estimated at

10% by the BBC British Class Survey (Savage et al. 2014)) who have the hat-trick of financial, social and cultural capital (Oliver Sterling, say by virtue of his holdings in Grey Gables.) At the bottom end and lacking all forms of capital, we have the introduction of 'The Horses', who are being criminally exploited by unlikely gangmaster Philip Moss (see Chapters 2 and 4.) The first clue in my mind that all was not well in this enterprise came when the Moss Building firm undercut Eddie Grundy for some small building jobs. This is a new low within the deepening downward curve of Ambridge inequalities. The Grundys are low paid and lack overheads so for a legitimate enterprise to be able to price more competitively would be strange. It is a strong theme in this book that social and cultural capital at birth in the village is defining in terms of both 'serious' life outcomes (see Chapters 11 and 12) as well as how more minor infractions and foibles are viewed – either punitively or with collective indulgence. Kate Madikane has less housing security at his point than both Tracey Horrobin and Emma Grundy but is presented as an annoying free spirit rather than another lone parent victim to the rural housing crisis. The differences are found in invisible but steel-strong class-based codes of conduct, which I will argue are delineated and policed by the matriarchs of the village.

THE SMALL WORLDS OF AMBRIDGE 2020: 'YOU LOT REALLY ARE ALL RELATED, AREN'T YOU?'

Interrogating the small worlds of the village demonstrates that 'Wherever human association is examined, we can see what can be described as thick spots – relatively unchanging clusters or collections of individuals who are linked by frequent interaction and often by sentimental ties' (Freeman &

Webster, 1994, p. 225.) So then, the thick spots, clusters, clans or cliques and their sentimental bonds with one another are the currency of the structure of the village. To view kinship networks as relatively stable, however, belies the possibilities of subtle change over time. The biggest changes to the structure of the village in recent years have been the introduction of forced labour in the building firm of Philip Moss, which serves to underpin the more regular precarity of the Grundys and Horrobins with the criminal exploitation of vulnerable others from beyond the village (see Chapters 2 and 4) and the loss of Home Farm by the Aldridges.

This was plotted impeccably as Jennifer Aldridge's domestic goddess identity was reaching pathological heights with the egregious Albion kitchen: 'Each of Jennifer's parties provides the opportunity for the other characters to play their social roles' (Medland, 2017, p. 354). It also serves to expose the ways in which minor criminal activity and negligence plays out for Aldridges, rather than for Grundys. The framing of an historic dodgy deal, this one many year previously on Brian's part leading to pollution of the River Am, environmental remediation and a huge fine. The fall out resulted in a radical down-sizing and the loss of 'Home' Farm. Alison Hindell, then-editor, confided to *Academic Archers* that they really struggled to ruin the Aldridges since they were so asset-rich, insured and protected (Headlam, 2019c, p. 15).

The poisoning of the Am is even more remarkable as it places Brian on the wrong side of the class divide raised by Steinem in the header quotation for this chapter: 'Rich people plan for three generations, poor people plan for Saturday night' (Steinem, 2019). By burying toxic waste on his own farm, Brian was showing more than merely poor judgement. It was a short-term fix that imperilled his social standing decades later. Short-term thinking is survival thinking, rooted in the stress of poverty, and there is emerging evidence from neuroscience that there are lifelong feedback loops between 'hot' and 'cold' cognition and the multiple relationships between cognition and childhood trauma. Anxiety disorders promote mechanisms associated with harm avoidance across multiple levels of cognition, from perception to attention to learning and executive function – a 'hot' cognitive function which can be both adaptive and maladaptive depending upon the circumstances. This mechanism comes at a cost to other functions such as working memory, but leaves some functions, such as planning, unperturbed. We also highlight a number of cognitive effects that differ across anxiety disorders and threat of shock. These discrepant effects are largely seen in 'cold' cognitive functions involving control mechanisms and may reveal boundaries between adaptive (e.g., response to threat) and maladaptive (e.g., pathological) anxiety (Robinson, Vytal, Cornwell, & Grillon, 2013). Such work, based on the notion that 'the body keeps the score' (Jour, 1994), shows how far negative experiences in early years can resonate for a lifetime. However, there are far more socially derived sources of comparative advantage, and these are rooted in the ways that intergenerational forms of capital are preserved or perish.

KIN-KEEPING AND THE TWIN MATRIARCHIES OF JILL AND PEGGY

The Granny power exercised by the twin matriarchies of Jill Archer and Peggy Woolley is of acute importance in the village. That both are financially secure, rich even, in the case of Peggy, means that there has been acute focus on their socio-emotional wealth preservation strategies and social structure are secured in the transition. Prior to the arrival of Rosie, the tribe of Peggy was the dominant clique in the village partly because Peggy is 10 years older than Jill and largely because her granddaughters, Kate and Helen Archer have several children (albeit both women suffering partnerships and marriages of limited longevity), as did Jon Archer before his death producing the long-lost and chipper Johnny to introduce some hybrid vigour into the Bridge Farm Archer gene pool. The tribe of Peggy now also boasts two conventionally-presented families of Ambridge's fourth generation. Despite the fact that their relationship seems perpetually in peril, James Bellamy and Leonie Snell have a legitimate heir (Mungo Bellamy) as do Iain Craig and Adam Macy (Xander). It has been part of a long-running interest in Queering Ambridge (Pitt, 2019) how profoundly heteronormative the Macy-Craig relationship has become, and by virtue of riding the relationship escalator with all the episodes in the right order they are a conventional nuclear family.

Marital fidelity and the legitimacy of offspring underlying property rights represent the foundational role of the marriage contract as a core function of the elision between property-owning democracy and bourgeois marriage. But not so much in the Home Farm Aldridges. Brian Aldridge has, over four decades in Ambridge, operationalised a highly differentiated set of mating strategies which may have threatened to fragment the Home Farm Aldridge legacy through sub-optimal strategy. Where there are risks, however, to the continuing dominance of the Aldridges in Ambridge it hasn't been Brian's fault. Prior to the arrival of Xander, the underactive mating strategies of the generation of Adam, Debbie Aldridge, Ruairi Donovan, and Alice and Chris Carter was notable. This lack of fecundity is countered by Kate who has two separate families and had been contemplating a fourth child with Jakob Hakansson. Further, the inheritance politics of the Aldridge family partnership will be significantly affected. I have long been frustrated by the seeming caprice with which Peggy's wealth is used to manipulate the younger members of the clan, but the way in which Jack Woolley's fortune is dispersed will be a gift that keeps on giving plot-wise.

HOME AS RITUAL AND NORM

In order to explore the roles of the matriarchies, I have familiarised myself with a new literature on 'kin-keeping' in order to more completely theorise the ways in which forms of capital are transmitted across generations in the village. The role of the Aldridges and Archers in Ambridge has been of settled and bourgeois landowning families. Their connectedness as 'cousins' underpins the routine co-operation necessary for life to run smoothly. However, as has been argued, the principal role of families of this type is as regards their ability to transmit capital across generations. So then, I have been guilty of viewing kin-keeping as a negative and controlling thing, an extension of emotional labour and of the women's work that I wrote about in *Custard, Culverts and Cake* (Headlam, 2019c). I am drawn to accounts which include the non-work work in the lives of women:

> *The work of kinship encompasses a variety of activities, including visits, letters, presents, cards, and telephone calls to kin; services, commodities, and money exchanges among kin; and the organization of holiday gatherings. It also includes the mental or administrative labor of the creation and maintenance of fictive kin ties, decisions to intensify or neglect ties, and the responsibility for monitoring and taking part in mass media and folk discourse concerning family and kinship.*
>
> (Leach & Braithwaite, 1997, p. 3)

Based on the work of Erving Goffman (1956) in the *Presentation of Self in Everyday Life*, feminist scholars Braithwaite and Baxter (1995) identified rituals as communicative events 'involving a structured sequence of symbolic acts in which homage is paid to some sacred object' (p. 179). Rituals function to preserve family identity and to maintain a family's belief system, and participation in rituals is related to the health of a family. Peggy and Jill are undoubtedly the performative matriarchs of Ambridge, active and enthusiastic about weaving ritual structures of both the role and status of their families and of the village itself. Such forms of 'soft power', the numerous and overlapping forms of embodied capital which create the layered norms and conventions of social life, can get particularly spiky in Ambridge when kin-keeping extends to combine with the Ambridge Fairy (see Chapter 12) as a provider of housing, or in sanctioning or gatekeeping for certain forms of romantic partners for their younger relations. Not only has Peggy housed hapless Kate but she has endorsed her relationship with Jakob; similarly, Peggy was keen on the coercive controller Rob Titchener due to superficial class signifiers being prominently displayed – like the bum of a public school baboon.

All these processes are complex because they operate within unstable frameworks and because they are intrinsically reflexive. All these levels interact between each other, and none of them are constant:

> *Just as marriages break and firms go bankrupt, so whole political societies may be recast or split through revolutions, wars, or the dissolution of empires. Individuals swim in waters now benign, now turbulent. Some may flourish in an inherited family niche, while others will starve in the same way. Against those who succeed or fail through transmission, we need to set those who choose to*

migrate in search of a better life, those who move to
escape an economic trap, or those driven to adapt by
the turmoil of revolution, fleeing from persecution or
war, and death. Change originates not only from
above, but equally from below, through the
initiatives of masses of people. Through having fewer
children or more, or through moving, voting with
their feet, they can transform the structures of social
space or demography.

(Mare, 2011, p. 6)

This extended quotation on the role of multigeneration inequalities is wonderfully allusive as regards the role of kin-keeping in fostering positive mentality and attitude. Faced by the same treatment, siblings may flourish or starve. Further, Mare affords agency to those who exercise their right of exit. We have had many long discussions at *Academic Archers* conferences about how far it is possible for women to thrive in Ambridge, and at the present time there does appear to be the exiting of the educated/childless/financially secure: for example, Hazel Woolley, though obstreperous is an independent woman with no interest in the village; Brenda Tucker recently took her talents elsewhere. Other young women have not fared well in terms of their ability to secure informal power bases from where they may transform the structures of social space.

The gendered work of kin-keeping, as well as maintaining informal networks and running families and careers may be just too much for the kin-keepers and civic-minded women of the village. I wrote in *Custard, Culverts and Cake: Academics on Life in The Archers* (Headlam, 2019a) about motivations underpinning voluntary activity exploring the internal and external motivations of women in volunteer, and informal roles are categorised as being characterised by, variously,

Self-Reliance, Solidaristic Activism, Lady Bountiful/NIMBYism
and lastly Benign (p)Maternalism. It may be that it is impossible for younger women to manage kin-keeping and informal
labour and that the village may be the poorer for it.

INCOMING: HOW ROSIE RUTH GRACE ARCHER KILLED THE HEADLAM HYPOTHESIS

When I dreamt it up *The Headlam Hypothesis 'The Archers
are dead long live The Archers'*, it was about the minor
families assuming more and more prominence in Ambridge at
the expense of the Brookfield branch of the line of Dan and
Doris Archer. At this time, their titular heading of the programme was jarring as the Brookfield Archers were all being
flaky in their deliberations to leave the village altogether as
The Route B debacle proposing a subdivision of their land
served as a literal beheading of the farm.

The Headlam Hypothesis was a response to the possibility
of the ravens leaving the tower (as it were.) It is fair to describe
the relationship of David and Ruth Archer as quite rocky over
the years. Despite their closeness as business partners and
husband and wife there has been a restlessness and resentment
expressed and acted upon by Ruth, who often seems miserable
in Ambridge. In essence, *The Headlam Hypothesis* has been
totally refuted by the arrival of baby Rosie. The Archer/
Fairbrother baby imperils *The Headlam Hypothesis* and
shores up the tribe of Jill both *vis à vis* the hitherto larger and
more powerful tribe of Peggy but also as regards the combined
network strength of the non-Archers who had been gathering
in strength by virtue of their multiple connections with one
another. Xander too joins Mungo as contributing to the
Granny power of Jennifer Aldridge.

Five years ago, despite having their name above the door (as it were), the Brookfield Archers - the tribe of Jill – had become a second-order clique within the structure of Ambridge. There were fewer members of the Jill clique than the Peggy one, and they were yet to deliver a fourth generation. Despite this, there were Brookfield Archers occupying much of the prime real estate in Ambridge; their landowning status the clique supported four independent households; Brookfield, Lower Loxley, The Stables and The Bull. It may only have been because Jill is 10 years younger than Peggy that the fourth generation of Brookfield Archers were yet to emerge. Indeed, I wrote that there was little hope of Pip Archer reproducing in the near future: 'the weight of expectation from her parents and grandparent as regards Pip's poor choices of companion make the future of the farm omnipresent in her romantic life' (Headlam, 2017, p. 4). Those complaining on social media about the circumstances of Pip's pregnancy (a second fraternal love triangle?? Please!) are howling in the wind as *The Archers* scriptwriter Keri Davies recently admitted on Twitter that the whole purpose of the Fairbrothers has been this storyline, and Davies (2014) further explains the backstory in a BBC blog. It is absolute genius on the part of the scriptwriters resurrecting this long-forgotten family shoring up the Archers of Brookfield and folding in long-dead connections within the family tree. Rosie by virtue of her Archer/Fairbrother genes at birth becomes the most connected Archer in Ambridge. This was not lost on Jill, whose interest in dynastic matters was far sharper than anyone else's. *Academic Archers* is also keeping a very close watch on the potential for another seemingly dead branch of the family tree, through a highly convoluted plot involving Aunt Laura who went to New Zealand.

OUTGOING: THE *ANNUS HORRIBILIS* OF
THE GRUNDYS

Another area in which network analysis has yielded conclusions which have not proved durable was my presentation at
the 2017 *Academic Archers* conference culminating in the
crowning of Ed Grundy as King of Ambridge: 'Ed (King of
Ambridge) [and] his wife Emma have exceptional brokerage
skills = they could, then, monetise these and create prosperity
and prestige for themselves' (Headlam, 2017).

Networks layered by both kinship ties and by legal and
contractual bonds are undermined by the fact that job security
as a contractor and the power dynamics of the landed families
will always end up trumping the strength of 'weaker' ties. How
far the lives of Ed and Emma – together and separately – have
lives defined by economic precarity is the subject of some
chapters in this volume: Claire Astbury's (Chapter 12)
masterful housing history of Emma Grundy shows the underlying insecurity which at times overwhelms her and Lalage
Cambell (Chapter 3) deconstructs the whole notion of economic and domestic security. Ed's dramatic fall from grace as
Ambridge's king merged into the Grundy *annus horibilis* –
where loss of their patriarch Joe Grundy capped a very rough
few years for the family; William Grundy coping with grief and
life as a widower, and Ed and Emma losing home, livelihood
and marriage after an extremely ill-judged criminal dalliance
with the dodgy Tim Oatey led to a severing of the network of
loose ties which had seemed so propitious previously. Could it
be that the Grundy disadvantage lies in the early death of 'my
Susan', Joe's wife? According to anthropological accounts on
the role of kin-keepers in framing the performance of family
could be at least as significant as their relative financial travails.

These motivations are all seen in the high levels of subtly
gendered activity undertaken in the informal realm (beyond the

structures of family or contractual relationships) whereby community power can truly be viewed as a form of 'women's work.' I would go so far as to describe the kin-keeping activities of Peggy and Jill in Ambridge to be one of policing the boundaries of the various hierarchies of the village, with material as well as emotional consequences for all concerned.

CONCLUSION: THE SMALL WORLDS OF AMBRIDGE 2020

So then, the arrivals of Rosie and Xander and the loss of Joe Grundy are significant because of the effects of their kinship connections. The village is still in thrall to the great Granny power of the twin matriarchies and their role in kin-keeping activities underpinning home and family, the dimensions of informal work and the economic consequences of class in Ambridge. However, due to the temporary nature of these connections, the analysis is only a point in time, and the ways in which all this intersects will land differently as the kaleidoscope of the village shifts and plays out in its patterns over time.

REFERENCES

Braithwaite, & Baxter. (1995). *Engaging theories in interpersonal communication: Multiple perspectives*. (L. A. Baxter & D. O. Braithwaite (Eds.) 2008). Thousand Oaks, CA: SAGE Publications.

Courage, C., & Headlam, N. (2017). Being academic Archers. In C. Courage & N. Headlam (Eds.), *Custard, culverts and cake: Academic Archers on life in Ambridge*. Bingley: Emerald Publishing Limited.

Courage, C., Headlam, N., & Matthews, P. (2017). Introduction to academic Archers: The birth of a new academic community. In C. Courage, N. Headlam, & P. Matthews (Eds.), *The Archers in fact and fiction*. Oxford: Peter Lang.

Davies, K. (2014). The death of Grace Archer. *BBC Blogs*, [online]. Retrieved from https://www.bbc.co.uk/blogs/the-archers/entries/0ca660a8-d03a-3479-9f82-8aeb73da7a69. Accessed on August 30, 2020.

Freeman, L. C., & Webster, C. M. (1994). Interpersonal proximity in social and cognitive space. *Social Cognition*, *12*, 223–247.

Friedman, S., & Laurison, D. (2019). *The class ceiling: Why it pays to be privileged*. Bristol: Policy Press.

Goffman, E. (1956). *The presentation of the self in everyday life*. New York, NY: Doubleday.

Headlam, N. (2017). Kinship networks in Ambridge. In C. Courage & N. Headlam (Eds.), *Custard, Culverts and Cake: Academic Archers on life in Ambridge*. Bingley: Emerald Publishing Limited.

Headlam, N. (2018a). *Can you catch the perpetrator of a hit and run in an ego-net?* Retrieved from https://static1.squarespace.com/static/589f1e875016e176237213e1/t/59fc7bdd0846652dc5c094e9/1509719008189/egonet+matt+blog.pdf. Accessed on August 30, 2020.

Headlam, N. (2018b). The tribes of Peggy and Jill. Retrieved from https://static1.squarespace.com/static/589f1e875016e176237213e1/t/5a721adcc83025b87bb0c983/1517427427404/peggy+jill+2018+blog+final.pdf. Accessed on August 30, 2020.

Headlam, N. (2019a). Women's work?: Civil society net-works for social stability or social change in Ambridge. In C. Courage & N. Headlam (Eds.), *Gender, sex and gossip; women in the Archers*. Bingley: Emerald Publishing Limited.

Headlam, N. (2019b). Interview with Alison Hindell. In C. Courage & N. Headlam (Eds.), *Gender, sex and gossip; women in the Archers*. Bingley: Emerald Publishing Limited.

Headlam, N. (2019c). Introduction. In C. Courage & N. Headlam (Eds.), *Gender, sex and gossip; women in the Archers*. Bingley: Emerald Publishing Limited.

JOUR van der Kolk, B. (1994). The body keeps the score: Memory and the evolving psychobiology of posttraumatic stress. *Harvard Review of Psychiatry*, *1*(5), 253–256.

Leach, M. S., & Braithwaite, D. O. (1996). A binding tie: Supportive communication of family kinkeepers, *Journal of Applied Communication Research*, *24*(3), 200–216. doi:10.1080/00909889609365451

Mare, R. D. (2011). A multigenerational view of inequality. *Demography*, *48*, 1–23.

Medland, A. (2017). Culinary coercion. In C. Courage & N. Headlam (Eds.), *Custard, culverts and cake: Academic Archers on life in Ambridge*. Bingley: Emerald Publishing Limited.

Pitt, B. (2019). What would the neighbours say? In C. Courage & N. Headlam (Eds.), *Custard, culverts and cake: Academic Archers on life in Ambridge*. Bingley: Emerald Publishing Limited.

Robinson, O. J., Vytal, K., Cornwell, B. R. & Grillon, C. (2013). The impact of anxiety upon cognition: Perspectives from human threat of shock studies. *Hum Neurosci*, 7, 203.

Savage, M., Devine, F., Cunningham, N., Taylor, M., Yaojun, L., Le Roux, B. … Miles, A. (2014). A new model of social class? Findings from the BBC's great British class Survey. *Experiment Sociology*, 47(2), 219–250.

Steinem, G. (2019). *The truth will set you free, but first it will piss you off: A lifetime of quotes.* Sydney; London: Murdoch Books.

Section 2

THE FALL OF THE HOUSE OF ALDRIDGE, THE RISE OF THE OPPRESSED GRUNDYS?

3

'IF YOU HAVE SECURITY, ED, THAT IS EVERYTHING': DECONSTRUCTING 'SECURITY' AS A BUFFER AGAINST LIFE'S CHALLENGES

Lalage Cambell

ABSTRACT

This paper presents a case study concerning the recovery of a young woman's wellbeing after a personal crisis in the summer of 2019. The analytical approach used draws on a conceptual model where wellbeing is a balance point between an individual's resources and the challenges they face. Therefore, stable wellbeing is when individuals have the physical, psychological and social resources they need to meet the physical, psychological and or social challenges they face. When individuals have more challenges than resources, the balance dips, along with their wellbeing, and vice versa. After outlining the theoretical base of the model, this paper presents a highly subjective analysis of the challenges faced by and resources available to the young woman in the case study. The daughter of a pig man and a Horrobin, she had worked three jobs in order to purchase a house for her young family. Her plans were precipitously destroyed leading to a breakdown in her marriage. This paper considers her path to recuperation in the aftermath of the crisis with a reference to her notion that 'security is everything.'

THEORETICAL BACKGROUND

Wellbeing is an interesting word; whilst it is commonly invoked by politicians, health and social care professionals, journalists and management, there is rarely a consensual definition. In fact, as we have remarked elsewhere (Dodge, Daly, Huyton, & Sanders, 2012), there is not even agreement on whether the word should be hyphenated. Wellbeing is a critical component of the definition of health given by The World Health Organisation (WHO) in its constitution: 'a state of complete physical, mental and social wellbeing and not merely the absence of disease or infirmity' (WHO, 1946). There is frequently a circularity of definition between 'health' and 'wellbeing' with the occasional addition of other components such as 'happiness' (Diener, 1984) or 'quality of life' (Stratham & Chase, 2010). Such attempts tend to focus on the experience of wellbeing, thereby either enumerating potential dimensions or describing just one. This tendency to confuse components with definitions has made the task of defining wellbeing 'conceptually muddy' (Morrow & Mayall, 2009, p. 221).

It may be that the nebulous nature of the notion is what makes it amendable to being bandied about as a concept, an ideal or, paradoxically, a politicised weapon (NEF, 2011). However, if wellbeing is to be measured, assessed or examined then a clear definition is a prerequisite. The definition my colleagues and I advanced in our paper on the challenge of defining wellbeing (Dodge et al., 2012) has gained considerable traction and is now frequently cited in both academic literature and health promotion materials. This indicates that the definition has an intuitive appeal and is readily understood. We proposed that wellbeing is conceptualised as the balance point between the resources available to, and the challenges faced by, an individual. In this context, resources and challenges comprise the physical, the psychological and the social. When either challenges or resources outweigh the other, the equilibrium is out of kilter and wellbeing is adversely affected.

The proposal that equilibrium is critical to wellbeing was first identified by Herzlich (1973) in her qualitative research into people's perception of health. Herzlich's respondents described equilibrium as an ideal state that it was quite rare and to be prized. In contrast, Headey and Wearing (1991) described the notion of dynamic equilibrium. They posited that for most of the time our subjective wellbeing is relatively stable because of this dynamic equilibrium between stock levels and income flows and demands and suggested that equilibrium is disturbed when external forces require a person deviating from their normal pattern of activities. Thus, wellbeing is dependent on three components: prior equilibrium, recent events and life events.

This theory was extended by Cummins (2010) who described homoeostasis as the state which may be affected

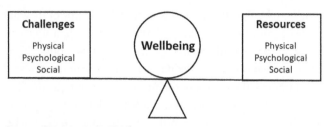

Source: (Dodge et al., 2012).

Fig. 3.1. The Definition of Wellbeing.

by incoming challenges. Cummins draws on the notion of a set point theory meaning wellbeing is stable when there are no challenges. Minor challenges will have only marginal effect on subjective wellbeing, but a serious challenge can overwhelm it entirely. This idea is also found in the work of Csikszentmihalyi (2002) who argued that for wellbeing it is necessary to consider the balance of challenges and existing skills. A similar theory is evident in Hendry and Kloep's (2002) lifespan model. This proposes that an individual grows through a continuing cycle of overcoming challenges and that process builds resources. Drawing on all these components, we propose the model below to illustrate our definition of wellbeing (Fig. 3.1).

CASE STUDY: EMMA GRUNDY

This paper will invoke our balance model of wellbeing as a framework for understanding the trajectory of Emma Grundy. What follows is a highly subjective assessment of Emma's circumstances over the period of the summer of 2019 to the end of Ambridge BC (Ambridge Before COVID-19).

The Crisis – 2019

Emma Grundy, *née* Carter, was born on 7 July 1984. In the summer of 2019, she and her second husband, Ed Grundy (the younger brother of her first husband, Will Grundy) had been living with his parents and were in the process of purchasing their own house. Despite the somewhat unorthodox and complex nature of these internecine Grundy relationships, there were times when this was a harmonious arrangement. However, it was a fine balancing act that was easily upset by external events.

Both Ed and Emma took multiple jobs in order to maximise their saving for the new house. Unfortunately, when Emma was told by Peggy Woolley that her services as a cleaner were no longer needed (5 April), Ed decided to moonlight with the somewhat dubious Tim Oatey (19 April), a job offer he had previously declined because he considered it suspect. The job in question turned out to be hauling unregistered and illegal chemicals. Unfortunately, a heated exchange between Ed, Will and Tim alerted Adam Macy, Ed's employer, to this nefarious activity, and Ed was summarily dismissed (26 July). Loss of job meant loss of mortgage and consequently loss of the longed-for house. On realising the devastating consequences of this chain of events, Emma was heard to wail (2 August): 'If you have security, Ed, that is everything' (BBC Radio 4, 2019a). We see here that, for Emma in this moment of crisis, security was synonymous with bricks and mortar. The idea that owning your own house is essential for wellbeing is linked to what Gurney (1999) describes as the normalisation of home ownership, a very British value. For Emma, losing the house is more than just a disappointment; it signifies a cataclysmic loss so great that it threatens every aspect of her future life.

Having set this context, this paper will now review the challenges that beset Emma and the resources upon which she drew throughout the latter part 2019 in each of the three spheres: physical, psychological and social. The aim is to identify what security really means for the wellbeing of this Ambridge resident.

Challenges and Resources: Physical Sphere

Initially it might be tempting to assume that Emma's problems arose entirely from a physical challenge, namely losing a house. Bricks and mortar are as physical as any commodity could be. However, Emma and Ed have never lived in a house of their own. They initially lived in what was described as a damp and, presumably, somewhat elderly caravan. They have since lived with her parents in Ambridge View, which Ed found quite challenging for some reason, and latterly with her in-laws at Grange Farm, where both were more relaxed, although still hankering after a house of their own. Having both sets of parents living in the village, in houses large enough to accommodate the next generation of the family if required, provided a safety net for the young couple. Therefore, losing the house on the new Beechwood develop-ment did not make them homeless. In terms of the wellbeing model, Emma's physical resources appear to counter-balance this challenge.

Acknowledging that purchasing their own house was going to stretch them financially, Emma had taken on an extra job in the chicken factory on top of her work with Fallon Rogers in the tearoom and cleaning for Peggy Woolley. By anyone's standards, this makes for a demanding lifestyle and potentially a physical challenge but one that Emma claimed to be able and willing to undertake. Such was her desire to own a house of their own, she was ready to tackle any physical challenge driven on by the tantalising lure of the perceived security of bricks and mortar.

Challenges and Resources: Psychological Sphere

It was not the physical impact of losing the house that devastated Emma; it was the crumbling of a dream. In order to understand the impact this had, we need to consider her background. Born Emma Carter, her family of origin could best be described as working class but with aspirations, at least on her mother's side. Her father, Neil Carter, is a pig man by training and trade who in February 2018, much to his own surprise, was appointed to a management position at Justin Elliott's new pig unit at Berrow Farm. This change in status has been a constant source of pride and delight for his wife, Susan Carter. She characteristically refers to her husband as having 'executive status in pig management' (BBC Radio 4, 2020b), or more colourfully, after excessive consumption of 'ron miel', she announced that he was 'high up in pigs' (BBC Radio 4, 2020a).

Susan was born a Horrobin, an extreme social disadvantage in this village given the family's uncertain reputation. Disparaging comments about this family are commonplace throughout the village, and many of Ambridge's leading socialites are reluctant to have any association with them (BBC Radio 4, 2010). Susan has done her best to distance herself from her roots and for many years nursed a desire to own her own bricks and mortar. This was eventually achieved when she and Neil built a house with the help of Mike Tucker. House ownership was a *leitmotif* of Emma's childhood, so it is little wonder that she cherished the same ambition. To this day, Susan remains openly aspirational in many respects and, whilst Emma sometimes teases her about her snobbishness, it is evident that she has not entirely escaped its influence.

Equally relevant to understanding the impact of the broken dream is Emma's role on the Parish Council. Two years previously, she had been elected to that role (23 November 2017) where she pressed for the establishment of an affordable housing development. It is unclear to what extent her joining the council was prompted by a sense of civic duty; it would be uncharitable to suggest (although some have) that it was born purely of self-interest. Once the anticipated development of such housing was agreed, she and Ed were quick to put their names down for a dwelling.

Given how long the dream of house ownership had held sway with Emma, how hard she had worked towards it and how physically and emotionally exhausted she must have been, it is not surprising that the psychological challenge of losing the dream when it had appeared within reach was so devastating. At that point, she did not have the psychological resources to cope. We can see this in her initial desperate response as she sought to borrow money by opportunistically approaching those in the village whom she perceived might be able to help (29 July). What she expected to achieve from this is unclear. Did she really believe, as she stated, that if she could borrow enough, she could increase their potential deposit and therefore the building society might relent and permit a lower mortgage? Or was her underlying hope that someone would be able to lend them funds equivalent to that previously available from the building society? The most likely explanation is that she, herself, did not think this through – that she acted on instinct at the prospect of losing the mortgage offer. Her desperate actions, however, presented a new challenge as this inappropriate begging showed no sense of dignity or self-respect. This was a fact that she eventually acknowledged and then had to live with the realisation of how she had behaved.

Then, as their personal crisis unfolded in the first week of August, Emma's predicament deteriorated further when Ed, feeling hopeless and helpless about their situation, terminated their relationship. He felt responsible for letting her down and trashing her dreams and believed that he would never be able to provide her with what she wanted most: a house of her own. If Emma was struggling to cope previously this further blow changed desperation to despair. Over the next few weeks, Emma exhibited signs of reactive depression (Showraki, 2019), disengaging with family and social relationships, disordered eating and sleeping and spending long periods of time alone in her bedroom in Ambridge View. It was evident that at this point, with the loss of the dream, of her reputation and of her marriage, her psychological challenges severely, but unsurprisingly, outweighed her psychological resources.

Challenges and Resources: Social Sphere

Arguably the biggest impact of this crisis was manifested in Emma's social relationships, which presented challenges on many fronts. Firstly, her relationship with her husband has been wrecked by events. He had been truly the love of her life even though she initially married his brother. Already, before that first wedding, she had formed a badly timed relationship with Ed which survived a series of dramatic events of Chekhovian proportions, which is more than can be said of the relationship between the two brothers, themselves. She had to face down her parents to be with him as they disapproved strongly in the early days. For him to say that their relationship was over, after all the twists and turns that had beset them, was a crushing blow. Learning to live life without Ed was arguably the biggest challenge she faced. Its devastating effect was clear in this outpouring (6 September):

> *I try and imagine the future and it's just hard to know how it will be without him .... We've been working together for so long, both of us, with this one dream of our own family in our own home. It's all either of us have wanted. Everything we've done, we did because of that and now it's all been ripped away.... It's like my whole world has fallen to bits around me and I don't even know who I am anymore. ~It's all so hopeless~.*

(BBC Radio 4, 2019c)

There are other relationships that present a challenge to Emma after the crisis. It may seem a relatively trivial point in comparison, but she had to face the rest of the village. Given how closely knit we understand this microcosm of English rural life to be, all the villagers, heard and unheard (see Chapter 17), were expecting her to move into Beechwood. She had, after all, not been hesitant in telling everyone of their plans. They were also likely to be shocked (and interested) in the breakup of the marriage. Such calamities are grist to the mill of village gossip. On the plus side, most village gossip usually passes through, or originates from, the village post-mistress who is uncharacteristically silent when it comes to her own daughter. Indeed, she is intolerant of others whom she wrongly believes to be gossiping about Emma (18 August). Although often perceived as a gossip, Susan prefers to think of herself as 'naturally interested in the world around her' (BBC Radio 4, 2019b). Susan became temporarily more cautious after a surprising drubbing down by her long-suffering hus-band about gossiping and being spiteful (16 August). This was an unexpected but thoroughly deserved diatribe that was caused mugs of chamomile tea to be lifted in cheery acknowledgement in many households. It may be assumed that in the immediate aftermath of this and to restore marital harmony, there was a need for generous portions of chilli.

Moreover, Emma had made a bad situation worse by importuning Jim Lloyd, Fallon Rogers and Peggy Woolley amongst others, a fool-hardy action which she had to live down. Whilst village opinion may seem an inconsequential issue, Emma is her mother's daughter and may not always be able to dismiss entirely how she is perceived by others. Facing the village after such daunting changes in her circumstances presented Emma with another stressful social challenge.

What social resources are available to Emma at this point in her life story? As a result of the break with Ed, along with George and Keira Grundy, Emma returned to live at Ambridge View and therefore had the support of her parents. Her father, Neil, is the quieter of the two, a bit of a worrier who lacks the aspirations manifest in his wife. Neil adores his daughter and wants to support her in his gentle, understated way. His attempts are occasionally undermined by the well-meaning but sometimes clumsy, and occasionally thoughtless, intervention of his wife. In the immediate aftermath of the crisis, Susan, bent on retribution for her daughter's wretched state, did not appear to Emma to be a receptive confidante. After Neil's chastisement for spite, however, Susan's demeanour changed, and the mother and daughter relationship harmonised. It was to a warm and sympathetic Susan that Emma eventually managed to pour out her feelings of grief and loss.

Another key figure in supporting Emma in the early days was Will. Will had troubles of his own concerning his children and stepchildren and for a while he and Emma found comfort in each other's company. Unfortunately, this led eventually to Will making an unwanted overture, much to her horror (27 August) and that triggered a dramatic series of events that are beyond the scope of this paper. However, given the emotional load that Emma was already carrying, this additional story line was yet another challenge for the poor, beleaguered woman. As the autumn drew on, Emma found that she could once again talk to Clarrie Grundy, who is simultaneously her erstwhile and current mother-in-law. The two women agreed that they missed each other's company (7 October) and were soon united in mourning the loss of the aged Joe (10 October). In the run up to Christmas, the two were heard baking mince pies together, bonding over the pastry and merrily united in their distaste for the culinary efforts that Ed and Will had thrown together (8 December). This represented a return to a previous harmonious co-existence that Clarrie had been lamenting only days earlier (5 December). By this stage, too, Emma was managing to have cordial conversations with Ed and had relented from her earlier proclamation that she did not want anything to do with him or his family ever again (3 September).

However, there was one social relationship that made the biggest difference for her throughout this trying period and that was with her aunt, the redoubtable Tracy Horrobin. Dubbed by someone as the 'tart with heart of gold', Tracy's approach to supporting her niece was strikingly different from that of her sister. This caused some tension between the Horrobin sisters but, undaunted, Tracy persisted in her straight-talking, no nonsense, feet first style of counselling. It was not always successful; when she enumerated Ed's faults, it simply reminded Emma of how much she missed him (15 August). But Emma found her aunt refreshing and began to accept her company at a time when she was otherwise choosing to be alone. Initially, Emma was prepared to discuss her feelings with Tracy when she refused to with her own mother, putting Susan's nose distinctly out of joint. Tracy believed that Emma should throw herself into having a good time as she was single again, but Emma was resistant. Although she does not always accept her aunt's advice, she did seem to find comfort with her in the early post-crisis days.

There are other villagers, voiced and unvoiced, from whom Emma could have sought support. As a Grundy, asking help of any member of the Archer family, allegedly the Grundy's oppressors (see Chapter 1), was an unlikely option. Throughout her trials and tribulations, Emma did not seem to turn to the friends of her own age group. It might have been different if sister-in-law Nic Grundy was still alive. There are other Ambridge residents, however, whom she might have approached. In the past, a young woman has found Lynda Snell to have an unexpectedly gracious ear and absorbent shoulder, despite an evident nasal drip. Usha Franks might have been able to offer legal advice, had she not lost her voice. A similar affliction has affected Kathy Perks who otherwise might have been able to sympathise with Emma given her own complex history of personal relationships. Even Sabrina Thwaite might have provided some comfort with her experience of being the subject of uncharitable (largely female) gossip about which she has stoically never been heard to utter a word of complaint. With the members of two families on which to draw for solace, arguably Emma has her own rich stock of social resources and needed to look no further.

Regaining Balance – 2020

As the year had drawn to its close it was evident that Emma had begun to show signs of returning equilibrium, and thereby developing a limited sense of wellbeing. Although stable, Emma seemed to be keeping a relatively low profile in the early months of 2020, but then on 4 March she stunned Ed by suggesting that they need to set about getting a divorce. It is believed that this statement caused one of the greatest number of stitches ever simultaneously dropped across the land. Tracy was equally horrified by this when she learned of it four days later. She was busy trying to persuade Emma of the error she was making when an explosion at Grey Gables interrupted their conversation and the subsequent fallout monopolised all discourse for weeks.

It was another month before Emma was heard to tell Ed that she did not want a divorce; far from it, she wanted them to get back together (6 April). His refusal, on the basis that nothing had changed, was yet another challenge for her to face. Whilst she was initially saddened by this rejection, this time it did not last long. Recent events may have provided her with a degree of resilience, a resource that can be a combination of personal characteristic and learned process (Hunter & Warren, 2015). It was just three days later (9 April) that once again the glorious Tracy intervened. Tracey told Emma to buck her ideas up and not to settle for 'no' as an answer from Ed. We began to suspect that this had had the desired effect when on 15 April she told Tracy that she had a plan to leave Ambridge View, and then the following day she asked Ed about using some of their savings as she planned to move. Our suspicions were confirmed when directly before COVID-19 hit Ambridge, Emma and Ed were together again in a mobile home of their own at Grange Farm. The resolution for Emma is, indeed, the home of their own that she had always wanted, but, in the end, it was not bricks and mortar but, presumably, pre-painted aluminium panels.

Emma's initial pre-occupation with owning the Beech-wood house was founded in the belief that homeownership was not just a pre-requisite for, but also a guarantee of, future happiness. If Emma had stopped to consider others in her village, she might have realised that this is not the case. There were two contemporaneous examples on which she could have drawn. Emma needed to have looked no further than her brother-in-law and ex-husband, Will Grundy. Thanks to his inheritance, he owns a house of his own (Number 1 The Green) which he did not even need so he rented it out. Will's wellbeing had been severely upset by the death of his wife, Nic, although it had already experienced a severe wobble when Emma left him for his brother. Will was in a wretched state in the summer of 2019 as Emma came to realise yet his bricks and mortar were no panacea.

At the same time that Emma's troubles came to a head, Jim Lloyd was experiencing trials of his own. In most respects, these two individuals are opposites. Emma is young, if not poorly educated then certainly under-educated, lacking material resources or financial backing. Jim is old, highly educated with no financial worries, a healthy income, a house of his own which he has subsequently begun to extend, suggesting no shortage of capital. Emma's crisis is a sudden and unpredicted turn of events when her dreams of homeownership are shattered. Jim's crisis dates from historical abuse, successfully suppressed over decades until coming face-to-face with the perpetrator. His material security could not insulate him against such trauma. The only common contextual factor is both are living in multi-generation households. What helped them both to come to terms with their challenges was the support of their nearest and dearest.

CONCLUSION

It is fitting that this story came to fruition after nine uncomfortable months for Emma, Ed and the children. Emma faced physical, psychological and social challenges, and the notional combined weight of these challenges inevitably upset the equilibrium, damaging her wellbeing. This paper contends that it was the extensive social resources that were available to her that eventually counterbalanced the challenges and facilitated her recovery. Emma was right when she said that security was everything. But what Emma came to realise over the course of Ambridge BC is that, for her, security is not bricks and mortar; it is family.

REFERENCES

BBC Radio 4. (2010). *The Archers*. 2 August 2010 [online]. Retrieved from https://www.bbc.co.uk/programmes/b00t6gzh. Accessed on August 28, 2020.

BBC Radio 4. (2019a). *The Archers*. 2 August 2019 [online]. Retrieved from https://www.bbc.co.uk/programmes/m00076 np. Accessed on August 28, 2020.

BBC Radio 4. (2019b). *The Archers*. 21 August 2019 [online]. Retrieved from https://www.bbc.co.uk/programmes/ m0007qf6. Accessed on August 28, 2020.

BBC Radio 4. (2019c). *The Archers*. 6 September 2019 [online]. Retrieved from https://www.bbc.co.uk/pro-grammes/m000843b. Accessed on August 28, 2020.

BBC Radio 4. (2020a). *The Archers*. 2 June 2020 [online]. Retrieved from https://www.bbc.co.uk/programmes/ m000jmmz. Accessed on August 28, 2020.

BBC Radio 4. (2020b). *The Archers*. 4 June 2020 [online]. Retrieved from https://www.bbc.co.uk/programmes/ m000jnb5. Accessed on August 28, 2020.

Csikszentmihalyi, M. (2002). *Flow: The classic work on how to achieve happiness*. London: Rider Books.

Cummins, R. (2010). Subjective wellbeing, homeostatically protected mood and depression: A synthesis. *Journal of Happiness Studies, 11*, 1–17.

Diener, E. (1984). Subjective well-being. *Psychological Bulletin, 95*, 542–575.

Dodge, R., Daly, A., Huyton, J., & Sanders, L. D. (2012). The challenge of defining wellbeing. *The International Journal of Wellbeing, 2*(3), 222–235.

Gurney, C. M. (1999). Pride and Prejudice: Discourses of normalisation in public and private accounts of home ownership. *Housing Studies, 14*(2), 163–183.

Headey, B. W., & Wearing, A. J. (1991). Subjective well-being: A stocks and flows framework. In F. Strack, M. Argyle, & N. Schwarz (Eds.), *International series in experimental social psychology, Vol. 21. Subjective wellbeing – an interdisciplinary perspective* (pp. 49–73). Oxford: Pergamon Press.

Hendry, L. B., & Kloep, M. (2002). *Lifespan development: Resources, challenges and risks*. London: Thomson Learning.

Herzlich, C. (1973). *Health and Illness – a social psychological analysis*. London: Academic Press.

Hunter, B., & Warren, L. (2015). Caring for ourselves: The key to resilience. In S. Byrom, & S. Downe (Eds.), *The roar behind the silence* (pp. 111–115). London: Pinter & Martin Ltd.

Morrow, V., & Mayall, B. (2009). What is wrong with children's well-being in the UK? Questions of meaning and measurement. *Journal of Social Welfare and Family Law, 31*(3), 217–229.

NEF. (2011). *The practical politics of wellbeing*. London: New Economics Foundation.

Showraki, M. (2019). Reactive depression: Lost in translation! *The Journal of Nervous and Mental Disease, 207*(9), 755–759.

Stratham, J., & Chase, E. (2010). *Childhood wellbeing – a brief overview*. London: Childhood Wellbeing Research Centre.

World Health Organisation. (1946). *Who we are*. Retrieved from https://www.who.int/about/who-we-are/constitution. Accessed on August 28, 2020.

4

'FEEDING THE HORSES': MODERN SLAVERY, THE DARK SIDE OF CONSTRUCTION HIDDEN IN PLAIN SIGHT IN AMBRIDGE

Nicola Headlam

ABSTRACT

The chapter explores how the recent storyline about modern slavery has landed in Ambridge, commending the writers and producers for the job they have done in engaging NGOs and pressure groups active in this area. It situates the plight of 'The Horses' as hidden in plain sight and probes the dark side of this important social issue in the context of how far the systematic exploitation of vulnerable people provides a ground floor within a profoundly unequal economy. Modern slavery speaks of a wider form of neoliberal necropolitics – in which logics of accumulation and hierarchies are played out on the bodies of workers. In this form of political economy social and emotional vulnerability and economic pre-carity combine together, trapping those unable to escape exploitation. It explored the policy context for the Modern Slavery Act and the assessment of how many people are enslaved in the UK. I also make the link from the extreme nature of modern slavery and connections with extractive and abusive employment situations throughout the economy. While Modern Slavery is an extreme form of precarity, where people are controlled and forced to work, scholarship on precarity shows us that it is a spectrum disorder, where economic aban-donment pushes people away from a liveable life.

> *Gavin (agitated): That's not how some people will see it, Dad...They'll say they are slaves.*
> *Philip (growls): Don't use that word.*
>   (*The Archers*, broadcast 22 May 2020)

Construction is a bipolar industry. On the public side, we create inspirational buildings, pushing the boundaries of architecture and technology; solving ever more difficult challenges. The dark side – the systematic exploitation of millions of vulnerable workers – is rarely acknowledged, even by the clients and multinationals that commission and create our shiny new cities. The sector is rife with human rights abuses. Bonded labour, delayed wages, abysmal working and living conditions, withholding of passports and lim-itations of movement are all forms of modern slavery. The business models must take a large part of the blame: the global trend towards outsourcing and cut-price contracting makes it easy for main contractors to duck out of their responsibilities. The plight of the most vulnerable gets lost among the long and complex supply chains (Blythe, Chartered Institute of Builders (CIOB), 2019).

I.

The Gangmasters Labour Authority has a chilling public information film about recruiting 'unfree' workers, *Trading*

the Horses (2019). In it a female voice describes how easy it is
to attract the vulnerable from drug rehab, homeless shelters
and prisons. *The Archers* has shown bravery in highlighting
this issue with such a long buildup (extended by the COVID-19
lockdown) and Philip growing in the village as a 'decent bloke'
despite his side-line as a gangmaster and exploiter of modern
slaves. It was telling that in exploring the truth underpinning
the storyline I have learnt some truly horrible things about the
dark side and how routine the exploitation of workers can be.
As the quotation from the chair of the CIOB above shows, in
the contemporary incarnation of the very guilds and trades
organisations which would have secured decent pay and conditions within early mercantilist capitalism, there are the
insidious tentacles of slavery within business models which
squeeze margins at every point in the supply chain. In
exploring how and why 'The Horses' have ended up in
Ambridge I followed the trail into the campaigning activities of
various non-governmental organisations (NGOs) and pressure
groups who have been highly effective in bringing these elements of the black and grey economy to light. However, this
chapter argues that the prevalence of modern slavery speaks
of a wider form of neoliberal necropolitics – in which logics of
accumulation and hierarchies are played out on the bodies of
workers. In this form of political economy social and
emotional vulnerability and economic precarity combine
together, trapping those unable to escape exploitation. Victims
may be of either gender, be British or from elsewhere and fall
through all the cracks and safeguards upon which we all rely. I
salute the scriptwriters for their careful examination of this
horrible corner of the economy, the backs of those upon whom
prosperity is built.

II.

As I Googled 'what are the signs of modern slavery?', the algo-rithm in my computer offered me the earlier Archers-prompted searches 'what are the signs of coercive control?' and 'what are the signs of sepsis?' The prompts made me smile, the big meaty public information storylines to have hit Ambridge in the past few years. All set up within long-standing characters, vast amounts of public information imparted and the inevitable tussle between credulity as regards characterisation or in service of the drama. As always, when deploying 'issues' the script-writers engage with the relevant pressure groups, victims' advocacy and NGOs in order to anchor the storyline. In this case they consulted the charity Hope for Justice for pointers on how to realistically portray modern slavery. Here their Chief Exec-utive Officer (CEO) explains their fundamental mission: 'Hope for Justice works with all victims of human trafficking. Whether it's a young girl sold for sex again and again in the city where she grew up or a father who's travelled overseas trying to support his family at home, we believe in the incredible value of every life.' (Cooley, 2019).

It is clear then that such sensitive social issues are researched and prepared for, such as it was in the example of the slow burn that the business methods of Philip's building firm are questionable. The reveal, cited above, that Philip and Gavin were colluding in using forced labour followed the accidental explosion in the kitchen at Grey Gables. Blake, the (then-nameless) worker on the spot had ignited a gas grill while using flammable chemicals as he was working on an empty stomach. 'The Horses', it emerged, are three vulnerable previously street homeless young men who the Mosses use as an unfree source of labour. They are British, with English as their first language, though talk with hesitancy and a lack of fluidity. They are highly vulnerable and have been 'rescued' from the ever-present dangers of rough sleeping. They are housed and fed by the Mosses (in this instance, not enough) and have been manipulated by them into believing that they should be grateful.

The International Labour Organisation (ILO, 2020) divides the issues into three broad categories: *unfree recruitment*, a deceptive recruitment, when a person is recruited with false promises about work and employment conditions, content or legality of employment contract; *forced recruitment*, when someone is forced to work for the employer against their will; and *work and life under duress*, an excessive volume of work, tasks that are beyond what can reasonably be expected within the framework of national labour law, situations of coercion, degrading living conditions; limitations on freedom, and forced overtime; impossibility of leaving an employer, being excessively dependent on one employer, use of threat or financial penalty that make it impossible to leave, and confiscation of identity papers/passport and travel documents. As the storyline was developed within Ambridge there was a major policy change in the EU and the Modern Slavery Act of 2015 shone a torch into this murkiest of corners of economic exploitation in the UK.

Modern slavery is where one person controls another by exploiting a vulnerability. It is often linked with human trafficking, where a person is forced into a service against their will – usually forced work or prostitution. The control can be physical, financial or psychological, which is defined as of four main types: *sexual exploitation*, a person trafficked for sex may be controlled by violence, threats, substance abuse, deception or grooming, with extreme physical or psychological domination; *forced labour*, work done under the threat of a penalty such as violence or harm to family, where victims are often further controlled by debt bondage; *domestic servitude*, when a person is forced to provide services with the obligation to live on or in a property without the possibility of changing those circumstances; and *organ harvesting*, a person who is trafficked and specifically chosen for the harvesting of organs or tissues, such as kidneys, liver etc. without consent, to be sold.

The Mosses' 'Horses' (Blake, Kenzie and Jordan) are victims of forced labour practices, and while not having to sell organs or being sexually exploited, their bodies and labour are being controlled under threat. These are the key signs, according to a Home Office–backed website: those being kept as slaves might have their movements restricted; often look injured and malnourished; have a lack of belongings; and avoid eye contact and are reluctant to talk to strangers.

Thinking about how these signs emerged within Ambridge, we see those being kept as slaves might have their movements restricted. It is not normal to never be able to leave the house on your own, or always having to follow strict instructions on where you are allowed to go and who you can talk to, but that is the reality for some people. This means those living like this may have a lack of knowledge of the area where they live and work. They may also be collected or dropped off to work at very unusual times to avoid being seen by members of the public. There is no question that transportation to and from sites was always controlled by Philip and Gavin. The constant vigilance associated with wrongdoing of this nature put both men constantly on edge. There was the time when, celebrating the completion of work on the playground, 'the lads' were invited to the pub as a thank you. Philip was panicky and evasive and made a series of excuses. We have no idea about the mental map of Ambridge in the minds of Blake, Kenzie and Jordan, but in order to keep them dependant it is unlikely that they have a clear picture of the lie of the land.

Some slaves are physically abused as a means of control, so regular bruising and injuries could suggest there are problems.

Victims are generally poorly cared for and living in over-crowded, dirty accommodation and given very little food which can lead to them appearing malnourished and ill. Although there was some superficial dispute between Philip and Prof Jim Lloyd concerning the building work being done on Jim's house, this was in the context of the fallout of Jim's childhood sexual exploitation coming to light. I am convinced that with emotions running high the Professor recognised the victimhood of 'The Horses'. Whether or not he was able to articulate it clearly or access it on a conscious level the outward expression of lack of care, illness or weakness would have broadcast clearly for Jim Lloyd and made him feel uneasy.

Further, a lack of belongings. We're not talking about not owning the latest smartphone but having items such as passports and personal identification taken from them to stop them having freedom to leave and work elsewhere. They may also wear the same clothes every day and these could be dirty and unsuitable for the weather or their work. I can't recall the clothes being openly discussed, but we can assume they must be scruffy. Lastly, avoiding eye contact and reluctance to talk to strangers. Victims may have been told lies about who they can trust or have been threatened by the people who are controlling them, resulting in them being unsure about who they should believe. A reluctance to seek help doesn't mean they don't want to; they might fear deportation or violence to them or their family. These behaviours came to the fore in the aftermath of the explosion, we heard numerous bullying interchanges and 'scripts' being agreed for what Blake was allowed to say and to whom. Blake was nervous at all times as was subject to a combination of threats and inducements to 'stick to the story'

but appeared anxious and panicky around all authority figures, from nurses to policemen.

III.

'Official' assessments of how many people are enslaved in the
UK vary widely. There have only been national statistics on
modern slavery since March 2020, and there are clear challenges in gathering statistics about such covert practices.
Victims are often hidden away, may be unable to leave their
situation or may not come forward because of fear or shame.
However, despite this many argue that modern slaves are
hidden in plain sight, in car washes, nail bars, in agriculture
and in the construction industries. Some public policy interventions focus on these settings, such as *The Safe Car Wash*
app, a tool that will enable the largest community intelligence
gathering exercise ever attempted in the UK. The data from
the app are shared with the National Crime Agency and the
Gangmasters and Labour Abuse Authority, two law enforce-
ment agencies who are leading on efforts to stamp out modern
slavery across the UK.

It is notable that the scriptwriters chose the setting of the
building trade, as such practices are also rife in farming itself.
Of course, the dilemma of showing modern slavery in the food
supply chain is that the main farms in Ambridge are family
businesses. Although they may suffer a dose of snobbery from
Jennifer Aldridge, the seasonal workers at Home Farm have
always been portrayed as well organised and powerful.
Introducing coercion right into the bosom of the main village
families may have been too much for regular listeners (the
same thing is levelled at portrayals of rape and sexual violence,
such things happen but perpetrators are 'from outside' – see,
Bilby, Chapter 11).

IV.

From a working baseline of 16,000 modern slaves in the UK in 2016, international NGO Unseen grabbed headlines by radically revising the estimate up by 10 times to 113,000. Statistics must of course be treated with caution as the covert nature of modern slavery defies official statistics. Since the Modern Slavery Act was made law there have been increases in criminal prosecutions. The Modern Slavery Helpline received a 68% increase in calls and submissions in the year ending December 2018, compared with the previous year and there were 5,144 modern slavery offences recorded by the police in England and Wales in the year ending March 2019, an increase of 51% from the previous year. Collecting legal evidence for modern slavery offences can be difficult, as discussed above, and the cases are among the most challenging and complex to prosecute. For example, there were 205 suspects of modern slavery flagged cases referred from the police to the Crown Prosecution Service (CPS) for a charging decision in England and Wales in the year ending March 2019, and over two-thirds (68%) of modern slavery related CPS prosecutions in England and Wales resulted in a conviction in the year ending March 2019. Modern slavery can affect anyone in society, with victims being exploited in a number of ways.

Almost one in four of those escaping are UK nationals like the Ambridge Horses. This shows that people are not only trapped by passports or lack of language skills, but that other, more complex vulnerabilities are in play. The scriptwriters had the clues 'hidden within plain sight' that there was something rotten in the employment practices of Moss and Son. However the extreme nature of modern slavery ought not to inure us to other forms of economic exploitation in Ambridge. There are profoundly extractive and abusive employment situations throughout the economy and once one scratches the surface of any supply chain the definitions and distinctions between the symbolic violence of the food system greatly muddy moral positions.

V.

While modern slavery is an extreme form of precarity, where people are controlled and forced to work, scholarship on precarity shows us that it is a spectrum disorder, where economic abandonment pushes people away from a liveable life. As we reach for descriptors on intensified social marginalization, the concept of precarity has come to name 'the politically induced condition in which certain populations suffer from failing social and economic networks... becoming differentially exposed to injury, violence, and death' (Butler, 2006, p. 25). Precarity has its roots in good old-fashioned economic exploitation (how far are Fagin's pickpockets different from Blake, Kenzie and Jordan?) and is further weaponised by the prevailing necropolitics of late capitalism (Mbembe, 2003) where some populations are made more grievable than others. Life is not valued for itself within the global circuits of exchange and stretched supply chains of the present moment. Or, that there is little equivalence between the lives of the consumers, voters and tax-payers within established democracies and the 'others' more marginal souls; economic migrants, the trafficked, the unfree, the sweatshop workers, the precariously housed and those wholly reliant on others. Within contemporary debates the nature of 'bare life' and of the 'cultural politics of disposability'. At times this logic produces apathy toward the suffering of others, as if they somehow deserve it, and dislodges responsibilities to care from broader social, political and economic institutions. In other instances, it produces forms of liberal empathy in which those with wealth and privilege engage in forms of humanitarianism that maintain, rather than challenge, the status quo. Examining the way precarity is created and how it is lived is therefore not only a means of critiquing the zones of exception on the margins of societies, but also a path to understanding how those who are thrown into precarious circumstances find ways to live otherwise. Henry Giroux (2006) accuses that the hyper-neoliberal 'racial state', since Reagan, has silently governed in the interests of 'Corporate America' at the expense of human lives by utilizing the repressive power of colour-blind ideology to implement policy reforms which increasingly silently neglect disadvantaged populations further into the margins, thereby permitting their disposability (letting them die) (p. 174). Thacker argues how it (bare life) is 'constantly rendered in its precariousness, a life that is always potentially under attack and therefore always an exceptional life' (2011, p. 158). In Thacker's *Necrologies* (2011), classical theorizations of what was called the 'body politic' are used to reconsider what we now think of as 'biopolitics', emphasizing the conceptual death of the body-political order and its recurrent resurrections. Thacker ultimately posits the contemporary biopolitical notion of what he calls 'whatever-life,'

> *...in which biology and sovereignty, or medicine and politics, continually inflect and fold onto each other. Whatever-life is the pervasive potential for life to be specified as that which must be protected, that which must be protected against, and as those forms of "nonhuman life."*

> (2011, p 160)

Themes which have crossed the Atlantic and landed in Paul Mason's (2019) polemic arguing that a radical defence of the

non-human – markets and machines – was necessary in
re-evaluating global humanism:

> *This is no longer a once-in-fifty years economic crisis,*
> *nor simply the fraying of the post-war global order.*
> *It is an all-out attack on values that have*
> *underpinned Western societies for 400 years. It can*
> *be fought, if we are prepared to conduct a radical*
> *defence of the human being: to reinvent humanism in*
> *a way that allows it to survive the attacks against*
> *race, gender and reason, the opponents of human*
> *rights. It means, fighting for universal rights, for*
> *human-centric institutions, and for the right to resist*
> *control of our lives by algorithms.*

For those who believe in the power of organisation of
labour forces to counter hegemonic neo-liberal narratives (as
Mason does) then the step from 'unorganised' to 'unfree'
exploitation of labour is not a big leap.

VI.

There are those who argue that the most exploited workers can
find social solidarity in organising to improve their terms and
conditions. This argument, that with precarity there exists an
emergent class waiting to claim legal rights, seems to be hard to
extend to the Ambridge Horses. Their route to improving their
conditions will only be to exit their current circumstances. In
this final section, I consider several different forms of precarious
labour in the village to demonstrate that there are *continua*
between feudal arrangements such as gamekeepers and vicars in
tied housing, as well as the vulnerabilities of the low paid when it
comes to paying housing costs (Table 4.1).

Table 4.1. Low Pay, Housing and Social Standing in Ambridge.

Group – Emergent Class?	Paid Minimum Wage?	Housing/ Shelter Tied or Contingent?	Type of Employment	Esteem
The Horses	No	Yes – housed together and driven to jobs and fed by Gavin	Forced labour – modern slavery	Abusive, threats of violence
Home Farm fruit pickers – work seasonal, casual and achieved using migrant labour	Yes	Yes – portacabins on site at Home Farm where pickers share	**Seasonal**, contracted summer harvest of 8-week period	Casual racism and some resentment. Work physically demanding and conditions basic.
William, (previously) Gamekeeper in with contractual relationship to Borchester Land	Yes	Yes – tied cottage tenancy with employer BL	**Stable and long term**.	Respected ingredient of rural land management economy
Rex in his uber-style minicab	Piecework	No – but own transport in good order	**Gig Economy** – top up job as farming	Source of shame for Rex that he needs to supplement

Table 4.1. (*Continued*)

Group – Emergent Class?	Paid Minimum Wage?	Housing/ Shelter Tied or Contingent?	Type of Employment	Esteem
			doesn't pay part of a mix of enterprises	income – temporary situation
Emma at the Turkey factory	Yes	No – wage clearly not sufficient to cover housing costs		Source of shame for Emma that she needs to supplement income – temporary situation (?) actual labour unpleasant, cold and nasty.

In this table we explore models for low-paid work and connect them with the housing and esteem hierarchies. As we can see as well as 'feeding the horses' and shining a light on employment practices that are both illegal and immoral those without family bolsters are engaged in various forms of insecure employment. Rex Fairbrother as a taxi driver is paid only for miles travelled with a fare on board; the pickers at Home Farm (in the pre-Brexit/COVID-19 years) were marginal and seasonal. Whereas for Emma Grundy, demeaning and physical labour created a third layer for her 'portfolio career' as cleaner, baker and mother; maybe we will only be able to change the underlying premises of the contemporary economy when we view all this too, the emotional labour and mental load associated with care and child rearing as a form of slavery. The horror of workers being exploited, then, must be seen as the modern slavery storyline has showed business practices both illegal and immoral, but that there are connections for the younger workers in the Ambridge economy who work without protection.

Insofar as we have an account from Philip of his actions – and this is surely to come in delicious melodrama as the compartmentalised spheres of his mind under which he is affable and generous in his domestic life but cruel and brutal to 'his' horses – we have only veiled allusions to previous financial difficulties. It is a matter of pride that Ambridge's gangmaster has been presented largely in the domestic setting which has been a completely separate sphere from the squalor and exploitation for which he is liable. The cracking open of all that is, at the time of writing, yet to come but some of the questions that this investigation has raised are not so easily answered; is modern slavery an inevitable dark side of neoliberalisation, that in pursuit of shrinking margins and stretched supply chains there are laying bare necropolitical forces in play whereby not all lives are mourned, not all lives matter? However the story ends for Philip Moss (and it must surely be in imprisonment and ignominy?) *The Archers* must be applauded for its complex portrayal of moral hazard and of the obscenity of modern slavery, at the very extreme end of the spectrum of precarious work, hidden in plain sight in England's green and pleasant land.

REFERENCES

Butler, J. (2006). *Precarious life: The power of mourning and violence*. New York, NY: Verso.

CIOB. (2019). The-Dark side-of-Construction. Retrieved from https://policy.ciob.org/wp-content/uploads/2016/02/CIOB-Research-The-Darkside-of-Construction.pdf?_ga=2.3080 112.1232147366.1580174800-192020260.1580174800. Accessed on August 30, 2020.

Cooley, B. (2019). Retrieved on from https://hope-forjustice.org/modern-slavery/. Accessed August 30, 2020.

Gangmasters Labour Authority. (2019). Trading the horses. Retrieved from https://vimeo.com/362492207. Accessed on August 30, 2020.

Giroux, H. A. (2006). Reading Hurricane Katrina: Race, class, and the biopolitics of disposability. *College Literature*, *33*(3), 171–196.

International labour Organisation. (2020). Typology of ILO publications, tools and services to better address constituents' needs in countries at different income levels. Retrieved from https://www.ilo.org/wcmsp5/groups/public/—dgreports/—dcomm/documents/publication/wcms_582092.pdf. Accessed on August 30, 2020.

Mason, P. (2019). *Clear bright future: A radical defence of the human being*. London: Penguin.

Mbembe, A. (2003). Necropolitics. *Public Culture*, *15*(1), 11–40.

Thacker, E. (2011). Necrologies or the death of the body politic. In Clough & Wilse (Eds.), *Beyond biopolitics*. Durham, NC; London: Duke University Press.

5

BORSETSHIRE BUSINESSMAN OR FECKLESS FARMER?

Christine Narramore

ABSTRACT

This chapter is an examination of what is meant by the term 'Good Farmer' and whether or not this is compatible with being a good businessperson. The term 'Feckless Farmer' is introduced to describe someone who is the opposite of a Good Farmer. And all of this is considered with reference to the farmers of the village of Ambridge in the West Midlands, with special emphasis on the practices of Brian Aldridge and his recent issues with contamination of his land and neighbouring watercourses. This work starts by defining key terms before moving on to consider the similarities and differences between farms and other types of businesses. The different philosophical paradigms that can underlie different definitions and practices of a Good Farmer are also explored. The ways that the economies of farms differ from most businesses will also be discussed. With some conclusions being drawn as to whether Mr Aldridge

is a Good Farmer or a Feckless one, and if he deserved to
be lauded as an award-winning businessperson.

Does being a successful businessperson in some way conflict
with being a 'Good Farmer'? Specifically, is there some
inherent conflict between the fundamental objectives and
philosophies of business and farming? Brian Aldridge and his
fellow farmers in Ambridge are used as examples to explore
these five questions: what is a good businessperson?; what
makes a good farmer?; can a good businessperson be a good
farmer?; is Brian Aldridge a Good Farmer?; and is he a good
businessperson? The meaning of a Good Farmer will be
expounded and the term 'Feckless Farmer' is introduced, as the
opposite of the 'Good Farmer.' The aim here is to reach some
final conclusions on evaluating successful farming and determine whether there is an inherent conflict with good business.

DEFINITIONS

It is important to be clear what is meant by certain key terms,
used here, so we need to start with some definitions.

What is a business? What do we mean by businessman/
businessperson?

Some definitions of the word business include: 'A business is
an organisation where people work together. In a business,
people work to make and sell products or services' (Wikipedia,
2020);

> *A business is defined as an organization or*
> *enterprising entity engaged in commercial, industrial,*
> *or professional activities....The term* business *also*
> *refers to the organized efforts and activities of*

> *individuals to produce and sell goods and services for profit' (Hayes, 2019); and 'the activity of buying and selling goods and services.*
>
> (Cambridge English Dictionary, 2019)

Furthermore, a businessperson can be defined as 'someone who works in business, especially one who has a high position in a company' (Cambridge English Dictionary, 2019) or 'a person engaged in commercial or industrial business, especially as an owner or executive' (Collins English Dictionary, 2020). From this it is clear that a business involves the production of goods and services and their sales. Whereas a businessperson is someone engaged in business, most commonly someone high up within the organisation with responsibility for the running and strategic direction of the business. An underlying assumption is that part of the motivation of such activities is to make a profit (see Chapter 6).

WHAT IS A FARM?

A farm is an area of land that is worked to raise crops or livestock: 'A farm is an area of land where livestock (animals) are raised and crops (plants) are grown for use as food, fiber, and fuel' (4H, 2019); 'a tract of land devoted to agricultural purposes' (Merriam Webster, 2019); and 'an area of land, esp. together with a house and other buildings, used for growing crops or keeping animals' (Cambridge English Dictionary, 2019). But what does a farm look like? Most people can picture a farm with its sheep, cows, pigs and maybe a tractor (a bit like the toy farm David Archer of Ambridge had as a child). Others may picture vast wheat fields.

However, is this enough to define a farm? It is expected that animals will end their life either being sold at market or on a journey to the slaughterhouse. The crops grown are only there for the growing season. Tractors and other farm equipment might in the future be completely replaced by small weed zapping robots (Small Robot, 2020). Just as modern machinery replaced the horse. And even the farm buildings can be destroyed (e.g. by arson) or sold off. But if a farm loses its animals, crops, machinery and buildings it would still *be* a farm. What remains? What truly makes a farm, a farm could be said to be the land.

WHAT IS MEANT BY LAND?

Meriam Webster (2019) has two definitions that are very useful, first: 'the solid part of the surface of the earth'. That is the land as opposed to the sea, and then, the secondary definition: 'ground or soil of a specified situation, nature, or quality.' Land then is not just the part of the Earth's surface that is not covered by water, but more specifically it can refer to a specific area of land, and area that can be characterised by its topology, geology, climate, microclimate, soil and the way it has been managed. A farm is a specific area of land that is worked to produce crops or animals, predominantly used to feed people.

WHAT IS A FARMER?

Similarly, some definitions of the word farmer include: 'a person who cultivates land or crops or raises animals (such as livestock or fish)' (Merriam Webster, 2019); 'a person who farms; person who operates a farm or cultivates land' (Dictionary.com, 2019); 'An individual whose primary job function involves livestock and/or agriculture' (Business Dictionary, 2020) and 'A farmer is a person who runs and works on a farm. Some *farmers* raise a variety of food crops, while others keep dairy cows and sell their milk' (Vocabulary, 2019). Thus, a farmer works a farm, raising crops or livestock.

It is not enough just to define what a business is, but to take this further and try to define what is a successful business? This is a question on which hundreds of thousands of business books have been written, so will only be considered to a very limited extent here. 'One of the most important aspects of business success is earning a profit' (Suttle, 2020). However, to be considered truly successful the business must have some degree of longevity. It is oft quoted that 60% of new businesses fail within their first three years (May, 2019). One measure of business success might be to receive an award, which an organisation is unlikely to gain until they have traded for some time. Therefore, overall a *successful* business both makes a profit and survives for some time.

FARMING AS A BUSINESS

A farm is usually run as a business, with a profit needed to provide the farmer with an income. However, farming is an unusual business sector as a lot of farms operate in a way that would cause most businesses to fail. If we consider farms in terms of their Farm Business Income (FBI), that is the net income of the farm, then: '14% of UK farms [failed] to make a positive FBI in 2017/18' while 'just under a third of UK farms had a FBI of over £50,000' (DEFRA, 2019). However even the 14% that made a negative FBI were not necessarily about to go out of business.

Prices in agricultural markets are often much more volatile than other industries. This is as Pettinger (2016) states, because: supply is price inelastic in the short term, taking a year to grow most crops; demand is price inelastic, as food is essential, and people are not usually put off by higher prices; and supply can vary due to climatic conditions. An underlying factor is that the produce of farms is not something that society can choose to do without: it is an essential for life. Hence governments often provide support in the form of subsidies or favourable borrowing conditions or other measures, to help farms continue through difficult times. Food security is seen as something that is important.

Another aspect that makes farming unusual as a business is that a farm may well have been owned/managed by the same family for decades if not centuries. Which is an unusual longevity of ownership. There is also the emotional and psychological attachment to farms and farming; whilst only about 1.5% of the population may be employed in agriculture (DEFRA, 2018), children are still introduced to the concept of farms at a young age. Whether visiting a Farm Park or singing 'Old MacDonald' with its farm noises or owning a toy farm; whereas they are unlikely to have a toy Blast Furnace or Coal Mine. Farming then is an unusual business and although remote from the lived experience of most of the population is one embedded in the national psyche.

THE GOOD FARMER

Farmers in this work will be judged as to whether they are 'Good Farmers' or not. Therefore, what is a Good Farmer? The one thing most authors (Burton, Forney, & Sutherland 2021; Farrell, 2018; Pettinger, 2016; Wilson et al., 2012) seem to agree on is that it is more than making a profit. For example, in the case of Ambridge, a former resident, Charlie

Thomas, who worked as a manager for 'Big Agriculture' once justified his motivation to Adam Macy as being about producing enough food to 'feed the world.' Even in the most 'industrial' of farming operations the underlying *raison d'être* is often more than just profit or longevity. Thompson (2017) in *The Spirit of the Soil* talks about four basic philosophical paradigms that can influence how someone farms: *Industrial/ Productionist*, which centres on a need for ever increasing food production to 'feed an ever increasing population'; *Agrarian Ideal*, which has a religious or quasi-religious notion of stewardship of the land, and that is taking care of what the Creator/ Mother Nature has provided; *Environmental/Ecological* approach, which focuses on the idea of the 'true cost of food', in terms of energy budgets, pollution and carbon budgets (for example, Raworth's (2018) *Doughnut Economics*) and *Holistic*, which aims to take into account the natural cycles (water cycle, carbon cycle, energy flow and mineral cycle) and community dynamics of the ecosystem. But is this approach able to provide enough food to feed the world?

Thompson would argue that a Good Farmer needs to balance all four philosophies, that is the need to feed the world, with the need to care for the natural world, to farm for the future, with the need to work with the land and ecosystems. To be a Good Farmer is a conscious attitude. However, it is possible that someone who is being a Good Farmer could also make a profit and would have a sustainable, long-lived 'business' and thus, it is not necessarily contradictory to be both a Good Farmer and a successful businessperson.

In this chapter the term 'Feckless Farmer' will be used to describe someone who is the opposite of the Good Farmer, being one who is at odds with all philosophical concepts of the Good Farmer, i.e. one who goes after short-term profit with no long-term view of stewardship, who neglects any environmental considerations, certainly does not work 'with' the land and even undermines long-term production goals. An interesting point to consider with this concept is who is the biggest Feckless Farmer? Is it the person who fells virgin forest in order to get a few years of high productivity from the land before it is so nutrient deprived and eroded as to give very poor yields? Or is it the farmer who is too lazy to work his land efficiently, and might well have some of it covered in old rusting farm machinery? (see Chapter 1).

AMBRIDGE FARMING TYPOLOGY AND GEOMORPHOLOGY

Ambridge is a small farming community in rural Borsetshire (between Warwickshire and Worcestershire) in the English Midlands. It was until the early 1990s mainly formed of four farms – Grange Farm, Bridge Farm, Brookfield and Home Farm – with other land in the area forming part of the Bellamy estate, which went on to became part of Borchester Land, partly owned by Damara Holdings, a large agro-investment company (Davies, 2019; Parkin, 1989). Of these, three farms now operate as traditional farms. As after mismanagement or bad luck (depending on who you speak to) the Grundy family lost the tenancy of the Grange Farm in 2000 and most of the land became part of the Borchester Land's holdings. Now the Grundy family only have a small amount of land they own and can use, their agricultural endeavours now being limited to breeding Texel sheep, raising Christmas turkeys and some agricultural contract work.

The other three farms offer an interesting contrast (all sizes come from Anthony Parkin's 1989 work). Bridge Farm is the smallest, at around 60 hectares in 1989, and is run on an organic basis. Its main crops are milk for its artisan dairy products, veg for veg boxes and a small beef herd. It has its own farm shop and plays host to a tearoom next door. Brookfield is larger (190 hectares in 1989) and is more a traditional mixed farm, with arable, sheep and dairy cows, and a small beef herd. It also lets out some farm buildings to some rural entrepreneurs, one of whom raises pigs, and another makes artisan gin. There are also some chickens and beehives on the farm, as well as a small orchard which produces fruit for personal use. Home farm is much larger again (about 650 hectares in 1989). It has a lot of land in arable production; and in the past it produced soft fruit in polytunnels but due to future labour issues has moved over to an aquaculture system of raising vegetables for salad and fish. Home Farm also has sheep, leases some land to Borchester Land for hunting and raises red deer for their meat.

Another interesting point is that all the main farmers of Ambridge, apart from Brian Aldridge, have deep roots in the area. There have been Archers in the village since at least the nineteenth century, if not longer, and there is evidence of the Grundy family being resident before that (along with such old families as the Forrests who inter-married with the Archers). However, in contrast, Brian Aldridge is an incomer. He sold his family land in Hertfordshire in the 1970s for housing and then invested in Home Farm and land from the Bellamy Estate to create the present Home Farm (Toye & Flynn, 2001). This could explain his generally more entrepreneurial attitude.

In summary, all the family farms in the area have diverse interests ranging from venison, shooting, arable, cows, pigs, chickens, sheep, to subletting land/buildings to local enterprises, to vegetable production, to a shop and a tearoom. All the farms have to consider how to provide for future generations and how control of the land will be distributed to them. Financial issues and uncertainty caused by ever changing government directives are also big factors in the way the land is managed, with each farm developing individual strategies and solutions.

Borsetshire's elevation is mainly under 300 metres, with the few hilltops exceeding that forming the Hasset Hills (North, 1999). As Aldridge, Tregorran and Smethurst (1981) put it, it is 'a land of quiet hills and slow-moving rivers'. The highest point in Ambridge is occupied by Lakey Hill, which seems to be an offshoot of the Clee and Malvern Hills. The geology is mixed from the ancient pre-Cambrian rocks of Lakey Hill, through limestones and clays, to sand and gravels deposited after the last ice age. The soil (like neighbouring Worcestershire and War-wickshire) is characterised by Keuper Marl or in modern terms, Mercia Mudstone group; overlaid with a topsoil of sandy gravel (BGS, NERC, 2020). The soils have long been known to be fertile and not too heavy on the whole (Parkin, 1989), and have been fought over through the ages by those who wished to possess its fertile land (Aldridge, et al., 1981).

The climate of the UK as a whole is maritime and influ-enced strongly by the Gulf Stream. Ambridge is in the west of the country so tends to be wetter than places in the east, so less prone to droughts, but silage or haymaking may struggle with summer rain (Borreani, Tabacco, Schmidt, Holmes, & Muck, 2018). The West Midlands as a region has the smallest average farm size of any of the English regions at 66 hectares (DEFRA, 2019). Bridge Farm is a little smaller than the average, but both Brookfield and Home Farm are bigger than average for the region. The West Midlands are unusual that 28% of the farmland is used for grazing, but also 25% is used for cereal crops. Mixed agriculture is still a pretty common form for this region (DEFRA, 2018) and the West Midlands is the third largest area for organic farming, with around 28,000 hectares in full organic production and another 5,000 in conversion (Wilson, 2018).

The microclimate varies considerably over the area. On the finest scale it will vary across even a modestly sized field. Knowledge of this variation in microclimate, such as the location of small 'frost pockets,' would have been well known to the farmers of 100 years ago. However, at a slightly more macro scale, areas such as the top of Lakey Hill are far more exposed to winds and weather than areas along the Am Valley, which may be more prone to flooding, whether the annual flooding of the water meadows to more extreme events such as those of 2015, which might well occur more frequently with climate change. Events around this extreme flood event are discussed in Courage and Headlam (2017). All of these factors should and do influence the ways that farmers in the area choose to manage their land. The affect of difference in this management was clearly seen after the flood. Brookfield had been inundated and struggled with their livestock until the ground dried out. Adam Macy observed much worse aftereffects at Home Farm, where there seemed to be large-scale erosion and soil loss.

THE GOOD AND FECKLESS FARMER IN AMBRIDGE

All of the Philosophical tenets (Industrial, Agrarian, Environmental and Holistic) have been demonstrated to some degree in the actions of farmers in Ambridge. Charlie Thomas and Brian Aldridge have demonstrated the Industrial Philosophy, with its emphasis on maximising yields. David Archer (and his father and grandfather before him) have tended to a more Agrarian approach, concerned with stewardship of the land and passing it on to the next generation. Organic farming can have either an Environmental or Holistic underpinning – in Bridge Farm it is probably closer to Environmental, as is Ruth Archer's decision to change the dairy herd at Brookfield to a grass management system and so reduce energy input to the farm by buying in less winter feed. Similarly, Ruth's aims to reduce carbon emissions, which she submitted for the Ambridge Conservation Trust award, come from an Environmental standpoint.

Adam Macy's 'mob grazing', herbal leys and no-till farming are all ideas that come from the Holistic approach to farming (Davies, 2019). Although a truly holistic approach would lead to a subdivision of Home Farm's vast fields and a return to farming the land in a more individualised way in line with its changing characteristics, this approach would not be suited to the big machinery used on Home Farm but might be more suited to the robots that Alice Carter (née Aldridge) was helping develop. The re-wilding project could be based upon this approach, although as yet its creators have communicated no clear philosophy.

The work of Burton et al. (2021) extends the concept of the Good Farmer into its cultural and identity concept and the presumed notions of what the word 'good' means and also places the concept in a historic context. All of which provides the basis to extend the concept out of a Western-centric view and encourages a deeper exploration of the underlying assumptions, including culture and symbolism in agriculture – something it would be interesting to question the farmers of Ambridge on – or, as David Farrell (2018), puts, on a farm there is a 'critical coupling... between a farmer and the farm, resulting in the emergence of often uncodified, site specific knowledge, solution and adaptations'. This sounds like the symbolism of the farmer from generations of farmers who are in tune with their land. However, Farrell goes on to say, 'agriculture represents the largest physical manifestation of negative anthropogenic impact on the planet – mankind's antagonistic relationship with planet Earth', which is full of rather more frightening symbolism, that of humankind fighting with nature.

THE CASE OF BRIAN ALDRIDGE OF AMBRIDGE

The Situation

As 2018 started Brian Aldridge of Home Farm was confi-
dently waiting for the Borsetshire Businessperson of the Year
awards, where he expected to receive the accolade and had
already given an interview to *Borsetshire Life* magazine in
anticipation. Brian was assured he was going to receive the
prize for his diverse agricultural-related business activities
centred on Home Farm, and his chairmanship of Borchester
Land. However just as 2018 started, Kirsty Miller (an
Ambridge resident and now volunteer manager for the Borsetshire Wildlife Trust) took part in the new tradition of a
New Year's Day wild swim in the River Am. This swim was
cut short when Kirsty discovered herself to be surrounded by
dead fish. An investigation by the Environmental Agency (EA)
followed, the result of which pinpointed the source of the
problem to be Home Farm: it was revealed that barrels of
chemicals had been dumped in a filled-in pond at the farm and
the subsequent remediation works, even before the EA's
decision to prosecute Brian Aldridge, led to the organisers
deciding to award the Borsetshire Businessperson of the year
to someone else.

This was not the first time that the River Am had been
affected by the actions of the local farms. In 2009, Bridge
Farm had been alerted to a contamination problem in Heydon
Brook, a tributary of the Am, seemingly caused by slurry run-
off from the farm. Subsequently, Bridge Farm introduced a
reed bed filtration system to prevent further effluent issues. In
1989, Phil Archer was responsible for a slurry leak which led
to the death of hundreds of fish (at least 1,000 brown and
1,000 rainbow trout at a local fish farm were killed, as well as
other water creatures) but Phil was not prosecuted. Big

Agriculture in the form of Borchester Land's Berrow Farm has been rumoured to be partially responsible for the extent of the Ambridge Floods in 2015, and there were further rumours about 'blocked culverts' and maybe a manager's involvement, although the bravery of Charlie Thomas in unblocking a culvert has to be acknowledged (Courage & Headlam, 2017). On the other hand, whilst talking to older residents of the village on an anonymised basis, there do not seem to be any specific pollution claims made against Grange Farm when the Grundy family farmed it: it looked 'untidy' with 'a lot of old machinery' but other than any fuel or other pollutants leaking from the old machinery, there seem to be few instances of pollution. The Grundys seemed to have been proud of the spring on their land – 'they tried to bottle the water and sell it once' (Toye & Flynn, 2001).

However, in the case of Home Farm, the full story that later emerged seemed to be one of complicity in the poisoning of his own land by Brian Aldridge. Not only had Brian allowed the dumping of builder's waste to fill in the unwanted pond on his land but also it also emerged that he knew that unidentified barrels of some kind were included. Furthermore, it appeared to be well known that the builder in question was less than scrupulous and had been approaching other farmers in the area to find somewhere to dump his waste. As Bert Fry has attested, he had 'heard all about it from Phil [Archer].'

Is Brian Aldridge a Good or Feckless Farmer?

The only way Mr Aldridge would himself judge his own farming is the Industrial model. He very much judges farming on its ability to produce food and the profit that can be made from it. He may have put land into 'set aside' when the subsidies made financial sense, or have been converted to leaving some field margins for skylarks when pushed into it by Pip Archer as a teenager, but as Adam Macy can testify it is the bottom line that is the most crucial for Brian. One of Brian's first actions when he arrived in Ambridge was to rip out ancient hedgerows to create mega fields suitable for the 'latest' large-scale methods and machinery (Sanderson, 1998), something that Shula Archer lamented at the time.

Brian is quite happy to invest in big machinery if it can add to the profitability of his farm and the reason he is a Brexiter is because he believes that Home Farm can make a larger profit after the UK leaves the EU. The effect of this on smaller and less industrial farms is of no real interest to him or may even be seen as a good thing. Brian's focus is very much on himself and his family, with his concern for others very much being linked to how much they affect him. Some of this attitude and behaviour may link back to just how 'connected' Brian is to Ambridge. Unlike the other farmers in Ambridge, Brian doesn't have a long established family connection to the area and it is worth noting that he was prepared to sell his family land and move, something that David Archer could not bring himself to do, even though at the time Brookfield was threatened with being cut in half by a road improvement scheme. It would be interesting to probe if there was more to the decision to sell the 'family land' in Hertfordshire than has been previously disclosed.

Even on just the industrial concept of the Good Farmer, can Brian Aldridge be seen as a good farmer? Brian's farming style seems to produce pretty high yields, although as his stepson worries, this could be at the long-term cost of degrading the soil and making erosion more likely, especially in extreme weather events. However, can any farmer who allows something that could poison his own land ever be considered a 'Good Farmer'? In allowing the barrels of chemicals of unknown or suspect origin to be buried on his land, purely for a short-term financial gain, Brian seems to have acted against any actions consistent with any model of the Good Farmer. Brian cannot be seen as totally Feckless, especially under the Industrial philosophy he would espouse: his farming does have high yields and works to improve these year on year and others have, at times, been able to persuade him of a more Agrarian, Environmental or even Holistic approach. However, none of these approaches seem to come naturally to him and he always seems more concerned about the bottom line than other factors. But it is quite clear from this example that he is *not* a Good Farmer, as allowing potential poisoning of land for short-term financial gain against all tenets of this concept.

Is Brian Aldridge a Good Businessman?

Brian is concerned with the bottom line and appears to consider agriculture as a business. But is he actually a good businessman? Eva Batzogianni (2018) lists five criteria of a good businessperson: 'to take risks, leadership skills, take initiative, good communication skills and to be seen as reliable.' How much Brian meets these criteria is subject to debate. Brian is good at taking initiative and risks, but his leadership style has often seemed more dictatorial than collaborative. His communication skills can be good when he bothers but may verge on the manipulative and his reputation for reliability has been fatally damaged by the Am pollution incident. This does lead to questions over what criteria were used to choose the Borsetshire Businessman of the year. Although it is rumoured that Brian Aldridge wasn't even the first choice for the award (it is said that Justin Elliot had turned it down.)

It is also worth examining the reason that Brian has given for agreeing to bury the barrels on his land in the first place. That is: that he was struggling with cash flow at the time, just after he married his wife Jennifer and took on the cost of educating her children privately, sending Adam to Sherborne and Debbie Aldridge to Cheltenham Ladies College (Toye & Flynn, 2001), two of the most prestigious fee paying schools. Brian does not seem to have economised in any way. Neither has Brian been willing to raise money on his main parcel of land. He bought the farm without a mortgage and even in the latest troubles was not willing to consider a mortgage on the farm, although he has at times taken out loans to purchase further parcels of land. This may be because, unlike a domestic mortgage, an agricultural mortgage is something that can pass down the generations. Is he particularly concerned with passing on debt to future generations? This reluctance to borrow has actually been observed quite widely in small and medium enterprises (SMEs) (Hunter, 2014) and has been identified as something that can lower growth in the economy as a whole. In farming it is noted (Wilson et al., 2012) that the top performing farms tend to have relatively low levels of borrowing. Maybe Brian's reluctance to borrow money is not that unusual, even though the alternative chosen in this case seems somewhat short-termist, surprising in a farmer.

CONCLUSION

On the whole whilst Brian Aldridge might seem an unusual choice for Businessperson of the Year, perhaps in a rural area like Borsetshire it might well seem diplomatic occasionally to give the award to a successful farmer and Brian does score well on the characteristics of a high-performing farm:

> *Common characteristics of high performing farms
> are: i) controlling costs; ii) paying attention to detail;
> iii) being open and flexible to new opportunities; iv)
> focus on margins and product quality to maximise
> profit, v) researching and using an appropriate range
> of marketing channels understanding the business
> attributes these provide; vi) improving business
> performance through enterprise change.*

(Wilson et al., 2012)

It may seem like misfortune that just as Brian was about to be given the accolade of Borsetshire Businessperson of the Year, being involved in a scandal would prevent him receiving the award, even if that scandal resulted from his past short-termist business decisions. Nevertheless, although previously Brian has on his own philosophical terms appeared to be a Good Farmer, the nature of this one decision does place him in the Feckless Farmer category. It seems even harder to under-stand as he had alternatives to any cash flow problems (borrowing money or sending his stepchildren to cheaper schools.) Although this seems to be an isolated incident, it does go against the fundamental principles of all models of the Good Farmer.

How should this affect agriculture outside Ambridge? Farmers in other places might like to judge how their business decisions and actions place them on the Good Farmer/Feckless Farmer spectrum, and how their neighbours would judge them. Hopefully it is clear that being a good businessman does not automatically make you a Feckless Farmer, although maybe a lack of connection with the land might predispose choices in that direction. It could be argued that Brian Aldridge is the most Feckless Farmer in Ambridge, a title that was long thought to have belonged to Joe Grundy.

REFERENCES

4 H. (2019). 4-H learning network. 4hlnet.extension.org. Retrieved from https://4hlnet.extension.org/what-is-a-farm/. Accessed on August 29, 2020.

Aldridge, J., Tregorran, J., & Smethurst, W. (1981). *Ambridge : An English village through the ages*. Borchester: Borchester Press in Association with Eyre Methuen PP.

Batzogianni, E. (2018). 'Project updates - five qualities of a good businessman - IED' in institute of entrepreneurship development. Retrieved from https://ied.eu/project-updates/five-qualities-good-businessman/. Accessed on August 29, 2020.

BGS, NERC. (2020). MySoil.

Borreani, G., Tabacco, E., Schmidt, R. J., Holmes, B. J., & Muck, R. E. (2018). Silage review: Factors affecting dry matter and quality losses in silages. *Journal of Dairy Science*, *101*(5), 3952–3979. doi:10.3168/jds.2017-13837

Burton, R., Forney, J., & Sutherland, L.-A. (2021). *The good farmer : Culture and identity in food and agriculture*. Abingdon: Routledge.

Business Dictionary. (2020). Farmer. Retrieved from http://www.businessdictionary.com/definition/farmer.html. Accessed on August 29, 2020.

Cambridge English Dictionary. (2019). Business. Retrieved from https://dictionary.cambridge.org/dictionary/english/business. Accessed on August 29, 2020.

Collins English Dictionary (2020). Businessperson. Retrieved from https://www.collinsdictionary.com/dictionary/english/businessperson. Accessed on August 29, 2020.

Courage, C., & Headlam, N. (2017). *Custard, culverts and cake: Academics on life in the Archers*. Bingley: Emerald Publishing Limited.

Davies, K. (2019). *The Archers: Year of food and farming*. London: Seven Dials.

DEFRA. (2018). Defra statistics: Agricultural facts -commercial holdings at June 2018 (unless stated). Retrieved from https:// assets.publishing.service.gov.uk/government/uploads/system/ uploads/attachment_data/file/866813/regionalstatistics_ westmidlands_20feb20.pdf. Accessed on August 29, 2020.

DEFRA. (2019). Department for environment, food and rural affairs department of agriculture, environment and rural affairs (Northern Ireland) Welsh government, knowledge and analytical services the Scottish government, rural and environment science and analytical service. Retrieved from https://assets.publishing.service.gov.uk/government/uploads/ system/uploads/attachment_data/file/848641/AUK_2018_ 09jul19a.pdf. Accessed on August 29, 2020.

Dictionary.com. (2019). Farmer. Retrieved from https:// www.dictionary.com/browse/farmer. Accessed on August 29, 2020.

Farrell, D. (2018). What makes a good farmer? Blue North. Retrieved from https://bluenorth.co.za/what-makes-a-good-farmer/. Accessed on August 29, 2020.

Hayes, A. (2019). Business definition. *Investopedia*. Retrieved from https://www.investopedia.com/terms/b/business.asp. Accessed on August 29, 2020.

Hunter, D. (2014). Small businesses reluctant to borrow. *Fresh Business Thinking*. Retrieved from https://www.fresh businessthinking.com/small-businesses-reluctant-to-borrow/. Accessed on August 29, 2020.

May, R. (2019). Start-ups across the UK are going bust - they need more careful management for our economy to boom. *The Telegraph*. Retrieved from https://www.tele-graph.co.uk/politics/2019/01/24/start-ups-across-uk-going-bust-need-careful-management-economy/. Accessed on August 29, 2020.

Merriam Webster. (2019). Farmer. Retrieved from https://www.merriam-webster.com/dictionary/farmer. Accessed on August 29, 2020.

North, M. (1999). *Ambridge and Borchester district*. London: Draughtsman Ltd.

Parkin, A. (1989). *The Archers book of farming and the countryside*. London: BBC Books.

Pettinger, T. (2016). Problems of agriculture – market failure - Economics help. *Economics Help*. Retrieved from https://www.economicshelp.org/blog/4977/economics/problems-of-agriculture-market-failure/. Accessed on August 29, 2020.

Raworth, K. (2018). What on earth is the Doughnut?... Retrieved from https://www.kateraworth.com/doughnut/. Accessed on August 29, 2020.

Sanderson, I. (1998). *The Archers anarchists A-Z*. London: Boxtree.

Small Robot. (2020). Small robot company. *Small Robot Company*. Retrieved from https://www.smallrobotcompany.com/. Accessed on August 29, 2020.

Suttle, R. (2020). What defines a successful business? *Small Business - Chron.com*. Retrieved from https://smallbusiness.chron.com/defines-successful-business-19029.html#:~:text= Successful companies are always attuned. Accessed on August 29, 2020.

Thompson, P. B. (2017). *The spirit of the soil agriculture and environmental ethics*. New York, NY: Routledge.

Toye, J., & Flynn, A. (2001). *The Archers encyclopaedia*. London: BBC Worldwide.

Vocabulary. (2019). Farmer. Retrieved from https://www.vocabulary.com/dictionary/farmer. Accessed on August 29, 2020.

Wikipedia. (2020). Business. Retrieved from https://simple.wikipedia.org/wiki/Business. Accessed on August 29, 2020.

Wilson, H. (2018). WMIC: Food, farming, environment. Retrieved from https://www.westmidlandsiep.gov.uk/news/article/19/wmic_food_farming_environment. Accessed on August 29, 2020.

Wilson, P., Lewis, M., Crane, R., Robertson, P., McHoul, H., Bonner, J., … Riley, M. (2012). Farm level performance: Identifying common factors determining levels of performance. *Rural Business Research*.

6

WHAT TO DO WHEN YOU'RE NO LONGER BORSETSHIRE'S BUSINESSPERSON OF THE YEAR, OR HOW TO HANDLE A SCANDAL

Olivia Vandyk

ABSTRACT

Many small businesses don't have the time or money to think about crisis communications, but latterly, events in Ambridge and surrounding areas have shown that even the smallest family enterprise can become headline news. This chapter illustrates how to inexpensively plan for the unforeseeable, how to project calm in the face of an agricultural storm and how to clear up the mess (toxic or otherwise) afterwards. The presentation studies known business-based issues in Ambridge such as the Low Mead incident and touches on individual communications calamities like Brian Aldridge's enforced retirement. It will also cover potential reputation management issues, for instance, the heir to a local hotel empire is arrested for dealing Class B narcotics. The session will provide

*valuable insight to anyone with an interest in the news,
local or national. In conclusion, with a small amount of
planning, the business people of Ambridge can ensure
that it doesn't have to be a literal case of closing the
stable door after the horse has bolted.*

Any business, at some point, will face some sort of a public
relations crisis, and the way you respond can go two ways:
you can either significantly damage your brand and alienate
your customer base, or if you can handle it well, positive
action under pressure can give you a much-needed image
boost. This chapter focuses on how a small business can get
ahead of a crisis with particular reference to Lower Loxley
and Home Farm. In my preparations, I wondered whether a
more accurate title would have been 'How not to handle a
scandal' because actually both Brian Aldridge and Elizabeth
Pargetter made a complete omnishambles of their respective
difficult situations.

CASE STUDY: HOME FARM/BRIAN ALDRIDGE

The first rule of crisis management is to avoid them. To do this
you need to assess from whence any problems may arise. By
undertaking a vulnerability audit, you will know your weaknesses and can prepare for the worst-case scenario. It is not
surprising that Brian had not undertaken such an audit –
because he is unlikely to admit to any weaknesses. Given that
Brian knew that there was waste at Low Mead, even if he
genuinely did not know how toxic it was, checks should have
been made – but of course to do so would be to tacitly admit
to the issue. A vulnerability audit would have allowed Home
Farm to have been more prepared for the potential damage,
both actual and reputational.

Sandman (2005) is keen to note the differences between a 'real' crisis – where there is justification for upset due to public safety being at risk and a 'reputational' crisis. In a 'real' crisis, when people are rightly upset about a situation that may genuinely endanger them (their health, safety, economic wellbeing, or whatever), apologising is secondary – even if you have things to apologise for. The core communication tasks in such cases are helping people bear the situation, helping them bear the strong feelings it arouses, and helping them make wise rather than unwise decisions about how to cope. Among the key crisis communication recommendations for a 'real' crisis: don't over-reassure, acknowledge uncertainty, validate people's fears and give people things to do. The Low Mead crisis was thus both.

Assuming the worst does happen, even if you have planned ahead, this handy CRISIS acronym (Agnes, 2018) creates a framework to help to control the situation: C-*Communicate*; R-*Respect*; I-*Initiate*; S-*Show*; I-*Issue-Manage*; and S-*Sustain*. The initial point is *Communicate*. Primarily, we need to recognise a crisis as an opportunity to strengthen relationship with stakeholders and communicate it as such. Brian did not communicate at all. Next is to *Respect* the feelings of those around you. This Brian fails to do – in fact he insisted that people trust him when there was no reason to do so, and in doing so, he ignored the feeling of locals and continued as though nothing was wrong. Kirsty Miller was incandescent with rage when she discovered what had happened – because there was a sense of danger to the environment not acknowledged by anyone at the Home Farm team. Then it is crucial to *Initiate* corrective action. Brian himself did not do anything publicly to redress his actions, and the toxic waste clean-up operation was only implemented under duress from the Environment Agency. The next point is to *Show* strong leadership skills by acting in a timely manner. Brian's ostrich-like tendencies created feelings of distrust towards his leadership. This ultimately resulted in further personal embarrassment by being stripped of the title Businessperson of the Year – the humiliation of which was compounded by this news becoming a story in *The Westbury Courier*. The penultimate point here is to *Issue-Manage*. The possibility of dumping more toxic waste in the future is solved by having a more ethical hand at the helm, reassessing of the corporate culture. This changed at Home Farm for Brian but not of his own volition, so where he could have had influence over the change, he lost that opportunity through inaction. The final point is that the business can be *Sustained* but only under new leadership in the form of his stepson Adam Macy, who has a different relationship both with the land and the locals (Elrhoul, 2015).

Once the news of a crisis has broken there is an immediate need for action. As in the medical world, in public relations parlance too, this is known as the 'golden hour'. Although of course in the world of communications it is not always literally 60 minutes, but when the news of a crisis breaks it is crucial to get the response right immediately. You need to be proactive, be transparent and be accountable. But Brian did not do any of this. Even if he had acted in time, Brian needs to remember that communication is now a two-way street, whether you want it to be or not and that any other members of the public (e.g. Kirsty, who discovered the toxicity) has just as much of a public voice as he does and can post or tweet online in a matter of seconds. The immediacy of having both a camera and social network on your person at all times means that it is commonplace for Joe Public to share their drama widely and immediately as standard now. Social media generally values emotion over fact, and so it is vital that the response to an issue is timely, open and honest. A real-time response is not just a suggestion but an expectation of your audience – research by Twitter emphasises not only the importance of the golden hour and a timely response but also the fact that positive communication buys trust. 60% of customers expect brands to respond to their queries within an hour. Our study found that when consumers have friendly customer service interaction – as defined by showing empathy and offering to help – they are more likely to recommend the brand. Therefore, it is imperative that the issue is shown as being treated seriously and as a priority, and the message is crafted in a language and tone that anyone can understand, relate to and appreciate.

What we actually want is what I have coined as the *4A response*: *Acknowledge* the incident; *Accept* responsibility; *Apologise*; and *Act* to avoid future disaster. If you can take care to be proactive online and offline with your messaging to all your stakeholders, you will be able to build your reputation and instill credibility forming a bank of community trust – so that if you find yourself in trouble, you can make a withdrawal from that bank. Greyser (2009) refers to this as a 'reputational reservoir' (perhaps not an ideal analogy in the context of a water pollution crisis), and it refers to an excellent foundation of corporate reputation on which to draw in a time of crisis:

> *In the event of brand reputational crisis, focus on forthrightness in communications, and on truly substantive credible responses in behaviour. These are the most likely avenues to rescue a brand in crisis. They may restore trust, although that is not guaranteed. The most important actions in a reputational crisis, however, can be the ones taken over time to build a 'reputational reservoir', a strong foundation for the corporate reputation. In some crises, a company can draw down on that reservoir.*
>
> (Greyser, 2009, p. 600)

If I could take a step back in time to before the spill was discovered, I would have encouraged Brian to have spoken about their business story on the Home Farm website. Talking about your values and showing that you are applying them is key to building up reputation. Adam took decisive action after the great floods of Ambridge, realising that the soil quality was low which was why there had been so much erosion. The installation of herbal leys would have been an opportunity to publish an advertorial in *The Borchester Echo* or *Borsetshire Life* explaining why the landscape of Home Farm had changed. Adam's commitment to the environment would have bought Home Farm some good will. Imagine the benefit of the doubt that could have been planted by regular honest communication. Anyone hearing allegations about toxicity would have given the Home Farm team a chance to put the record straight.

If you have invested time in this way, then you will know instinctively to whom you can turn to act as an advocate for you. Financier Warren Buffett (Miles, 2014), who has plenty of experience in damage control, says: 'It takes 20 years to build a reputation and five minutes to ruin it.' Brian, alas, had not done this. We know from previous research from Headlam (Courage & Headlam, 2017) that Brian's power network is not as strong as he thinks:

> *Brian Aldridge has, over four decades in Ambridge, operationalised a highly differentiated set of mating strategies which may have threatened to fragment the Home Farm Aldridge legacy through sub-optimal strategy.*

(p. 199)

In short, he is not the King of Ambridge that he believes himself to be. In fact, Brian has a long history of acting

selfishly and not learning from previous crises; the Grange
Spinney housing development; battles on the Borsetshire Land
board with Martyn Gibson and anything to do with Matt
Crawford.

In terms of reputation management, it is also worth noting
that others are impacted by events too. The toxic dumping did
not just affect Brian: 'Crises can also harm stakeholders – be it
physically, financially or emotionally' (Salvador & Ikeda,
2018, p. 76). The ripple effect in this situation was marked.
Adam lost out on a soft fruit contract because word had got
out. Additionally, Adam's opportunity to be involved in a new
collaborative conversation on soil qualities fell through, all
because Brian's reputation preceded him. Much as Brian may
have scoffed at daughter Kate Madikane's yurts, the business
was her baby, and the toxic chemicals clearly affected sales of
yoga classes and retreats. His wife Jennifer Aldridge had of
course been affected personally too – following a 'paparazzi'
photo of her having a lovely spa day while the river still flowed
with toxicity. As a direct consequence, she and Brian have
become local social pariahs, excluded from dinners with the
smart set which had been their previous domain. In the end,
they were reduced to kitchen supper with the Carters. Ruairi
Donovan too, is affected: due to financial constraints, Brian
will have to pull him out of boarding school for him to attend
the local college for sixth form.

The fact that *The Westbury Courier* had run a feature
describing Brian as a 'tainted businessman' should not have
come as a surprise to him, but it did. Brian should be listening
more than he broadcasts. It is not realistic to expect an agribusiness enterprise like Home Farm to have its own public
relations team, but a simple Google news alert to stay on track
of what is being said would have sufficed for a business of that
size. For bigger brands, software packages such can assist with
monitoring. Virality maps created by such software can chart

how a single remark on Twitter can trigger commentary across a variety of different social networks over time which emphasises the importance of controlling the story as soon as you can. It is possible that Brian was avoiding making any kind of apology in order maintain credible deniability. What he overlooked was that apologies certainly act as social lubricant, and until an apology is made it is impossible to move forward and change the narrative.

Brian finally came clean and admitted guilt only at his trial. This came about by virtue of an angst-ridden conversation about guilt and family with Joe Grundy. In terms of the compensation and redress, he considers his humble pie has been duly eaten in the form of the £120,000 fine and the indignity of having to sell the farmhouse they love so much to live (albeit temporarily) at Willow Cottage. And yet he is still trying to shirk out of supporting some kind of village cele-bration which he previously promised. If he were to do so, it would feed into our crisis framework of building, strength-ening and maintaining relationships with stakeholders. So while I think it's unlikely that Brian will publicly apologise, one thing I would recommend is for him to throw open his – now smaller – wallet and cough up for some kind of village hoopla to start replenishing the levels of the reputational reservoir.

CASE STUDY: LOWER LOXLEY/ELIZABETH PARGETTER

A vulnerability audit would have been less use to the team at Lower Loxley because Freddie Pargetter, the ultimate cause of their problems, would not have been considered as a signifi-cant risk factor. From a business viewpoint, there do not really seem to have many financial or reputational issues really since the death of Nigel Pargetter in early 2011. The conference and wedding venue bookings, in addition to the many events, were all providing no cause for alarm. Going back to the crisis framework (Agnes, 2018) and Elizabeth Pargetter's bank of trust or reputational reservoir was actually in pretty good repair. However, since Freddie's arrest for being discovered with intent to supply, Lower Loxley has been in a chronic state of crisis – with Elizabeth's attention elsewhere – it is fair to say that the TripAdvisor reviews would not have been up to par.

When Freddie was arrested, Elizabeth panicked. She procrastinated and prevaricated and so missed the golden hour of opportunity to contain the story and its damage. Of course, the details of Freddie's arrest was going to come out and even the local British press loves a 'toff does drugs' story. While it does seem to be an Archer family trait to run away from one's problems (witness Kenton Archer literally hiding from David Archer when he was in debt to him) in Elizabeth's case it is easier for the listener to forgive because we know that she was struggling with her mental health. However, her paying customers would not be so kind, as they would have no knowledge of this.

Although Elizabeth took some post-event action; for instance, installing CCTV in the darker corners of the estate, the Lower Loxley alcohol licence was revoked because of the drugs bust. The impact of this loss should have been the wake-up call Elizabeth needed in order to recognise all of the issues. One of the keys to handling a situation like this is to grip it and focus on it, fully identify the problem and its cause, then define a solution. But because Elizabeth was so distracted by Freddie's woes, concentrating on what he needed, she did not focus on the lack of license, which is what the business required. Her mental health was starting to deteriorate at this point, leading her to become unable focus on anything and thus unable to help either her son or her business. This resulted in a nervous breakdown at a later date.

Until the October half-term, Lower Loxley limped on because Elizabeth had a fairly good team around her. But when Geraldine the manager booked a replacement act for the *Halloween Spookalicious Gardens*, she did not check whether they were family-friendly. Families from the whole county who rely on Lower Loxley for a day out when the kids are off school turned up in their droves expecting a Scooby Doo style spooky event. Instead, the act was much more horror-based. This easily avoided mistake resulted in terrifying the little ones and leaving them crying and traumatised. Where there are members of the public with smartphones in their pockets, it is inevitable that the press will get wind of something. I am sure the 'Borsetshire Mummies' Facebook group was awash with gossip and complaints. But instead of taking action to control the damage, Elizabeth was dismissive of Roy Tucker who was merely trying to help her when standing in the car park, attempting to take details in order to make the crucial apology to visitors. What is extraordinary about this is that Roy no longer worked there but was acting out of basic human kindness and empathy, traits which Elizabeth failed to display. With basic monitoring, the story about the Halloween fiasco in *The Borchester Echo* should not have come as a surprise to Elizabeth, but it clearly was. Elizabeth's lack of focus was further demonstrated when she drafted a press release that mostly referred to Freddie's arrest and forthcoming court case and thus not relevant to her customers who were seeking apology and compensation for the event. Whilst it is to her credit that she tried to engage with the media, her demands for Geraldine to appear on Radio Borsetshire and talk about Freddie rather than the Halloween fiasco were a complete disaster. Geraldine refused and then quit. Whether Elizabeth went on the radio herself was not clear, but the Lower Loxley team as a whole would be well-advised to work on repairing their relationship with the local radio station in addition to their customer base.

What should Elizabeth do now? From a commercial perspective, she should immediately address any further concerns over the alcohol licence and work to get it back. *Deck the Hall* without mulled wine must have been unthinkable, not to mention unprofitable. Whilst Elizabeth and her team are taking steps to restore the fortunes of the business with family-friendly events, she needs to work harder on her stakeholder relations. For example, hosting a lunch for the very hardworking volunteer tour guides in The Orangery; inviting local press with the full red-carpet treatment for the previously snubbed Radio Borsetshire journalist and welcoming local mummy influencers to build on their family-friendly branding. In terms of the sustainability of the business, if the outlook for the return of the alcohol licence is looking bleak, an alternative might be to consider rebranding as a teetotal haven. With an increased understanding of mental health issues, it may not be too much of a stretch to imagine Lower Loxley becoming Borsetshire's answer to the Priory. Certainly, they need to think about the long-term future because a conference centre without alcohol is most likely unviable.

CONCLUSION

In the midst of a crisis, it is of course incredibly challenging to do and say the right thing under time pressure and stakeholder scrutiny. An improper crisis response can exacerbate the situation. What both Brian and Elizabeth also failed to do was remember to be human while recognising the mistakes that have been made. It is worth noting too that neither Brian nor Elizabeth is alone in this, and the same has befallen much larger businesses. Tony Hayward, CEO of BP, dealing with the fallout of the Deepwater Horizon oil disaster in 2010 quipped in frustration to journalists, 'I'm sorry. We're sorry for the massive disruption it's caused their lives. There's no one who wants this over more than I do. I'd like my life back' (Kanter, 2010). Understandably, he was heavily criticised for this. If an organisation fails to adequately deal with a crisis, the public considers that the organisation is not in control of the situation and thus must be responsible for the accident. And because this is a 'reputational' crisis Sandman (2005) emphasises the imperative of an apology. When making an apology, the only consideration should be what's best for the institution and its stakeholders. Saying 'we'll look into this' shows a lack of considering for the emotion involved. If you say, 'we are concerned and will work on making things better', you are showing much more empathy. Sandman (2005) explains further:

> *You have to back your apology with two kinds of efforts to 'make it right' – compensation for those who were hurt by what you did, and policy improvements so it's less likely to happen again (not 'to ensure that it will never happen again'; that's over-promising). Note that compensation and improvement should come after you apologize, not instead of apologizing.*

In a 2018 study by Deloitte (Cuerden, 2018) of over 500 senior crisis management executives, 60% said that their firms face more crises than they did a decade ago. The same study showed 90% of those who had conducted a crisis review had only done so after the event. Businesses are less motivated by the fear of a potential crisis than they are by preventing a repeat of a previous crisis and Deloitte stated:

> *A life cycle approach to managing crises fortifies an organization's ability to avoid crises by focusing proactively on detection and risk management as well as on readiness and response. It also recognizes that crises can present opportunities for organizations to emerge stronger, enabling them to build more effective capabilities at all stages of the crisis life cycle.*

(Cuerden, 2018)

Had either Elizabeth or Brian responded quickly, honestly, constructively and empathetically to their crisis, they may both have been given the benefit of the doubt. Instead, they found themselves caught in the headlights of public distrust with little obvious place to turn. For Brian and Elizabeth, the key strategies needed to manage crises in today's digital world are still as they used to be. I would commend them both to: acknowledge what has happened, accept responsibility, apologise and act to ensure the future and reputation of both businesses.

REFERENCES

Agnes, M. (2018). *Crisis ready*. Herndon, VA: Mascot Books.

Courage, C., & Headlam, N. (2017). *Custard, culverts and cake: Academics on life in The Archers* (pp. 199–200). Bingley: Emerald Publishing Limited.

Cuerden, S. (2018). 2018 Global crisis management survey. Deloitte, UK. Retrieved from https://www2.deloitte.com/uk/en/pages/risk/articles/2018-global-crisis-management-survey.html. Accessed on June 28, 2020.

Elrhoul, M. (2015). Research: Four ways brands can build customer service relationships on Twitter. [online] 30 June 2015. Retrieved from https://blog.twitter.com/en_us/a/2015/research-four-ways-brands-can-build-customer-service-relationships-on-twitter.html. Accessed on June 28, 2020.

Greyser, S. A. (2009). Corporate brand reputation and brand crisis management. *Management Decision*, 47(4), 590–602.

Kanter, R. M. (2010). BP's Tony Hayward and the failure of leadership accountability. *Harvard Business Review*. [online] 23 July 2014. Retrieved from https://hbr.org/2010/06/bps-tony-hayward-and-the-failu.html. Accessed on June 28, 2020.

Miles, R. P. (2014). *Warren Buffett wealth : Principles and practical methods used by the world's greatest investor*. Hoboken, NJ: John Wiley & Sons.

Salvador, A., & Ikeda, A. (2018). Brand crisis management: The use of information for prevention, identification and management. *Review of Business Management*, 20, 74–91.

Sandman, P. (2005). The role of apologizing in crisis situations (Peter M. Sandman website). Retrieved from http://www.psandman.com/articles/busters.htm. Accessed on June 28, 2020.

Section 3

FAMILY FUNCTION AND DYSFUNCTION

7

CONTEMPORARY SOCIAL PROBLEMS IN A RURAL SETTING: USING *THE ARCHERS* IN SOCIAL WORK EDUCATION

Helen M Burrows

ABSTRACT

Social Work education has seen some changes since my first paper on how The Archers *could be used to enhance a student's understanding of service user experiences (Burrows, 2016). Social Work students still, however, need to understand the difficulties that their future service users may experience; learning is developed through lectures, seminars and workshops, and most of all through practice experience, but a real challenge for educators is how to show students the constant lived reality of families and communities who have complex difficulties. A visit to a household only gives a snapshot of their life, and service users may be guarded in their behaviour during a professional visit. My original paper considered the educational value of the 'fly-on-the-wall' perspective of* The Archers, *in catching unguarded*

moments and drawing attention to issues in the com-
munity. From the impact of rural poverty and unaf-
fordable housing, through issues of mental health,
hospital discharge, to adult survivors of child sexual
abuse and the tangled webs of modern slavery, these
issues will resonate with any social worker, in Adult,
Children and Families or Mental Health fields. These are
not just issues in a rural setting; professionals in more
urban settings will recognise these as things the families
and individuals they work with must deal with from time
to time.

INTRODUCTION

A common stereotype of a social worker is *the Guardian*
reading, BBC Radio 4 listener; whilst stereotyping is
anathema to us, many of us have been known to sit in car
parks between visits to listen to the lunchtime broadcast. In
2016, I wrote a paper (Burrows, 2016) to show how
listening to *The Archers* can contribute to social work
education, with reference to the story of Helen (née, Archer)
and Rob Titchener's dysfunctional relationship. The idea for
this came up when a student I was supervising on placement
wanted to learn more about domestic violence. I talked to
him about Helen and Rob and realised how much he and
other students and professionals could learn if they started
to listen in. On being asked to revise and update the chapter
to look at how things have changed in the last years, I have
also looked at other issues relevant to social work and how
they could be used in the current forms of social work
education.

THE ROLE AND STRUCTURE OF SOCIAL
WORK EDUCATION

In 2016, most social workers qualified through a three-year first degree or two-year Masters course, combined with practice placements across Children's, Adult, and Mental Health services. Now, in 2020, they have more options: as well as full- or part-time undergraduate or postgraduate courses, students can undertake a social work degree apprenticeship and alternative training routes and courses. As suggested by the 'apprenticeship' route, much of their learning is 'on the job', earning as they work. As an example, *Frontline* is an employment-based route to qualification for students who want to work with children and families, who already hold a good 2.1 or above first degree. It starts with the Summer Institute, a five-week residential study block at the University of Warwick, and continuing over two years where students work in a local authority in groups of ideally four, led by an experienced social worker and supported by practice tutors, at the same time working towards the initial 120 credits of a Masters degree, then working in the second year as a newly qualified social worker, and continuing to work towards a Masters Degree in Advanced Relationship Based Social Work Practice. They benefit from leadership development, and end up joining the *Frontline Fellowship*, a practice community working to pursue wider social justice and change for vulnerable children and families (Frontline, 2020).

Education and training standards (SWE, 2019b) set out the expectations of opportunities for the development and assessment of skills, knowledge and behaviours that meet the Professional Standards for Social Work (SWE, 2019a). For example, to meet standard 4.7 – 'The delivery of the course will support and develop autonomous and reflective thinking' (SWE, 2019c, p. 27) – a variety of approaches can be used including discussion groups, workshops, practice simulation and debriefing; reflective diaries or logs. It is in this area that I think *The Archers* can be of most use.

Social Work students encounter many different family and individual situations during their training and need to understand the difficulties that their future service users may experience. None of us have experienced all the problems that may be met in social work practice, so what do social work students learn and how does this learning take place? In addition to lectures and seminars, the social work placement (or their work-based group) is maybe the most important learning opportunity for social work students (Domakin, 2015); they are supervised by a qualified practice educator given the opportunity to apply classroom learning to real-life practice in skill development. One of the reasons for the growth in work-based qualifying programmes such as *Frontline*, and its Mental Health equivalent, *Think Ahead*, is that as Irvine, Molyneux, and Gillman (2015) suggest, experiential learning has more of a lasting impression than other methods of teaching and learning. Working with service users and carers enables students to learn about procedures and legislation and to apply these sensitively and carefully, for it is real lives that they are dealing with.

Despite this, work-based learning does not necessarily enable students to fully understand the lived experience of individuals and families. Service users may be wary of professionals, who can have the power to provide or refuse services, and in some cases impose conditions on how families live, including compulsory admissions to hospital, or the removal of children into care. On a standard university placement, it can be difficult for people to trust a student who they know will be 'handing them on' to someone else when their placement ends. Even with the best working relationships, an hour's visit can only ever provide a snapshot of how people are living and interacting. As professionals, we will rarely see life as it is lived all the time. This is where *The Archers* can come into its own, in allowing us to catch unguarded moments which a professional would never see (or hear.)

WHAT CAN *THE ARCHERS* TEACH SOCIAL WORKERS?

The Archers gives us a fly-on-the-wall insight into the daily lives of the residents of Ambridge, which – whilst it may have its strange aspects, like a lack of BBC Radio 4, and having its own micro-climate – is in itself a microcosm of English society, with all its strengths and wonderful eccentricities, and reflects the issues that can be found in the majority of communities. Whilst the programme no longer has the remit to educate farmers on new agricultural practices – it is now 'contemporary drama in a rural setting' – a number of social issues have been addressed; amongst other things racism, rural poverty, homelessness, medical conditions, addictions such as alcohol, drugs and gambling, and rural crime have all been addressed in recent years, alongside the yearly cycle of the agricultural and village social calendar. I intend to focus on five main issues (though other factors will come into them): Helen and Rob's ongoing story of domestic abuse and its consequences; parenting under pressure and complicated relationships (see Chapter 8); housing; adult survivors of sexual abuse; and modern slavery (see Chapter 4).

CONTINUING HELEN AND ROB'S EXPERIENCES

At the time I initially wrote my paper for the first *Academic Archers* conference in February 2016, the domestic abuse by

Rob against Helen was still ongoing – it was not until early April 2016 that Helen snapped and stabbed him. My student would have learned about tools to assess domestic abuse, the legal framework including the Serious Crime Act 2015 which framed the concept of coercive control, support networks, how friends and families of survivors can be drawn into collusion with abusers. He would have learned about victim/survivor perspectives, the dynamics of domestic violence, and we would have looked at the impact on the children, Henry Archer and Jack/Gideon Titchener. With Helen on remand for attempted murder, we had a fantastic opportunity to look at the criminal law framework and mechanisms, issues of advocacy, social and moral justice, and children in prison.

By September 2016 when the case came to court, and later, in December, when custody was decided in the family court (following social work assessments and a psychological assessment of Rob), we had even more opportunity to look at Family Law, Human Rights, morals and ethics, and at a level you rarely can observe in a student placement. Rob's attempted abduction of Jack in early February 2017 raised further issues around safeguarding and ongoing control from ex-partners. There have been many comments in fan forums about the possible impact of the domestic abuse on Henry (see Chapter 10), so discussions on child development and Adverse Childhood Experiences (ACEs) (Wade et al., 2016) have been facilitated.

Helen appeared to have made a really good recovery from the trauma of her relationship with Rob – but more recently, in the 'lockdown' format of *The Archers*, it is evident that she is still deeply affected, and this is likely to impact on her, and Henry, for years to come, so again this will be rich material for looking at developmental issues through the life course.

PARENTING AND COMPLICATED RELATIONSHIPS

Helen was truly parenting under pressure in her marriage to Rob, but the millennial, younger adult generation of the Grundy clan provides an interesting case study in parenting in adversity and within complicated relationships. Will and Ed Grundy both grew up with some difficult circumstances, where money was always tight, and in their teens found their family being evicted from their tenancy, Grange Farm, through bankruptcy. However, their parents, Clarrie and Eddie Grundy, provided a stable and loving family which also supported Eddie's father Joe until his death, back at his beloved Grange Farm, in October 2019. They had a potentially bad influence in their lives in their extended family, with Eddie's brother Alf Grundy being a career criminal who has spent significant time in prison.

Emma Grundy, daughter of Susan and Neil Carter, grew up alongside the boys, and has been married to both. Currently she is married to, and living with, Ed, their daughter Keira Grundy, aged nine, and her son George Grundy, aged 15, in Little Grange, a static caravan in the grounds of Grange Farm (though without planning permission). George's father is Will – though initially Ed believed he was the father, and it took a DNA test to prove otherwise. Will's other child is Poppy Grundy, aged six, through his now-deceased wife Nic Grundy – and he has two older stepchildren, Jake and Mia Grundy, who moved to live with their father Andrew after Nic's death.

There have been many points in Will, Emma and Ed's journeys so far in parenting, where professional help might have been helpful. Fairly early on in Will's relationship with Nic, there were some concerns about her treatment of George when she hit him. If he had disclosed this at nursery or school then safeguarding procedures would have been instigated; Nic was filled with remorse, and moved out of the household, so a useful vignette for looking at threshold criteria for safeguarding. More recently, there have been many points where there have been safeguarding concerns in respect of Poppy – with Will taking her out working at night with him, causing her to be overtired at school, leaving Mia to care for her (neglecting all the children's needs in the wake of Nic's death, if truth be told) and then his attempted suicide with the resultant damage to Poppy's room from the shotgun being fired. Luckily Poppy was not there – but this highlighted Will's deteriorating mental health.

This incident would also give the opportunity to explore working with parents with poor mental health who will not seek professional/medical support and the tactics that can be used in intervention with threatened suicide (Kourgiantakis et al., 2019). Like Helen, Will seems to have recovered remarkably quickly, but again like Helen, we must wonder what lies ahead for him in the years to come. Linked to this are the concerns that George, Poppy, Jake and Mia got nothing significant in the way of bereavement support after Nic's death, and Mia could have also benefitted from support as a young carer.

Emma's relationship with Ed has been on/off and has been the cause of a lot of tension and animosity between the Grundy brothers. Generally though, through all of this, and even with the tremendous financial pressures they have been under, with Emma working three jobs and Ed having had bad losses with his livestock, the two of them have still put the interests of the children first, and have tried to keep lines of communication open when they have been apart. We must remember though that much of this has been facilitated by both Ed and Emma's parents – both sets of parents have provided places for them and the children to live and have looked after the children as a 'given.' It is helpful to reflect on how things may have gone if the children did not have two sets of supportive and local grandparents and to reflect on how much such support mitigates against the difficulties and pressures of parenting. The whole family's situation over the years can also be read as a case study of parenting in poverty, with strengths, difficulties and resilience demonstrated throughout (Katz, Corlyon, La Placa, & Hunter, 2007).

Discussion of aspects of the Grundys' ongoing story (and at the time of writing we have yet to see what pressures might be placed on them in lockdown through the COVID-19 pandemic) can lead us to consider the different practice models and tools that we might employ should social work intervention be required. For example, from earlier on in their story, we might want to look at the point that Will and Nic decided to change Jake and Mia's family name to Grundy. This may have had impact on their identity, relevant again recently when following Nic's death and Will's deteriorating ability to care for the children, Jake and Mia both moved back to live with their father Andrew – we might ask whether stepparent adoption by Will could have been an option at either point, and consider the complex negotiations that this involves when a birth parent (Andrew, in this case) is likely to object to losing their parental responsibility for the child/ren. We had an example of stepparent adoption being facilitated by a social worker some years ago, when Alistair Lloyd married Shula (Hebden-Lloyd, née Archer) and adopted her son, Daniel. However, Daniel's father, Mark Hebden, had died before Daniel's birth, so the matter was relatively straightforward.

Considering the (luckily, relatively few) safeguarding concerns over the years, the Signs of Safety approach (Turnell & Edwards, 1999) could be applied. This focuses on building partnerships with parents and significant other family members and applying solution-focused approaches to turning points of risk and danger into strengths and safety. This approach would have considered the family holistically, so concerns over

George's behaviour at times (for example, having unexplained money, potentially radical religious beliefs) could have been addressed. If Clarrie and Eddie and Neil and Susan had not always voluntarily taken up care for the children when the younger parents were struggling, then Family Group Conferencing would have been an option, giving both the children and the adults a voice. Both approaches fit in with the systemic approach used in many local authorities.

Signs of Safety has its own practice tools, both for assessment and for direct work with children, and another tool that could be used to look at the impact on the children of the family problems and dynamics would be genograms. These 'enhanced' family tree diagrams map the strengths and difficulties, the areas of conflict and the areas where positive alliances can be built, and can go a long way towards mapping and understanding dysfunction and difficulties within families, as Burrows and Gillies (2017) demonstrated with their application to the Aldridge and Horrobin families in Ambridge. Genograms are used extensively in social work practice, but rarely to their full extent, so practice during training improves their later use by practitioners.

HOUSING

Why is understanding housing issues important for social workers? As Simcock and Machin (2019) rightly point out, access to affordable and appropriate housing is a matter of social justice, and housing security and poverty should be an integral part of social work assessments.

The Grundy family gives us a fairly comprehensive case study for looking at how housing can impact on families. Originally tenant farmers at Grange Farm, they became homeless in 2000 and moved into emergency housing, a council flat at Meadow Rise, Borchester. Will Grundy was by then living in a flat provided for him by his godmother, but Clarrie and Eddie were worried that Ed would 'meet the wrong sort' on the Meadow Rise estate. The move had a bad impact on Joe's mental health; at one point he killed his pet ferrets in despair and went into a decline that saw him wandering disorientated. There was no social work intervention at this point, although it could be well argued that the family could have benefitted from support from Adult Social Care, or Mental Health support for Joe. If there had been then they could have expected advocacy with the Local Authority Housing Department to assist them to find somewhere more appropriate for long-term accommodation. The legislation current at the time (Housing Act 1996) gave clear guidance on the duties around rehousing homeless families, and since then further legislation (Homelessness Act 2002; Localism Act 2011; Homelessness Reduction Act 2017) has added to this imperative. Housing officers recognise the link between housing and wellbeing and work with tenants to address problems such as domestic abuse, fuel poverty, disability and debt but with austerity measures hitting all areas of local authority work, sensitive and assertive advocacy is often helpful, and as Sillman (2018) makes clear, appropriateness of housing can exacerbate or help to resolve other social needs.

The Grundys were able to move back to Ambridge when Keeper's Cottage became available, and this was their home, albeit in cramped conditions that saw Ed, when he was there, having to share a room with Joe, until 2015 when the Ambridge Flood again made them homeless. At this point, the local authority might have been expected to rehouse them again, but they were accommodated temporarily at Grey Gables, so were able to stay in the village, and in one of those 'Ambridge Fairy' moments (see Chapter 12) Oliver Sterling gave them Grange Farm to live in. Eventually, of course, Joe died there, in his beloved farmhouse which by then was accommodating the whole extended family including Will and Poppy. Rich material indeed here to consider the importance of place for older service users, and the strengths of family networks, the need to take a 'Think Family' approach for social workers in all sectors, and the role of the social worker as advocate. Rich material to work on critical reflection when looking at assessment and analysis of need (Karlsson, 2020).

ADULT SURVIVORS OF CHILD SEXUAL ABUSE

One story in 2019 that was handled sensitively, and which prompted a lot of discussion on fan forums on Facebook, was Prof. Jim Lloyd's disclosure of having experienced child sexual abuse (CSA). Typically, such stories relate to female characters, which are understandable given that most instances of sexual abuse are perpetrated by males against females (Nelson, 2009), so this was of particular significance, highlighting the under-reporting of male-on-male incidents, and the shame felt by male survivors. Marsh (2019) explains that one of the reasons for underreporting is the dominant discourses of masculinity; the myths which say that males are strong and should be able to fight off an abuser, or the myth that suggests that if most abusers were themselves abused, anyone who was abused will go on to become an abuser. Internalised homophobia also affects disclosure rates and sadly I have had to challenge attitudes in this area with students on a number of occasions. So, whilst hard to listen to, Jim's story provides especially useful material for discussion of gender issues and anti-oppressive practice.

MODERN SLAVERY

Philip Moss, a building contractor, was first employed in Ambridge in March 2017, when he quoted Shula for the repair of the Hunt kennels roof which had collapsed. He came across as an amiable man with an interest in wildlife, and he made friends in the village. Through their mutual interest in bird-watching, Philip got together with Kirsty Miller in February 2018, and eventually they moved in together to a house on the new Beechwood estate, with plans to marry. Moss's son Gavin later moved in with them when his fiancée left him. Moss continued to do work around the village, and in early March 2020, he took on some repair work to Grey Gables' kitchen floor, quickly followed by the explosion that nearly killed Lynda Snell and the workman Blake.

It fairly soon transpired, through the conversations between Moss and Gavin, who was supposed to be have been super-vising Blake that day, that Blake and other workmen were being kept by the Mosses in modern slavery (see Chapters 2 and 4). Moss spells out to Gavin that this is what people will call it, and it appears that the explosion was caused by Blake having been provided with petrol to use as a solvent, and, starving, using the grill to try to make toast because Gavin hadn't fed him. Moss continued to exert a lot of control and pressure on Blake, with threats and coercion as he lay in hos-pital, attempts to stop Blake being interviewed by the police without Moss being there, and finally removing Blake from the hospital (disguised as 'self-discharge') and pretending to have driven him to Norfolk to his family. To date (still under COVID-19 restrictions in the UK), there has been no social work intervention in any of this situation, and no one knows how the truth might be revealed as the story unfolds. But how might we use this to teach?

Modern slavery is an issue that must be clearly understood by any social worker, whether in Adult or Children's Services. Vulnerable adults and teens can be drawn into many kinds of exploitation and abuse, of which modern slavery is one – and one that is rarely talked about in the media in general – so that this story line provides some really useful material to discuss. The idea of modern slavery is often related to human trafficking, and this sometimes carries assumptions that cross-border migration is usually involved. Most of us will probably have seen reports of people being tricked by the promise of work into migration to the UK from Eastern Europe, war zones, or areas such as the Philippines, and coming at great financial and human cost to find themselves in forced labour. This covers areas such as domestic labour, the sex industry, and, as here, manual trades such as construction or agricultural labouring.

What the Moss storyline brings out is that this also happens to people from within the UK, often adults who are vulnerable through street homelessness, with mental health or learning disabilities. For many reasons (Shaw & Greenhow, 2019) young people leaving care are particularly likely to be exploited in this way, and it is vital that social workers are able to recognise abuse such as forced labour, domestic servitude, sexual exploitation (such as escort work, prostitution and pornography), debt bondage, being forced to work to pay off debts that realistically they never will be able to. Possible indicators of modern slavery include:

> ...*signs of physical or emotional abuse, appearing to be malnourished, unkempt or withdrawn, isolation from the community, seeming under the control or influence of others, living in dirty, cramped or overcrowded accommodation and/or living and working at the same address, lack of personal effects or identification documents, always wearing the same clothes, avoidance of eye contact, appearing frightened or hesitant to talk to strangers, fear of law enforcers.*

(SCIE, 2020)

So much of this can be seen in the case of Blake, Kenzie and Jordan, and much can be gained from consideration of the attitudes and actions of Moss and Gavin towards the 'horses' as they refer to them, discussion around the police process and looking at what guidance there is for professionals, highlighting the National Referral Mechanism for victims of modern slavery (Gov.UK, 2020). Police procedure here is particularly relevant; one might have expected Sgt. Harrison Burns to have identified Blake as a vulnerable adult and insisted on an Appropriate Adult to assist Blake in his witness interviews. This is a role often played by social workers and gives the opportunity to explore support and advocacy under the Police and Criminal Evidence Act (PACE) 1984.

CONCLUSION – LEARNING THROUGH NARRATIVE AND DISCUSSION AND THE IMPACT OF COVID-19 AND SOCIAL DISTANCING

Dramatic narrative has been used in social work education in a variety of ways in recent years (Duffy, Montgomery, Murphy, Davidson, & Bunting, 2020). Our relationships with the characters in dramas can be intensely personal, so exploring these, and facilitating the expression and exploration of emotion is key. Such interactive and immersive learning experiences (Dodds, Heslop, & Meredith, 2018), asking the question, 'so what would you do in this situation?', is a valuable method for enabling students to consider and develop their practice skills in the classroom, linking knowledge, skills and understanding, both of a service user's position and of their own selves as practitioners. The exploration of emotion in learning for practice is particularly important in developing understanding of the self as a practitioner, a point that Dore (2019) makes eloquently.

Helen Walmsley-Johnson (2016) wrote in *The New States-man* of the Helen and Rob story, 'Storylines like this are really best covered by the soap genre because they allow an almost real-time development of the plot.' This is as true of the Moss modern slavery storyline as it was of Rob and Helen's rela-tionship. We need to remember that insights into the real-life experience of a particular issue can not necessarily be generalised to all people experiencing something similar, but we can start to recognise patterns that fit certain common behavioural traits.

Given the difficulties that social distancing placed on class-room learning, online discussion is likely to be a teaching and learning tool used widely in the coming years. The use of well-managed online discussion is widely understood to be an effec-tive online teaching method in terms of meeting students' diverse learning needs and styles (Madoc-Jones & Parrott, 2005), and in creating communities of practice (Moore, 2008) and commu-nities of learning (Gillingham, 2009). This is something which *Academic Archers* has had much success in facilitating through the initial COVID-19 pandemic lockdown, in their Saturday Omnibus sessions (Academic Archers, 2020), where the learning community is multi-disciplinary, and the discussion is as deep as it is broad. It is not only social work students who can learn from listening to *The Archers*.

REFERENCES

Academic Archers. (2020). The Saturday Omnibus podcasts. Retrieved from https://academicarchers.buzzsprout.com/. Accessed on August 29, 2020.

Burrows, H. M. (2016). An everyday story of dysfunctional families: Using the Archers in social work education. In C. Courage, N. Headlam, & P. Matthews (Eds.), *The*

Archers in fact and fiction: Academic analyses of life in rural Borsetshire. Oxford: Peter Lang.

Burrows, H. M., & Gillies, L. (2017). A case study in the use of genograms to assess family dysfunction and social class: To the Manor Born versus Shameless. In C. Courage & N. Headlam (Eds.), *Custard, culverts and cake: Academics on life in the Archers.* Bingley: Emerald Publishing Limited.

Dodds, C., Heslop, P., & Meredith, C. (2018). Using simulation-based education to help social work students prepare for practice. *Social Work Education, 37*(5), 597–602.

Domakin, A. (2015). The importance of practice learning in social work: Do we practice what we preach? *Social Work Education, 34*(4), 399–413.

Dore, I. (2019). Talking about emotion: How are conversations about emotion enabled in the context of social work practice education? *Social Work Education, 38*(7), 846–860.

Duffy, J., Montgomery, L., Murphy, P., Davidson, G., & Bunting, L. (2020). Differing knowledges: Comparing the contribution of drama students and service users in role-plays preparing social work students for practice. *Social Work Education.* doi:10.1080/02615479.2020.1717461

Frontline. (2020). Our programmes. Retrieved from https://thefrontline.org.uk/our-programmes/frontline-programme/. Accessed on August 29, 2020.

Gillingham, P. (2009). Ghosts in the machine: Student participation and grade attainment in a web-assisted social work course. *Social Work Education, 28*(4), 423–435.

Gov.UK. (2020). National referral mechanism. Retrieved from https://www.gov.uk/government/publications/human-trafficking-victims-referral-and-assessment-forms/guidance-on-the-national-referral-mechanism-for-potential-adult-victims-of-modern-slavery-england-and-wales. Accessed on August 29, 2020.

Irvine, J., Molyneux, J., & Gillman, M. (2015). Providing a link with the real world: Learning from the student experience of service user and carer involvement in social work education. *Social Work Education*, *34*(2), 138–150.

Karlsson, S. G. (2020). Looking for elderly people's needs: Teaching critical reflection in Swedish social work education. *Social Work Education*, *39*(2), 227–240.

Katz, I., Corlyon, J., La Placa, V., & Hunter, S. (2007). *The relationship between parenting and poverty*. Policy Research Bureau. York: Joseph Rowntree Foundation.

Kourgiantakis, T., Sewell, K. M., Lee, E., Adamson, K., McCormick, M., Kuehl, D., & Bogo, M. (2019). Enhancing social work education in mental health, addictions, and suicide risk assessment: A teaching note. *Journal of Social Work Education*, *56*(3), 587–594.

Marsh, N. (2019). Sexual abuse of boys continues to be missed: What social workers can do. *Community Care*, March 18, 2019. Retrieved from https://www.communitycare.co.uk/2019/03/18/sexual-abuse-boys-continues-missed-social-workers-can/. Accessed on July 6, 2020.

Madoc-Jones, I., & Parrott, L. (2005). Virtual social work education - theory and experience. *Social Work Education*, *24*(7), 755–768.

Moore, B. (2008). Using technology to promote communities of practice (CoP) in social work education. *Social Work Education*, *27*(6), 592–600.

Nelson, S. (2009). *Care and support needs of men who survived childhood sexual abuse: Report of a qualitative research project*. Edinburgh: Centre for Research on Families and Relationships.

Sillman, D. (2018). Families of four or five were living in one room: How social work and the housing crisis intersect. *Community Care*, September 10, 2018. Retrieved from http://www.communitycare.co.uk/2018/09/10/families-four-five-living-one-room-social-work-housing-crisis-intersect. Accessed on July 6, 2020.

Simcock, P., & Machin, R. (2019). It's not just about where someone lives: educating student social workers about housing-related matters to promote an understanding of social justice. *Social Work Education*, *38*(8), 1041–1053.

Shaw, J., & Greenhow, S. (2019). Children in care: Exploitation, offending and the denial of victimhood in a prosecution-led culture of practice. *British Journal of Social Work*, *50*(5), 1551–1569.

Social Care Institute for Excellence (SCIE). (2020). Retrieved from https://www.scie.org.uk/safeguarding/adults/introduction/types-and-indicators-of-abuse#modern-slavery. Accessed on August 29, 2020.

Social Work England (SWE). (2019a). *Professional standards*. Sheffield: Social Work England. Retrieved from https://www.socialworkengland.org.uk/media/1640/1227_socialworkengland_standards_prof_standards_final-aw.pdf. Accessed on August 29, 2020.

Social Work England (SWE). (2019b). Qualifying education and training standards 2019. Sheffield: Social Work England. Retrieved from https://www.socialworkengland.org.uk/media/1641/socialworkengland_ed-training-standards-2019_final.pdf. Accessed on August 29, 2020.

Social Work England (SWE). (2019c). Qualifying education and training standards 2019 guidance. Sheffield: Social Work England. Retrieved from https://www.socialworkengland.org.uk/media/1528/education-and-training-standards-guidance-designed-2019_final.pdf. Accessed on August 29, 2020.

Turnell, A., & Edwards, S. (1999). *Signs of safety: A solution and safety oriented approach to child protection casework*. London: W. W. Norton & Company.

Wade, R., Cronholm, P. F., Fein, J. A., Forke, C. M., Davis, M. B., Harkins-Schwarz, M. ... Bair-Merritt, M. H. (2016). Household and community-level adverse childhood experiences and adult health outcomes in a diverse urban population. *Child Abuse & Neglect*, 52, 135–145.

Walmsley-Johnson, H. (2016). Helen's story of abuse in the Archers reminds me of my own – so I'm willing her to leave. *New Statesman*. February 2, 2016. Retrieved from http://www.newstatesman.com/politics/feminism/2016/02/helen-s-story-abuse-archers-reminds-me-my-own-so-i-m-willing-her-leave. Accessed on August 29, 2020.

8

ACADEMIC ARCHERS ASSEMBLY: PUTTING THE PARENTS ON TRIAL

Cara Courage

ABSTRACT

The parenting styles, or perhaps lack thereof, of Ambridge families is a much-talked about topic among The Archers *listeners. This has been brought into keen focus recently with the parental role in, and reaction to, Ed and Emma Grundy's separation, and the intra- and inter-family dynamics of the Archers clans brought about by Peggy Woolley's Ambridge Conservation Trust. This chapter presents an Archers Assembly, based on the Citizens' Assembly model, to pass judgement on the parenting styles of the matriarchs and family heads of key Ambridge clans. The Archers Assembly crowdsourced (through the Academic Archers Facebook group) considerations on: The Matriarchs, Peggy and Gill Archer; David and Ruth Archer; Pat and Tony Archer; Susan and Neil Carter; Jenny and Brian Aldridge; and Clarrie and Eddy Grundy. The chapter offers the evidence on each set, with a list of 'for' and 'against' cases, and quotes, from respondents.*

INTRODUCTION

The parenting styles of those in Ambridge is a perennial
conversation topic among *The Archers* listeners and at the
2020 *Academic Archers* conference at University of Reading a
selection of eight of the parenting sets in the village were put
on 'trial', posed against the question, 'Are [parent/s] an
example of good parenting?' and using an adapted Citizens'
Assembly model to make this deliberation. This chapter
presents the findings of the (very informal) research on The
Matriarchs, Peggy and Jill Archer, and on David and Ruth
Archer, Pat and Tony Archer, Susan and Neil Carter, Jennifer
and Brian Aldridge, Clarrie and Eddie Grundy, Helen Archer,
and Emma, Ed and Will Grundy. It will first outline the
Citizens' Assembly model and the *Academic Archers* adapta-
tion of that, and then present data findings from the *Academic
Archers* Facebook page on each parenting set.

THE CITIZENS' ASSEMBLY MODEL

A Citizens' Assembly is a cross-section of citizens of a state who
are brought together to discuss an issue or issues of local or
national importance, often dealing with divisive and highly
politicised issues such as same-sex marriage, abortion and
climate and ecological emergency, and reach a conclusion about
what they think should happen. The membership of a Citizens'
Assembly is randomly selected to be broadly representative of
the population, and a group will be composed of between 50 to
250 participants. The method and model have been used in the
United Kingdom, Australia, Canada, the United States and
Republic of Ireland and gives members of the public the time and
opportunity to learn about and discuss a topic, using a variety of
various methods of inquiry, such as directly questioning experts,

before reaching conclusions and workable recommendations (Citizens Assembly, n.d). In many cases, the state will require these proposals to be accepted by the general public through a referendum before becoming law (Parliament.uk, n.d).

Citizens' Assemblies are used to both give decision-makers a detailed understanding of informed public opinion on complex issues and open up the space for political consensus to be found. The method is used most effectively when the goal is to examine broad policy objectives or create new ideas and propose solutions; assess policy and develop recommendations; and to gain insight from the public about existing policy and practice. A three-step process of learning, deliberation and decision-making is applied, supported by a team of impartial facilitators who guide participants through the process. Participants learn about the topic from experts in the field and additional learning materials. The second phase, deliberation, encourages participants to explore their own opinions based on what they have learnt and to develop nuanced positions on the issues at hand, before the third and final stage, decision-making. This involves participants coming to some conclusions on what they have learnt through the assembly process (Citizens Assembly, n.d).

The process can bring attention to an issue, surface diverse opinions on an issue, decision-makers are brought face to face with the populace and it offers policy makers an insight on public opinion. However, the process can be time and resource-heavy (and thus, expensive) and it is a complex process to run, with a danger of it being utilised as a publicity stunt if real outcomes are blocked (Citizens Assembly, n.d; Involve, n.d; Parliament.uk, n.d).

ACADEMIC ARCHERS ASSEMBLY METHOD

All expense spared for the *Academic Archers* Assembly, however, with the data gathering being done via the group

Facebook page. Furthermore, the selection was far from random, with all participants self-selecting listeners to *The Archers*, and deliberation was a curtailed process as most participants presented a fixed mindset on all parent sets. However, as all *Academic Archers* 'members' are attributed Research Fellow status, all information submitted to the Assembly was from an expert. The parenting sets were: The Matriarchs, Peggy and Jill Archer, David and Ruth Archer, Pat and Tony Archer, Susan and Neil Carter, Jennifer and Brian Aldridge, Clarrie and Eddie Grundy, Helen Archer, and Emma, Ed and Will Grundy.

Data were gathered over a period of two weeks in 2020, with a total of 253 data points submitted, a selection of which presented here anonymously. A Facebook post per parenting set per day was presented to the c2,500 (at the time) members of the *Academic Archers* Facebook page, with the question, 'Are [parent/s] an example of good parenting?' Participants then submitted their evidence and opinion in the comments section. This was analysed and collated and then presented at the 2021 *Academic Archers* conference at the University of Reading, and each set of parents set to a 'yes/no' vote by the assembled Fellows. One response was banned from the start: the recommendation that any of the parents undergo psychotherapy, as this is a given for all residents of Ambridge.

Archers Assembly 1: The Matriarchs, Peggy and Jill Archer

Sixty-four responses were submitted to the question 'Are Peggy Wolley and Jill Archer good parents?', garnering not only just the most responses of all parenting sets but also some of the most acerbic. Peggy and Jill were described as 'the epitome of smug, complacent, conservative (with both small and large C)' and 'self-obsessed.' Both were thought to be over-controlling in their own ways, resulting in keeping their children tied to apron-strings. Conversely, some thought them 'Just ordinary women of their generation', not perfect, but products of different times.

Many respondents cited Peggy's manipulative and divisive use of her money as a parenting style, 'She's a bit too fond of playing Lady Bountiful,' and is mischief-making, and, it was noted in particular what this has done to Tony Archer, as he has been side-lined and belittled by his mother. There was some sympathy for Peggy though, her first marriage cited here and the emotional and literal heavy lifting she had to do in this relationship. However, on the whole, Peggy was seen as 'too honest', for example, letting one child or grandchild know the other is preferred; and also as a bad judge of character, her fawning over Rob and all his outward attributes of class and breeding she saw cited here. There were some positive mentions of Peggy: for example, her taking in granddaughter Kate Madikane, how she has the measure of Kate and has put some boundaries in place in her relation to Kate, which arguably Kate's parents haven't been able to; the inheritance-gate situation with Tony resulting in him getting some backbone; and that she raised two very capable daughters.

There was less barbed vitriol for Jill from respondents, but she was criticised for her 'smothercare' of David Archer in particular, which was also seen to have an impact on his parenting of Jill's grandchildren. Jill was seen to use emotion to manipulate her children into doing what she wants; many mentioned her lack of support for Shula Hebden-Lloyd when divorcing; and also, her capacity to ignore the emotional politics and dynamics between her children, between David and Kenton Archer, for example, and not do what is in her gift to resolve this. Sympathy was however expressed for Jill around her living in the shadow of Grace Archer, and happiness for her for finding a new love which was seen as releasing her from the Brookfield kitchen and freeing her from her trait of putting others first, which some saw as a positive trait, others not.

With both though, as one commentator stated, what is the correlation between feeling some sympathy for their lives, and their capacity to parent? In sum, there was more on the 'for' side than the 'against', but the weighting of the evidence presented perhaps skews this reading.

For

1. Both, difficult pasts; typical of their generation

2. Jill – Leonard's liberation of; putting others first?

3. Peggy – Kate/Tony success

4. Less about them as mothers than as women?

5. Next generation 'pretty much OK'; grown up, mistakes their own

Against

1. Smug, self-obsessed and over-controlling

2. Peggy – financial manipulation

3. Jill – smothercare, passive-aggressive manipulation and wilful ignorance

4. Both, children still on apron-strings

Archers Assembly 2: David and Ruth Archer

Those children of theirs...While there was no unanimous praise for any of their offspring, the Brookfield Archer children were largely seen to have been actively damaged by their parents. From David's shock at Pip Archer wanting to move as far away as Rickyard Cottage to their passive-aggressive to aggressive-aggressive attitude to Josh Archer, and any non-farming interest being openly scorned and positioned as inferior. Interestingly, it was with the Brook-field Archers that we got the most 'who are we to pass judgement/I wasn't a perfect parent' responses, and some saying they are a normal family – does this mean that the Brookfield Archers are the most relatable as parents, if they engender such sympathy? One commenter sums up the majority response:

> *They both have a childish petulant streak a mile wide that speaks to being indulged to excess by Jill and Heather pet. Their failure as parents comes from their own spiteful immaturity. When they're not in huff and puff mode, I think they do alright as parents.*

Pip has never been an easy character for *The Archers* listeners, and some saw this as being a result of the Jekyll and Hyde parenting of her – David in particular putting her on a pedestal, only for Ruth in particular to whip that away from her and punish her at the slightest thing, resulting in Pip's arrogance, insecurity and indecision. It was also commented that while Pip is praised for being an excellent mother, what we hear most often is Rosie Archer being cared for by others.

With Josh, the sustained, undermining and belittling of him and an open lack of celebration in his success or pride in his aptitude to see his own opportunities was cited often by respondents. Overall, as irritating as many find Josh and as many struggle to maintain sympathy for him, it was felt that Josh can't win: it was made clear he can't have a paid job on the farm and when he brings his own business to it, he is treated like a third party, yet when Pip fails, he is expected to step in. While it was Josh and Josh alone that got him in a police cell overnight, David and Ruth are not seen as business role models themselves, nor as having taken an active and nurturing interest in Josh as a young adult or in his business, is it at all surprising he has made some serious mistakes?

Thus, we must ask do, do David and Ruth pass muster as parents? Or, is being called 'normal' being damned by faint praise and are they a living parenting nightmare?

For

1. Gave Ed Grundy advice when he was struggling – but Ed is not their child

2. 'they're fine'

3. 'who are we to judge?'

4. 'well-balanced, happy and normal family'

Against

1. Jekyll and Hyde parenting

2. Often divided as parents

3. Not business or emotional role models, 'emotionally stunted'

4. Passive-aggressive/aggressive-aggressive – Ruth's ruthlessness

5. Bias towards farming and keeping children at Brookfield for life

Archers Assembly 3: Pat and Tony Archer

Pat and Tony Archer only got 34 comments in total, so clear, agreed and quick was the response. Again here, as with their matriarch, Peggy, there was some sympathy for some of the trials of life they have been through. However, there was almost unanimous acknowledgement they have raised some of the most obnoxious children ever known: John Archer in particular was disliked by respondents, being a ruthless womaniser gaining him no sympathy. One commentator sums it up: 'Are Pat and Tony good parents? Their two surviving children are both awful, so no. Also, John was pretty horrid.'

If a volume of business plans written is a measure of good parenting, then Pat and Tony come and collect your gold medal. That does not speak of the success of those business plans – as one commentator said, 'who can say success is withdrawing a product from market just as it gets big in the supermarkets?' Nor does it speak of the emotional integrity of their offspring, Helen and Tom Archer both cited as selfish, horrid and dysfunctional, and as a family, enmeshed. As one respondent put it: 'I've often wondered, in life as well as in *The Archers*, how an extremely united, devoted couple can produce offspring with such poor abilities to form relationships.' One person did speak up for Pat and Tony: 'Running a family business which binds you into ongoing daily contact with adult children puts a lot of extra strain on family relationships, and the Bridge Farmers manage this surprisingly well' and others saying that they did at least provide stability in their children's lives and are clearly devoted to family life. It would seem then that one person's family devotion is another's enmeshed family dysfunction.

For

1. Their children can churn cheese as well as churn out business plans

2. They are devoted to the family

3. Provided stability in early years

Against

1. Infantilising

2. All their children disliked – 'Jonny, get out while you can'

3. 'Misery is the dominant gene in the Bridgers'

4. No self-awareness as parents

5. Enmeshed in each other's lives – unhealthy

6. Poor communicators

7. Don't set strong boundaries

Archers Assembly 4: Susan and Neil Carter

There were only 15 comments made on Susan and Neil Carter, and these were largely all in accord. Susan's social climbing was mentioned, wanting to go from pig farmer's wife to Lady of the Manor, and this social climbing was commented on a causal with regards to daughter Emma Grundy and the dissatisfaction with her life that has led to her restlessness and status fixation. But is Emma not just like her mother in wanting something more to her life than what has been allotted to her, and in wanting to provide stability and social acceptance for her family (see, Headlam and Courage, this volume)? Chris Carter was also seen very much as his father's son, wanting to avoid emotional confrontation around in particular wife Alice Carter, her drinking and their difference of opinion in wanting to have children. On that issue of course, Susan did stand up for Alice when she was being brow-beaten by her mother. Gossiping aside, Susan was seen to be a good listener and a good defender of people. There was a lot of love for Neil, and for Susan and Neil as a couple: as one person said, 'they are kind and loving, and can be relied upon in a crisis. They have a good sense of fun, and of empathy.' Another commented: 'Definitely two of the best parents probably because they are not Archers.' Thus, this is the first set of parents that had more on the 'for' side than on the 'against'.

For

1. Susan – a good listener and advocate

2. 'kind, loving, loyal and supportive parents, who have raised kind children'

3. Can be relied upon in a crisis

4. Empathetic

5. Other parents could learn a lot from them

Against

1. Susan's social climbing – led to Emma's downfall?

2. Neil – avoidance of emotional confrontation

Archers Assembly 5: Jennifer and Brian Aldridge

This couple divided people: to some, they are 'toxic' as parents, to others they have created and sustained a blended family that is collectively resilient, if not emotionally functional, and also show a level of genuine affection for each other, though not consistently. It is fair to say that across Peggy, Lillian Bellamy, Jennifer Aldridge and Kate, we have three generations of women in the Aldridge orbit that are all, in some way, remarkable, and it was the women of this clan that got most of the comments. Debbie Aldridge was – unsurprisingly to an *Archers* listener singled out as the exception to prove the Aldridge rule. But is her success down to her parents as role models? However, both Kate and Alice have had their 'moments', Alice struggling with alcohol and suffering from putting her father on a pedestal and feeling lost in life partly as a result, and Kate and her complete lack of self-awareness and her own parenting faults. A lot of this was attributed to Jennifer – she was often described as indulging, too quick to forgive, a helicopter parent and also inconsistent. But there was a push/pull response to Jennifer, respondents conversely citing her as holding the family together as a positive, and that all of her children like her and have a deep fondness and love for her. Jennifer of course stepped up to be Ruairi's mother, and protected him in the most part from the hurt this has caused her, and she was somewhat admired for how she handled that. However, the storyline of her as the forgiving wife was thought to be somewhat anachronistic. Respondents asked us also to not forget either that both Jennifer and Brian were ignorant and seemingly surprised by Ruairi Donovan's interest in his mother. Ruairi has had some teenage adventures to date, and respondents asked if this was a sign of a difficult adulthood to come, or just youthful arrogance? How Ruairi was with Mia Grundy showed a surprising Aldridge depth of character and empathy, and it was in Ruairi that respondents placed their greater hope. However, no respondents attributed this to either Brian or Jennifer.

With Brian, thoughts on his parenting were less complex. Brian's affairs and what effect this might have had on the children was the top comment. For example, Adam Macy has put husband Iain Craig through the fidelity wringer, and that's just with what Iain does know – is this the outcome of Adam having seen Brian have desire wander outside their marriage? Does it also explain Kate's struggle with commitment and inconsistency in her own parenting, and Alice's adoration of her father, despite evidence to the contrary of his conduct? Brian was also called out for being slow to accept Adam's sexuality, and of having fixed notions of his children which they are unable to alter: 'Alice a pretty little poppet, Kate totally useless, Adam stubborn and deliberately provocative, Debbie saintly and all-knowing' and that his answer to every problem is, or perhaps was, to throw money at it.

For

1. Genuine affection

2. Ruairi – emotional depth

3. Debbie – but also, the exception to the Aldridge rule?

4. Collective resilience as a family

Against

1. Philandering Brian

2. Brian not an active parent, throws money at problems, slow to accept Adam's sexuality

3. Jennifer a helicopter parent, and indulging and too quick to forgive

4. A 'toxic' parenting duo

Archers Assembly 6: Clarrie and Eddie Grundy

Unanimously, the most common response for Clarrie Grundy was that she is the centre of the family and has pulled it together through many a hurdle, and that the younger generations of the Grundys have an older generation they love and feel loved by. But, as respondents pointed out, there have been years of their sons at loggerheads, with all sorts of repercussions of this in all directions within the family, and, of Eddie Grundy's making, all sorts of ups and downs for the family. Eddie and Clarrie were noted as being very much present for their children and supportive of them through their difficult times – and Eddie was the only father noted to have been emotionally open with his children. Clarrie was also viewed as indulgent, putting William Grundy on a pedestal, for example, and an enabler of all of the family and their faults. In the main, Clarrie and Eddie were seen to have come good in respondents' eyes – from a perhaps shaky start and Eddie's wavering moral compass, and Clarrie's domestic and emotional servitude, the two have nonetheless risen in estimation. Their house has always been open, they have unconditionally supported their children, Eddie has come into an emotional maturity, and there is a deep emotional love across the generations of this family.

For

1. Clarrie – strong anchor point

2. Neil – emotionally open

3. Intergenerational love and regard

4. Supportive and emotionally stable parents

Against

1. Clarrie's indulgence and enabling

2. Eddie's moral compass

3. Children put on a pedestal

4. William – no boundaries set by his parents

Archers Assembly 7: Helen Archer

Forty-five responses to the question, 'Is Helen Archer a good parent?', just two behind David and Ruth, who were second to Peggy and Jill. Helen has had her problems in life, but respondents were all agreed that she is hard to like. As one commented: 'Nothing excuses her treatment by Rob [Titchener], but I would shed few tears if she had a nasty fatal accident with a combine harvester.' But, if we reference back to the comments on Pat and Tony as parents, was Helen ever equipped for life in the first place? Like Pip, Helen has benefitted from a family to co-parent and have on tap as baby-sitters, but so far, she has raised 'King Henry.' Helen was viewed essentially as a self-centred character. Some saw her as a protective parent, others as over-protective, over-anxious and controlling. At the *Academic Archers* convenings, it has been asked many times if Helen is a neglectful parent, by not getting Henry or herself into counselling, but that was not thought an issue for some, saying that her love will win out in the end. Helen was also thought of as a bully – of Tom Archer, into taking the blame for running over Mike Tucker, for example. She was described too as brittle, 'not very bright' and 'better at cheeses' than being a parent.

For

1. Protective mother

Against

1. Over-protective, controlling

2. King Henry and had Henry so 'someone would always love her'

3. Counselling – neglectful, of sons and self

4. Self-centred, lack of empathy, a bully

5. 'Better at cheeses'

Archers Assembly 8: Emma, Ed and Will Grundy

This trio was added by popular demand from the *Academic Archers* Fellows, but surprisingly little was actually commented about them – could this be that on the surface, Emma, Ed and Will Grundy are considered to be a contentious family, but that in reality, they are now a noncontentious blended family unit? The consensus in the respondents' posts was largely of praise and celebration. With an initial confusion of who Emma should be married to in this generation of Grundys, the Grundy brothers were at war for a great many of their children's formative years, and respondents wondered how this would affect the next generation in the long run – it was asked, even if a peace has been reached now, how long will it last? Since the deaths of Nick and Joe Grundy, the family is seen as being in a state of harmony. Many commented on how Emma has stepped into a maternal role with Mia Grundy were some of the most touching scenes of her parenting style. However, comment was made about the heteronormativity of the role models in this family, referencing back to Mia making the pink and blue cup cakes with Clarrie.

For

1. Familial peace reached

2. Emma stepping into maternal role with Mia

3. Positive example of a blended family

4. Hardworking family

5. Children not spoilt

Against

1. Destructive formative years for the fourth generation

2. Heteronormative role models

CONCLUSION

To the regular *Archers* listener, the comments on the parenting styles may not be a surprise, but to see each other's comments in the Facebook survey as composite did open up considered nuance and some unexpected sympathy for Ambridge residents. While the *Academic Archers* Citizens' Assembly was a truncated, unorthodox and somewhat wry exercise, it did engender some deep discussion about parenting in general, respondents reflecting on their own parenting experiences and styles, as much as commenting on those in Ambridge, which became a bonding exercise in the Facebook group.

REFERENCES

Citizens Assembly. (n.d). Retrieved from https://citizensassembly.co.uk/. Accessed on June 16, 2020.

Involve. (n.d). Citizens Assembly. Retrieved from https://www.involve.org.uk/resources/methods/citizens-assembly. Accessed on June 16, 2020.

Parliament.uk. (n.d). What is a Citizen's Assembly? Retrieved from https://www.parliament.uk/business/committees/committees-a-z/commons-select/housing-communities-and-local-government-committee/citizens-assembly-faq-17-19/. Accessed on June 16, 2020.

9

ACCENT AND IDENTITY IN AMBRIDGE: THE LINK BETWEEN HOW WE SPEAK AND WHO WE ARE

Rob Drummond

ABSTRACT

This chapter explores the fascinating relationship between the way we speak (our accents) and who we are (our identities) by investigating the ways in which accent is used in The Archers *in the process of characterisation. It begins by describing the link between accent and identity in everyday life, arguing for a perspective in which the way we speak is seen as contributing to the active performance of our identities rather than something through which our identities are passively reflected. The main part of the chapter describes two small studies into the ways in which* The Archers *both uses and reinforces existing language-based stereotypes in order to help in its presentation of clear and recognisable characters.*

ACCENT AND IDENTITY

Spoken language and identity are inextricably connected. It is often the case that we see spoken language as somehow reflecting people's identities, allowing us to gain insights and make judgements about somebody on the basis of the way they speak. We might infer where somebody is from, or their social class, or how friendly they are, simply by listening to their voice. This would perhaps suggest that our identity is something inside us; something relatively fixed, and able to be reflected in a consistent way. But of course, 'who we are' changes depending on the situations in which we find ourselves. In the course of a single day the same individual might be a parent, a manager, an employee, a customer, a frustrated commuter, a friend, a shoulder to cry on, a partner and many other things. All different versions of the one person, and all representing slightly different identities. More broadly, we are likely to have gender, ethnic and sexuality identities, each of which may be more or less important to us as individuals, or as parts of social groups, depending on where we are and who we are with. How can spoken language possibly reflect all this?

Another way to think about it is not to see spoken language as reflecting our identities, but rather as helping to create them in the first place. We are all aware of speaking slightly differently depending on who we are speaking to and where we are – there are some situations where we may be very conscious not to swear, or very aware of the need to speak more carefully and clearly. And we have all heard somebody we know put on their 'phone voice', even if we think we don't have one ourselves. These are examples of us actively adjusting the way we speak in order to emphasise a particular aspect of ourselves or to make us appear a certain way. In other words, we don't speak the way we do *because* of x, y and z; rather, we *perform* our x- , y- and z-ness through the way we speak. This way of thinking doesn't see our identity as something fixed inside of us which is then reflected in our speech and behaviour, it sees our identities as multiple, fluid and dynamic, able to be created and negotiated within the interactions in which we engage. When we find ourselves in those different situations, we are performing subtly (or not so subtly) different identities, and part of the way we do this is through the way we speak. We use language alongside other resources such as the way we dress, the way we behave, our make-up, jewellery and so on, in order to enact or perform whatever identity is needed, wanted, expected or allowed in a particular context. We are all aware of being slightly different people when we are, for example, teaching in front of a class, speaking to our parents, taking part in a protest, being interviewed for a job or helping a child or grandchild draw a picture. And when we start to think along the lines of identity performance, we begin to appreciate some of the mechanisms behind the process. We are actively creating different versions of ourselves through the 'stylistic practice' combination of our behaviour, and, crucially, our speech.

Obviously, when it comes to spoken language, there are certain limitations in terms of the extent to which we can manipulate how we sound. Most of us naturally acquire the accent of the place(s) where we grew up and of the people around us, and this accent is made up of particular ways of pronouncing certain sounds. For example, if we grew up in Bolton, we are naturally going to have a Bolton 'sound system', and it might sound odd if we suddenly started speaking like the Queen. However, even within the constraints of a Bolton sound system, it is quite possible to switch between sounding 'very Bolton' and sounding simply 'vaguely northern English'. And the same is true for any accent – we are all able to adjust our speech to either emphasise or de-emphasise

particular local features. Most of us quite naturally do this all
the time, often quite unconsciously, but also consciously and
strategically, depending on who we are speaking to, the situation we are in and how we would like to be perceived by
others.

ACCENT, IDENTITY AND ATTITUDES

Of course, the way in which we use spoken language in order
to perform particular identities is not entirely within our
control. Whatever identity we *intend* to perform, it will
necessarily be shaped by the perception and understanding of
those around us. The linguist Penny Eckert talks of style (and
by association, identity) as being 'not in the intent but in the
intersubjective space between production and perception'
(Eckert, 2016, p. 79). In other words, identities are a mixture
of what is intended by Person A (production) and what is
actually perceived by Person B (perception). And this
perception is determined to some extent by Person B's own
experiences and awareness, and the extent to which the 'social
meaning' of particular practices are recognised. For example,
somebody might be dressing in a certain way, or using
particular accessories in a certain way, or speaking in a certain
way in an attempt to project a particular identity or show
alignment with a social group. But if that symbolic gesture
isn't picked up by the people around them, then they will not
make that link, and the identity performance will not be
perceived as intended.

However, the social meaning of some social practices are
shared widely, and accent is one of these. Within any society,
there is a shared understanding of how particular accents
and ways of speaking are perceived and subsequently evaluated in relation to social factors such as social class,

friendliness, trustworthiness, intelligence and so on. This is especially the case in the UK, where we have a particularly broad range of accents, coupled with a historically strong system of social class and status. The result of this combination is a society which tends to have very strong feelings about the way people speak; people are very quick to make judgements about an individual's (or a group's) personality and character on the basis of their accent. Stereotypes around accents sounding 'posh', 'uneducated', 'friendly', 'trustworthy', 'unintelligent' abound, and people are generally free to state their preferences and, if we're being honest, prejudices.

ACCENT IN DRAMA

Film, television and radio drama routinely uses the strong associations people make between speech and personality in order to help in the process of characterisation. An example that is often used to illustrate this practice is animated films, where often non-human characters are given particular accents in order to help portray particular traits. For example, in the original *Lion King* (Hahn, D. (Producer), Allers, R., & Minkoff, R. (Directors), 1994) film, the two main characters, Mufasa and Scar, are given strikingly different accents, despite being brothers in the story. Heroic and trustworthy Mufasa has a rich, deep, American accent (voiced by James Earl Jones), while evil and cynical Scar has an effete British Received Pronunciation-type accent, the latter following and feeding a tradition of Hollywood villains being given an accent which is seen to combine both intelligence and treachery (and see Lippi-Green (1997) for an excellent discussion of accent stereotyping in film.) Closer to home, we only have to remember *Auf Wiedersehen, Pet*

(McKeown, 1983–1986) from the 1980s. This classic BBC
TV comedy-drama series followed a group of British construction workers as they leave the UK in order to find work
overseas. Characterisation in the series relied quite heavily on
regional accent stereotypes in the form of the tough Geordie,
the crafty Cockney, the ex-con Scouser and dull, boring
Barry from the Black Country.

But while film and TV drama is able to draw on a range of
resources to create character – the way the person looks, the
way they are dressed, the way they move and behave all
combine with the way they speak to produce the desired result
– radio drama naturally has less to work with. Without the
visual aspects, radio relies much more heavily on voice in the
process of characterisation. Of course, *what* a character says
will have a great bearing on how they are perceived, but *how*
they say it is just as important. Going back to the points made
at the beginning of this chapter – actors in a radio drama are
quite literally enacting and performing identities through
spoken language, and accent plays an important part in this
process.

ACCENT IN *THE ARCHERS*

In 2018, I ran a small pilot study with the aim of investigating
the role that accent plays in the creation of character in *The
Archers*. I did this by using traditional sociolinguistic methods
of eliciting attitudes towards recordings of voices, in which
participants are asked to rate the voices on scales relating to
social factors such as 'intelligence', 'kindness' and 'friendliness'. The recordings consisted of short clips selected from
episodes of *The Archers*, representing a range of characters. In
order to separate accent from all the other character-making
devices (such as content of speech, behaviour, actions,

relationships, etc.) it was important to a) find participants who were not familiar with *The Archers* and b) use clips that did not give anything away regarding the personalities or status of the characters. In order to satisfy the first condition I asked some students to take part, on the presumption that most of them, given their age, were unlikely to be listeners. In order to satisfy the second condition I carefully selected clips that were no longer than 10 seconds and which only contained everyday conversation that gave nothing away with regard to storylines or character motivation. I used clips of 12 speakers: Brian Aldridge, Clarrie Grundy, Emma Grundy, Eddie Grundy, Ian Craig, Jazzer McCreary, Jennifer Aldridge, Jim Lloyd, Lynda Snell, Matt Crawford, Ruth Archer and Susan Carter; and participants were asked to evaluate the voices in terms of the extent to which they sounded: posh, educated, intelligent, kind, friendly and trustworthy. The first of these three characteristics are seen as measures of 'status' and the second three as measures of 'solidarity'. Thirty-six people took part: 26 women and 10 men, aged between 18 and 46. Twenty-seven of the participants had English as a first language, and nine had a different first language (these were overseas students who did not grow up in the UK). The process was simple – participants were played a clip, and then they immediately evaluated the voice in the clip by putting a mark on a scale from 'posh' to 'not posh', and from 'educated' to 'not educated' and so on.

Perhaps unsurprisingly, there was a distinct pattern with regard to how 'posh' characters sounded. The left panel in Fig. 9.1 shows this pattern. In the chart, when the blocks of colour are to the right, this shows that a character was rated as 'posh', and when they are to the left, they were rated as 'not posh'. The blocks themselves represent the middle 50% of the ratings for a particular character, which means that when they are narrow, the ratings for this character were bunched together consistently, and when they are wide, there was a broader spread of opinions. The chart tells us that Brian, Jennifer, Jim and Lynda were all rated as sounding the most 'posh'. The chart is less clear when it comes to 'not posh', although interestingly, some of the more distinctly 'regional' accents such as Emma, Ian and Jazzer, are quite firmly over at that side. Incidentally, 'regional' is in scare quotes here because I have an issue with the idea of 'regional accents'. 'Regional' in this sense really only means 'not Southeast England', which is, of course a region itself, so the term is used as a way of 'othering' those accents (and therefore speakers) which don't share the arbitrary prestige of the RP-like accents often found in the Southeast. The right panel in Fig. 9.1 shows the ratings for how 'friendly' the characters sounded. Here there is a lot more variation, with some characters such as Brian, Jim, Lynda and Matt receiving ratings from right across the scale. However, there is a something of a pattern when we compare the two charts, as several of the characters who were judged as sounding the least posh are subsequently rated highly in terms of friendliness (especially

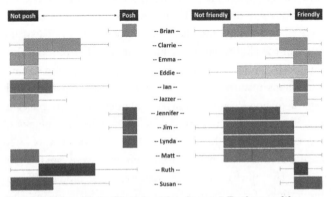

Fig. 9.1. Box Plots Showing the Accent Ratings with Regard to 'Posh' and 'Friendly'. First Language English-Speaking Participants Only.

Emma, Ian, Jazzer and Susan). This is not unexpected, as such measures of status and solidarity are often inversely related in these kids of studies more broadly.

The two groups (participants with and without English as a first language) were separated due to the fact that their responses predictably differed. Participants without English as a first language demonstrated a wide range of responses for most characters. This is interesting, as it begins to demonstrate the fact that we tend to use acquired stereotypes in order to judge accents –the participants who did not grow up in the UK simply do not have the same stereotypical judgements. However, due to the small number of participants, and the restrictions of this chapter, I will not go into any more detail on this point.

Given the context of Ambridge, we can begin to see the beginnings of a class/status distinction, with the higher status individuals displaying 'posher' accents. 'Status' can come from various sources, for example: land ownership (Brian), marriage (Jennifer), education (Jim) or perceived cultural sophistication (Lynda). Remember, the people rating the accents have no idea as to the actual characters and will have been unable to discern anything meaningful from the clip itself. Of course, in some ways, the choice of accent for each character could be argued to reflect 'real life' outside of Ambridge; people do have different accents, and these often relate to social class. But perhaps a more interesting and useful way to look at it is by seeing the accent choice as a way of 'performing' a particular character by drawing on existing associations. Even if we *are* inclined to see the accent choice as reflecting real life, it is only reflecting the natural performance of identity through language along the lines of the process described at the beginning of this chapter. In other words, however we choose to view it, the accents are being used as part of the process of characterisation. *The Archers* is drawing on heavily entrenched accent stereotypes in order to set up broad distinctions between those characters who are high status, eloquent and urbane (e.g. Brain, Jim and Lynda) and those who are lower-status, less eloquent and markedly rural (e.g. Emma, Eddie and Jazzer).

THE GRUNDYS

The lowest status family of all in *The Archers* is, of course, the Grundys. They are also, not coincidentally, the family who most strongly evoke the sense of traditional English 'working-class rural'. They invoke this rurality through almost everything they do – their work, their hobbies, their apparent attitudes and values, and crucially, the way they speak. Barras (2017) does an excellent job of describing the use of rhoticity and hyper-rhoticity in *The Archers* in order to present a generic rural speech style. Rhoticity is the term given to accents which pronounce the 'r' sound in words such as 'farm' or 'car', a feature that is disappearing in England, but still clinging on in areas of the south-west and the north-west; however, as Barras points out, it would not be expected in the area in which we generally believe Ambridge to be. Hyper-rhoticity refers to the pronunciation of 'r' even when it doesn't exist in the spelling, resulting in an exaggerated pronunciation by Eddie of 'Lyndar'. It is no coincidence that among fan commentary of the programme, 'Emmurr' is a regular nickname for Emma Grundy.

The Grundys are a good example of the use of rhoticity in the performance of rurality; however, this is not the only speech feature at their disposal. There are several vowel sounds which also have the potential to signal their rural (and class) status. In the following description I'm going to use the system of 'lexical sets' to discuss the vowels in question. This is a system designed by the phonetician John Wells (1982), and creates a straightforward way to refer to similarities and differences between particular vowel sounds in different accents, as each set contains words which will have the same vowel sound in a given variety of English. I'm going to look at five vowel sounds here: the TRAP vowel (the vowel sound in words such as *trap, map* and *mat*), the BATH vowel (the vowel sound in words such as *bath, path* and *grass*), the LOT vowel (*lot, stop, pot*), the MOUTH vowel (*mouth, loud, now*), and the PRICE vowel (*price, my, fine*). Each of these five vowels has what might be called a 'dictionary standard' version and a 'Grundy' version. The 'dictionary standard' version is what you would see if you looked up words which use that vowel sound in a dictionary, a pronunciation based on the accent of Southeast England. The 'Grundy' version is what we hear various members of the Grundy family using (although interestingly, to different degrees), and, like the rhoticity, invokes a sense of rurality, even if the combination of sounds doesn't necessarily match any specific regional accent.

I should point out here that when we talk about differences in vowel sounds between accents, we are often discussing very small variations between the two. It only takes a slight adjustment in vowel length, or vowel quality, to make a noticeable difference in the way speech sounds. You can try this out for yourselves. Say the sentence 'I'm quite happy' out loud. Depending on the accent you have, the vowel in the second syllable of 'happy' will sound slightly different. It might be a long sound like the sound in *pea*, it might be a short sound, like the sound in *pin*, or it might even be more like the sound in *pet*. Whatever your natural pronunciation is, try saying the sentence aloud using one of the other pronunciations just mentioned. See how it immediately changes the nature of the accent?

The following descriptions of the Grundy vowels use phonetic transcription alongside more general illustrations and explanations, so hopefully they make sense whatever your linguistic experience:

TRAP. Longer than dictionary standard. Words like *chat* and *back* have [æː] rather than [æ] (imagine *chaaat*).

BATH. Midlands/northern England variant, so *bath* and *bat* rhyme. Words like *past* and *glass* have [æ] rather than [ɑː]. But they can also be longer (see TRAP above), so [æː].

LOT. Longer than dictionary standard and also pronounced with the mouth more open and the lips less rounded. So words like *lot* and *shop* have something closer to [ɑː] (the dictionary standard vowel sound in *sharp*) than [ɒ].

MOUTH. Sounds more like dictionary standard *goat*. So words like *out* and *now* sound like dictionary standard *oat* and *no* using [əʊ] rather than [aʊ].

PRICE. Sounds more like dictionary standard *choice*. Words like *my* and *nice* use something closer to [ɔɪ] than [aɪ].

Initially, I decided to look at the speech of the Grundy males only. The reason for this is that Joe Grundy, Eddie Grundy, Will Grundy and Ed Grundy provide a unique (in Ambridge) example of three generations of speakers of the same gender, raised and living in the same location. This is always of interest in sociolinguistic studies, as it gives us a way to explore language change through what we call an 'apparent time' study. The thinking is that our accents do not actually change that much after puberty and throughout adulthood, especially if we stay in the same geographical place. This means that any differences in the speech of older members and younger members of the same family, coming from the same social background and living in the same region, can be viewed as illustrating changes in the accent over time. In other words, 98-year-old Joe's accent is much the same as it was when he was 68 or when he was 35. So if we compare the speech of 98-year-old Joe with that of 68-year-old Eddie and that of 35-year-old Ed, given that they all live in the same place and are from the same social background, the differences between their accents can be interpreted as a change in the accent itself. For the purposes of this study, I investigated the speech of Joe, Eddie, Will, Ed and Jake. Jake is a bit of a linguistic outsider, given that he hasn't always lived full-time with the Grundys, but he at least gives us a small insight into a modern local accent. George would have provided a more useful picture, but he simply doesn't appear enough.

There are two ways to approach the analysis of vowel sounds: acoustic analysis and auditory analysis. Acoustic analysis involves the use of specialist software which helps us measure the frequencies of the speech sounds, helping us to categorise them according to what we are investigating. Auditory analysis relies on the listener's own (well-trained) ear to do the same. In a more comprehensive study, we would aim to collect an extensive range of recordings from each character and carry out a quantitative analysis of each speech feature under investigation. This would involve, for example, looking at each time Joe used a word containing a TRAP vowel and then measuring the length of each of those example vowels (either acoustically or auditorily) in order to determine if it should be classified as a 'standard' variant or as a 'Grundy' variant. This would allow us to see a proportion or percentage of standard vs Grundy for each feature and each speaker. Given the small-scale nature of this study, I relied on a simpler categorisation system, noting whether for each speaker a particular feature was realised as (1) mostly or always 'dictionary standard'; (2) mostly or always 'Grundy'; (3) a mixture of the two. The samples were taken from a range of recent (2018 and 2019) episodes.

Due to the fact that all accents change over time, we would naturally expect older speakers to have stronger 'regional' features. This is not to say that accents are 'disappearing', simply that those features traditionally associated with particular accents will start to die out, possibly to be replaced with others in younger speakers. In our context, we would expect the order of accent strength to be Joe > Eddie > Will and Ed > Jake. However, see Table 9.1.

As you can see from the table, the 'Grundyest' accent among all the speakers belongs to Will. For four of the five features, at least in the recordings that were analysed, Will uses the Grundy variant all or most of the time, more than any other speaker. Jake, perhaps unexpectedly, uses no Grundy variants. The difference between Will and Ed is interesting, given that they are brothers, have had the same upbringing, and move in the same circles. However, it is perhaps not unexpected, given the differences in life experiences. Will has had a much narrower life experience than Ed; he is (or was, prior to Nic's death) settled, more stable and has been relatively content with his life. Until recently, he had a solid position in the hierarchy of rural life as gamekeeper.

Table 9.1. Use of 'Grundy' Variants of the Five Vowel Sounds by Each Speaker. ✔ = Mostly or Always 'Grundy; X = Mostly or Always 'Dictionary Standard'; ✔X = Mixed.

	TRAP	BATH	LOT	MOUTH	PRICE
Joe	✗	✔ ✗	✔ ✗	✔	✔
Eddie	✔ ✗	✔ ✗	✗	✔	✔
Will	✔	✔	✔	✗	✔
Ed	✗	✗	✗	✗	✔ ✗
Jake	✗	✗	✗	✗	✗

Ed, on the other hand, had a far more adventurous adolescence and has never really found his place in Ambridge
society as an adult. He is also under constant pressure from
Emma, who continually seeks higher status in the community, to better himself. The fact that Will is more Grundy in
speech than Joe and Eddie is also very interesting and might
also be put down to his (until recently) fixed position in the
social hierarchy, with a clear 'superior' in Brian, to whom he
was willing to show due deference and respect.

However, there is one Grundy who out-Grundys them all,
and that is Mia Grundy. Although not included in the original
analysis due to the focus being on the stable male generational
line, her accent is hard to ignore. Mia has all the Grundy
features, including the one that Will doesn't seem to have.
Moreover, the variants she uses are even more extreme than
those displayed by the Grundy men. The strength of Mia's
accent is hard to explain from a sociolinguistic perspective –
she is young, has familial influence outside of the Grundys and
seems to be fully engaged with the world around her (and all
the linguistic variation this brings). That said, the fact that she
shows more Grundy variants than her brother, Jake, is not at
all surprising. At the time of the study, Mia was consciously
engaging with Ambridge life to a far greater extent than Jake.
She consciously chose to be with Will, and she was extremely
close to Clarrie and Emma (both strong users of Grundyese).
But the extreme nature of her Grundy vowels is still surprising. Why should this be?

THE ELEPHANT IN THE ROOM

Here, we have to address the elephant in the room: the fact
that we are listening to the voices of actors and not people
who have actually grown up in Ambridge. In the course of

carrying out the research, I had a brief online chat with the actor Barry Farrimond, who plays Ed. I asked him what direction he was given with regard to Ed's accent, and he revealed that he couldn't recall ever receiving any specific guidance, although he did say it was a long time ago when he started the role. This would suggest that the actors were left to their own devices to find the voice of their characters, which goes some way to explaining both the generic rurality, and the variation between speakers. However, it is unlikely that this lack of direction is still the case. Sean O'Connor, the show's editor from 2013–16, made the well-publicised decision to professionalise the cast by replacing some of the younger characters who were played by untrained actors, with drama-schooled alternatives. Within this context, it is very likely that a new era of professionalism developed, one in which something as crucial as a character's accent was not left to chance. This is speculation on my part, but I do wonder if Mia's overt Grundyness came as the result of specific direction. It might be that she ultimately over-delivered when compared to the rest of the family, but the underlying decision for her to use this accent was perhaps a conscious choice.

CONCLUSION

You might well be reading this thinking 'So what? These are characters in a drama, and we shouldn't read too much into the accents they use'. This is of course true, to an extent. Accents in drama only work if they resonate with our real-life experiences outside of the drama. The very fact that the characters in *The Archers* are presented as having different accents and that there is a consistency within those accents (e.g. between families, or between groups of people) means that those accents are being used in the process of characterisation. Otherwise, why not simply let every actor use their own voice? By exploring the use of accent in drama, we can begin to gain insights into how the hierarchy of accents pervades our everyday lives. The two studies described here are very small and can only ever serve as a tentative illustration of the importance and relevance of accents in how we perceive ourselves and others, but they hopefully offer the opportunity for the debate to be had. Because dramas such as *The Archers* are not innocent in all of this. By using accent stereotypes in the development of character, they are at the same time reinforcing those stereotypes. By using a perceived link between a particular way of speaking and a person's levels of intelligence, trustworthiness or loyalty in the minds of the listeners, they are reinforcing that link in the minds of people outside Ambridge. And the more these stereotypes are reinforced and seen as part of everyday life, the more acceptable it is, or continues to be, to judge others on the basis of the way they speak. It is fine to have accent and voice preferences – we all do. But when we start to use those preferences as a way to negatively stereotype other people, we need to reflect on what we are doing. Because criticism of the way someone speaks is almost always about something more than speech.

REFERENCES

Barras, W. (2017). Rural Voices: What can Borsetshire tell us about accent change?. In C. Courage, N. Headlam, & P. Matthews (Eds.), *The Archers in fact and fiction: Academic analyses of life in rural Borsetshire*. Oxford: Peter Lang.

Eckert, P. (2016). Variation, meaning and social change. In N. Coupland (Ed.), *Sociolinguistics: Theoretical debates* (pp. 69–85). Cambridge: Cambridge University Press.

Hahn, D. (Producer), Allers, R., & Minkoff, R. (Directors). (1994). *The lion king* [motion picture]. USA: Walt Disney Pictures.

Lippi-Green, R. (1997). *English with an accent*. Abingdon: Routledge.

McKeown, A. (Director). (1983–1986). *Auf Wiedersehen, Pet* [Television series]. England: Central Independent Television.

Wells, J. (1982). *Accents of English*. Cambridge: Cambridge University Press.

10

'WE SHOULD HAVE CALLED HIM DAMIEN': A DISCUSSION OF THE IMPACT OF HENRY ARCHER'S EARLY YEARS ON POTENTIAL CRIMES OF THE FUTURE

Nicola Maxfield

ABSTRACT

Much discussion has taken place in real life and in cyber space about the future of Henry Archer. He has been the subject of gossip, with the nature of his conception, and then gained a stepfather, seemingly a gentleman, who cared for both Henry and his mother. Coercive control came to dominate the relation between Rob Titchener and Helen Archer, giving an outward appearance of perfection in all aspects of family life. Henry experienced the gaslighting along with Helen and having seen his mum stab his new adoptive father, Henry was left without his mum, and in the care of evil Rob, effectively prevented from contact with his staid, and consistently caring grandparents. This paper will consider the impact of the trauma on Henry's potential psychological self as an older child and adolescent, looking at the impact of attachment, disparate parenting styles, social learning theory and domestic violence. There is also a comparison to a case study which could illustrate Henry's future, should he decide to begin a career in serial killing.

Henry Archer has had an interesting life to date. He was born on 2 January 2011, in a dramatic manner, needing to be delivered by emergency caesarean section six weeks early after Helen Archer developed pre-eclampsia. Even his conception was controversial, with Helen deciding to go it alone, using donor insemination. A cosy life with Helen and his grandparents ensued until Henry was two years old and Rob Titchener arrived, and Henry's life was to change spectacularly. From then on, Henry saw his mother bullied and was in turn bullied himself by an outwardly charming man. The style of parenting that he was subjected to vary daily and eventually the tinned custard turned the worm. Helen stabbed Rob and was arrested. Helen went to prison and Henry spent more time with Rob, and with Rob's manipulative parents, Bruce and Ursula Titchener. Poor Henry had to then deal with the arrival of a new brother, and the disappearance of Rob who then reappears to take away the new baby and leave him.

Will these events cause psychological damage to Henry Archer? On the face of it, the disruption to the mother-child attachment would ring warning bells for later in the child's life. The basis of attachment theory links the lack of maternal bond to affectionless psychopathy in later life; this is what every psychology student learns from the *Forty-four Juvenile Thieves* (Bowlby, 1944). However, there are many more influences on Henry's life than Rob and Helen's time in prison. This paper will examine the other theories which may help foresee whether Henry becomes a tedious fan of tractors like Grandad Tony Archer or a psychopath in the manner of Frank Cauldhame in Iain Banks' *Wasp Factory* (Banks, 2013).

There are several aspects of Henry's life to consider, the wrenching from him of Helen when she was detained on remand, the coercion and domestic violence he witnessed along with bullying he experienced at the hand of his step-father Rob. The perils implicated by these incidents will be considered, along with his circumstances which may mitigate the dangers. John Bowlby's work is the starting point for this look at Henry's potential issues. Bowlby's traditional attach-ment theory states that a child that does not have a beneficial bond with their mother may become an offender (Bowlby, 1944); Henry was denied his mum for time when she was in prison on remand, and he was deprived of Rob. Rob dis-appeared off to the United States in February 2017 without any explanation given to Henry that we heard. Bowlby developed the term 'affectionless psychopathy' which he stated was created when there is a sustained separation from mother or persistent rejection from her. The result being that the child, Henry, may be unable to show love or concern for others, he might act on impulse and not care about the con-sequences (Bowlby, 1944). Papagathonikou (2020) expands on previous work on attachment, that positive relationships are vital for the development of emotional and reasoning skills. By bonding well with Helen, Henry will be able to create scaffolding to allow him to understand how to relate to others throughout his life, he will see what she does and imitate her actions.

Research has demonstrated that if initial bonds are good (Schaffer, 1964), then it does not matter who the attachment is with. It could be Pat Archer, Tony Archer or even Tom Archer. Henry and Helen lived at Bridge Farm much of the time pre-Rob and therefore Henry spent as much time with his maternal grandparents as with his mum. Both grandparents were caregivers (babysitters) for Henry to allow Helen to play at shops with Ambridge Organics. It can be stated that Henry bonded with more than one adult which enabled him to have a stable base. This may negate the impact of Helen's forcible removal from Henry at the age of four.

The type of attachment is crucial for the outcomes for the child as aggressive and disruptive behaviour is associated with pathologies of attachment (Papagathonikou, 2020). There are four types of attachment: *avoidant insecure*, wherein mothers sometimes ignored their child; *securely attached*, wherein the mothers were considerate to their child's emotions; *resistant insecure*, wherein mothers were ambivalent toward their child; and *disorganized*, wherein mothers were unpredictable and likely to be abusive. For Henry to have an avoidant attachment, Helen would have had to be unresponsive to his needs and be emotionally unavailable, promoting hasty independence. It appears to be more common in boys to develop an avoidant attachment (Hoeve et al., 2012). The consequences of such poor attachment include sexual violence and sexually coercive behaviour, cruelty and the possibility of borderline personality disorder (Papagathonikou, 2020). Hoeve discusses Hirschi's 1969 premise which links poor attachment to criminal behaviours (Hoeve et al., 2012). Hirschi developed Bowlby's theory and considered that a child who had strong affective bonds to a parent or other figure would be more likely to have anxiety over breaking their parent's expectations and wish to reflect their values and norms. This is 'indirect parental control' according to Hoeve et al. (2012).

If there is one known in this instance, it is that Helen is always emotionally available, and is very responsive to anything Henry wants or needs. Indeed, she has been soundly criticised via social media for her over-protectiveness and mollycoddling of Henry (see Chapter 8). Henry does have extremely strong bonds with not only Helen but also Pat and Tony and possibly even his uncle, Tom Archer. Henry did not lack maternal care. He will have internalised the norms and values of the Archer clan and society. He is likely to have to consider those he respects before starting a campaign of violence. It is that internal indirect influence from parents and significant carers that stops children and young adults from offending, in many cases it continues long into adulthood. For children with poor attachment, antisocial or criminal behaviour is more likely. In Henry's case, the attachment appears sound and the risk of offending behaviour in this respect is low.

In terms of Rob's influence on Henry's attachments, there may be a different outcome. Henry experienced inconsistent care from Rob. Rob did not always have time for Henry. Consider when Henry began to wet his bed: Helen was forbidden by Rob from attending to Henry and a soft toy that Henry was attached to was removed by Rob. This behaviour was confusing for Henry and caused him anxiety. Rob displays insecure attachment in his behaviours such as being hypercritical of others and unable to ask for or anticipate help from others (Bender, 2015). Even someone with a poor imagination can suppose that Ursula was an inattentive mother, inconsistent and afraid to put her sons first. In August of 2016, with Helen in prison, Rob is relying on Emma Grundy to help him look after Henry, his parenting style is contrasted with Emma's when Henry is asked to put his sandals on. Emma completes the task for Henry, almost making it a game, but Rob insists that Henry can do it by himself. Emma is gently encouraging, a figure of safety and warmth, distinct from Rob's firmness. This must have been confusing for Henry, although in a sense Emma had replaced Helen's nurturing manner, giving some form of continuity.

It is likely that Henry has secure attachment; his relationship with his mum and extended family is healthy and was
until he was about four years old. He was able to explore his
surroundings in safety, given time to play, lots of adult
attention and made to take responsibility for his actions (apart
from kicking Johnny Phillips in the googlies and not being
disciplined.) Just before the stabbing, Helen and Pat watch
with anticipation as Henry cautiously approaches a piglet,
clutching Thomas the rabbit. Johnny is patient in encouraging
Henry to get close to the piglet, while great-grandmother
Peggy Wolley is disparaging, even commentating that he
should not have a cuddly toy (different if he was a girl) and
judgemental that Henry is nervous. Henry's mum and
grandma are very encouraging and celebrate when he does get
to the piglet. Henry continues to investigate his environment
in safety, knowing he is protected. There is a beneficial effect
of the steadiness (boringness) of Pat and Tony. Maternal care
was not distorted as Helen did not neglect Henry, he is very
close with his grandparents, Tom and other members of the
extended Archer family; these relationships all allowed him to
maintain equilibrium when Helen was in prison. Henry's close
bonds with others in his early years will also support his
stability, although Helen's previous mental ill health, the
anorexia and depression need to be considered and that could
be a symptom of unresolved issues from her childhood which
may unconsciously affect him.

The implications of a secure attachment for Henry will be
demonstrated in the future by him being able to have strong
adult relationships without substantial jealousy or criticism.
As Henry becomes an adolescent, the parent-child bond will
be tested as he interacts with and is influenced by his peers.
Henry may have issues with intimacy if his attachment style is
avoidant, he could have a vision of the perfect relationship
and be hypercritical of potential future partners. Just as Rob

was of Helen, and Bruce Titchener of everyone he meets. This can be contrasted with some of the apron strings which have not been cut in Bridge Farm. Tom is still running back to mum and dad, as is Helen. If Henry had avoidant attachment because of trauma, he is more likely to become very competitive and belligerent, and this was shown in his attitude at karate lessons. The criticism of this view is that the quality of parental care giving has a greater influence, especially with boys, and the wholesomeness of the Archers clan could counter that effect. However, theory states that the impact of family strain is greater on boys than girls because of gender expectations and experiences of social control; this combined with exposure to domestic violence will increase delinquency risk factors and make Henry more vulnerable (Hay, 2003). However, the Walton's style righteousness of Bridge Farm may cancel that out. Tony's ability to plod on, no matter what has happened will give Henry the resilience and stability to grow up as a typical Archer.

The separation from Helen when she was sent on remand no doubt has affected Henry. He was five when she went to prison. This may be key in whether he becomes a psychopathic serial killer. However, the staidness of Pat and Tony strikes again. In 1964, a longitudinal study considered attachments in babies up to 18 months old (Schaffer, 1964). This determined that children were able to form multiple attachments from 10 months old and therefore in Henry's case he formed especially close bonds with his extended family. It could therefore be believed that Helen's disappearance was mitigated for Henry by his relationship with Pat and Tony. Another piece of research asserts that the replacement carer should be considered, their bond and whether the child must move house too (Howard, 2011). Again, Pat and Tony were (eventually) the replacement care givers, and Henry went back to the house he had known very well for his whole life, diminishing any potential impact. Along with Jean Mercer's assertion that 'attachment is probably most easily observed in infants and toddlers from about eight months to two years' (Mercer, 2005, p. 3). It may be claimed that as Henry was much older when Helen, left the impact was lessened. Conversely, a study found that a child who was parted from their parents for more than a month was at higher risk of indicators of Borderline Personality Disorder (Howard, 2011).

There are some implications for the changes that Henry experienced at home. While many incidences of a parent being taken from their child is likely to take place in a household where there are other characteristics of a chaotic household, such as overcrowding and noise, it is obvious that this did not happen in Henry's case. The consequences however may impact intellectual progress. Although, had he lived at Brookfield with its variability of bedrooms, it may have been a different matter. Changes to who a child has living at home could have implications for Henry, this again links to intellectual concerns and even experimenting with sex at an earlier age (Howard, 2011). Helen may become a granny quite early. The number of comings and goings at Bridge Farm cannot be disregarded. It should be a stable home for Henry, having seen some of the issues at Blossom Hill Cottage, he does need stability. However, Tom and Johnny have come and gone like yoyos, although they are always a part of the family, importantly they are always welcome back into the household at Bridge Farm. This gives a sense of belonging and openness, no judgement given, there is always a home with Pat and Tony, although as seen later in this chapter this may not be a good move for them in the light of the case of Edward Kemper.

Eric Ericsson developed a series of psychosocial stages which show the potential outcomes for each stage of development. Mooney (2013) asserts that the early stages of development can 'wire' the brain for various dilemmas experienced by the child. One of the dilemmas critical to Henry's development is trust versus mistrust. If an adult regularly fulfils an infant's needs, the child will develop trust, if they are not met the child will cultivate mistrust (Mooney, 2013). If Rob had been on the scene, Henry may have become mistrustful and insecure, developing anxiety and feelings of worthlessness. Rob and Helen became a consistent item at the end of 2013, Henry was nearly three at this time. For Erikson, the quandary at this age (one year to three years) is autonomy versus shame and doubt. Henry did have autonomy for much of this period, he did appear to call the shots a lot of the time – consider Helen waiting for him to finish feeding the pigs or jump in puddles. Did Rob tip the balance to humiliation and uncertainty? According to Erikson, a toddler may become manipulative if they are not supported at this stage. They may acquire 'precocious conscience', thinking they are more in control than they really are (Graves, 2006). This might manifest itself in Henry becoming very bossy and expecting adults to conform to his will. The child might consistently test the boundaries, and this does apply to Henry, however, other than Rob, the adults around him have always been consistent in their responses to untoward behaviour. It could be claimed that Helen has created the right balance in allowing him to explore his environment and test his boundaries, while giving him clear guidance about what is and is not acceptable. Helen and the extended Archer family have allowed Henry to make choices. These actions are positive for Henry to develop health autonomy. Graves and Larkin further acknowledge that lack of autonomy at this stage can lead to low self-esteem, they continue by stating that:

> *Shame is usually thought of as being exposed, caught with one's pants down, sinking into the ground, or being invisible. In other words, according to Erikson,*

> *the term means to be completely exposed but not*
> *ready to be looked at – self-conscious. Too much*
> *shame in a young child's life may lead to a strong*
> *determination to get away with things, or worse, it*
> *may lead to defiance and shamelessness*

(Graves, 2006, p. 65).

Aspects of these behaviours were seen in Henry's behaviours at school, when he was caught bullying girls and karate, as he tried to dominate others.

The crucial stage for Henry was Erikson's stage of initiative versus guilt, important for children aged three to six years old. As Henry grows in physical ability and intellectual capacity, he will be eager to test himself, and any mistakes will, in the ideal environment be met with care and support. This sympathetic approach adopted mainly by Helen and the Archer clan will lead Henry to be caring and thoughtful. However, with Rob in his life, Henry had to deal with aggression and anger when he made mistakes. It has been seen in Henry's dealings with other children that he had some issues with sharing and interacting with other children, this is quite normal for his age and stage of development, but a parent snapping at him and making him feel guilt at such events can lead to consequences later on in life. Such guilt can lead to lack of confidence, initiative and creativity in later life along with the risk of anti-social and asocial behaviour. Furthermore, there may be 'an unresolved sense of wrongness, a reservoir of guilt that affects the whole personality...repressed regret and hurt feelings may trigger a self-preservation reaction...blunts or defends against guilt' (Linsey, 1999, p. 52). What does this mean for Henry? He may be perfectly normal, and the effect of Pat and Tony has negated any malign influence from Rob. There may be problems with Henry being unable to show guilt and he might tell lies and become manipulative to prevent people from finding him out. Overall, low self-esteem is a likely consequence. In situations where parents had tried to provoke guilt in their child, there was an increase in fire setting (Singer, 2004). Rob certainly did try to make Henry feel guilty on occasion and further risk factors will be considered later in this discussion.

Parenting has a direct effect on the future psychology of a child. O'Connor and Scott (O'Connor, 2007) discuss that both Social Learning Theory (SLT) and parenting style impact on children. Albert Bandura pointed out that children are influenced by those around them, particularly those to whom a child looks up, such as Henry to Rob. With SLT the child's role model shapes their behaviour. Henry revered Rob and this was palpable in how Henry's behaviour towards Rob at cricket, with both Pat and Tom commenting that he 'hero worshipped' Rob. Because of this, Henry would take on the characteristics of the object of his adoration, including the aggressiveness Rob displayed at the cricket matches, where he would stop at nothing to win. Also, at cricket Rob made homophobic comments to Adam Macy, it may be implied that had Henry spent more time with Rob, these values may have been transmitted to Henry. Henry may have developed an understanding of stereotypes from Rob. He saw his mother increasingly relegated to a role purely in the home and unable to drive. Pat in hindsight stated that Rob 'was obviously a chauvinist', it is remarkable that as a feminist in previous times, she did not notice this earlier. Henry was being conditioned into thinking that women were inferior to men. Only a fly on the wall knows what was said to Henry when he spent time with Rob and Ursula, however, if, as many suspect, there were consistent derogatory attitudes voiced by them would drip feed into Henry's mind, and he would take on their views.

Further to SLT, Wright and Hensley discuss Dallard and Miller's assertion that 'every individual is socialised to seek affection and approval from those they love' (Wright & Hensley, 2003, p. 74). This lack of love can lead to humiliation which then may cause frustration. This degradation becomes internalised and the child begins to await further humiliation. To restore their sense of self-worth, the individual may then take their bitterness out on others, animals or something more dire. For example, should Rob humiliate Henry for some reason, Henry may feel that he cannot hit back at Rob, therefore he will find someone weaker on which to vent his resentment. This vulnerable object might be an animal or a smaller child, both accessible to Henry on the farm. There is one case study in the literature which might be pertinent. Edward Kemper was humiliated by a parent (mother, but it could be Rob in Henry's case), he was locked up in a cellar, his resentment and anger was gratified by killing cats. He was eventually sent to live with his grandparents (substitute, Pat and Tony) and later killed them both. Kemper went on to kill six more individuals (Wright & Hensley, 2003). This trajectory is unlikely now Henry has no contact with Rob, but it is possible that Henry may have had a life parallel to Kemper if he had stayed with his stepfather. It is worth noting that a study found that around 8% of convicted serial killers had been adopted, a percentage higher than in the general population, and links to the theory of children internalising the effects of rejection by birth parents (Fox, 2018). While Henry was not rejected by a birth parent, he was discarded by Rob, who only wanted his biological son when leaving Ambridge.

Henry began wetting the bed during the period that Rob was piling on the pressure, and ERIC, the enuresis charity, had an article entitled 'Why is Henry wetting the bed on *The Archers*?' (Favero, n.d.). It considers that Henry's bed wetting is linked to anxiety linked to changes and stress is in life. Henry had just started school; his mum was about to have another baby and his parents were on edge. However, the author does acknowledge that domestic violence can be a trigger as it causes heightened levels of fear and anxiety. Some researchers link enuresis and domestic violence, humiliation associated with bed wetting and with finding a victim torturing animals or fellow humans. MacDonald (Wright & Hensley, 2003) called this a triad, further to this there are several behaviours to look for in Henry in the future such anger management issues, deceitfulness and bullying. Henry has already demonstrated each of these to a small degree. Wright and Hensley (2003) continue by considering animal cruelty in the triad. Stating that the FBI judge animal cruelty to be a sign of later serial murder. Why does this happen?

There are links between parenting style and outcomes for children later in life (see Chapter 8). Diana Baumrind began by looking at parental approaches to their children. Baumrind identified four attitudes to children two of which apply to this. Authoritative parenting is the ideal, with parents showing lots of warmth and who are positive in their discipline, showing fairness and understanding. This is in line with Helen's approach to Henry, as well as Pat and Tony's. Authoritarian parents show little warmth to their children, might be very critical of the child and have high levels of control, even using physical punishment. This could be Rob at times. Building up to the stabbing in April 2016, Rob was increasingly controlling with both Henry and Helen. He commanded Henry to put Thomas the rabbit into the bin when caught sneaking chocolate, he does not let Helen go to comfort Henry and is aggressive in how he tells Henry to go back to bed. This was typical of Rob's attitude to Henry when he was not compliant. The permissive style of parenting is where there is little control exerted by the parent, but lots of warmth, like Kate Madikane's nurturing, while Tracy Horrobin's childcare approach could have been described as neglectful or disengaged at times.

The implications for Henry in terms of Rob's parenting could be anti-social behaviour in the future (Schaffer, 2009). Hoeve et al. (2012) state 'parenting styles are configurations of attitudes and behaviours of parents towards their child and create a context or a climate for the parents' (Hoeve, 2008, p. 224) and children from authoritarian parents are more likely to be involved in offending. The children are likely to rebel and become aggressive, show offending conduct and anxiety. This is like the effects of insecure attachments. Rob did show some genuine concern for Henry, and when Ursula had collected Henry from school, about a month after the stabbing incident, Rob was anxious to know how Henry had got on, who he'd played with and expresses that he hopes Henry settles back in well. Looking back to the disposal of Thomas the rabbit, Rob showed a lack of understanding and empathy with Henry and a mistake was punished harshly. Another example of inconsistency of parenting style can be seen as Rob makes a point of commenting about Henry getting dirty when being looked after by Emma in August 2016, with Emma commenting to Ed that Rob doesn't 'allow Henry to be a child' (O'Connor, 2016). Later that week Rob appears not to care about this and engages in a water fight with Henry. This seesawing of parenting styles is confusing for the child and such lack of consistency can be linked to unwanted behaviours in children (Meteyer, 2009). Schaffer discusses the evidence from research for antisocial behaviours and parenting approaches. These risk factors include 'low parental warmth, inconsistency and parental rejection', all which Henry experienced by Rob at some time in their time together (Schaffer, 2009, p. 52).

The World Health Organisation defines intimate partner violence as 'behaviour by an intimate partner or ex-partner that causes physical, sexual or psychological harm, including physical aggression, sexual coercion, psychological abuse and controlling behaviours' (WHO, 2017). Helen experienced intimate partner violence; there is no controversy in this. However, there is debate about how much violence Henry witnessed. It will be assumed here that Henry saw an amount of violence and intimidation at home. Psychology students are introduced to Bandura's 'Bobo' doll: children watch an inflatable doll being beaten, and then copy the behaviour of the adult to show the mechanism of the social learning theory and how children will imitate those they think are role models. Could Rob have transmitted his values and aggression to Henry?:

> *Social learning theory suggests that when a child is exposed to violence in the home, he or she will cognitively replicate the situations in which it occurred, and the negative emotions attached to the past experiences will result in violent behaviour.*

> (Anderson & Kras, 2005, p. 107)

Henry may have begun to see that when Rob bullied his mother that things happened, his mother acquiesced. He could then feel that this was the way to deal with things. Henry would see that the way to deal with traumatic circumstances is by using anger, aggression and violence. Children may not learn the norms and values of society, but the norms and values of their particular family, even if it is dysfunctional. The child is unlikely to learn how to deal with confrontation or stress in a helpful way, they will remember what worked for their parent.

Anderson and Kras reflect Dutton's premise that abused boys are likely to identify with and copy their abuser, this in Henry's case could mean that he will consider it acceptable for Rob to smack or verbally abuse him as he hero-worshipped him. He may then repeat this behaviour when he has a girlfriend and

there is a disagreement (Anderson & Kras, 2005). After Rob
had been stabbed, he decided to coach Johnny in cricket. Johnny
revered Rob and when told to sledge the opposing team he did
so, demonstrating that even an older teenager was willing to
verbally abuse others when asked to do so by a potential role
model. Anderson and Kras state that

> *Family members model violent conflict resolution, as*
> *well as victimize the observer, and this experience is*
> *transmitted to the child, which the child then repeats.*
> *A generation of violent socially learned behaviour*
> *has been sustained.*

(2005, p. 107)

There is the potential for Henry to continue the fear and
violence he saw committed by someone he loved and was
presented to him as a good influence and his new daddy.
However, the period that Henry was affected by Rob was
brief; there may not be the impact that will cause harm.
Henry's role model did disparage women, with Pat exclaiming
that Rob was 'obviously a chauvinist' (O'Connor, 2016),
while much can be said of the wonder of hindsight, transmission of Rob's values may impact Henry. When Rob's
father, Bruce, appeared it was evident that his values had been
transmitted to Rob, he also was discriminatory and disparaging of women, very aggressive and judgemental. There is a
risk that these views could have passed on to Henry:
'Observation of violence as a child also has a direct effect on
approval of violence and a negative effect on sex-role egali-
tarianism' (Stith, 1993, p. 188).

It would be difficult for a young child to make sense of
what happened in the kitchen when Rob was stabbed by
Helen and therefore Henry may have a skewed perception of

the events and precursors. Indeed this is put well by Anderson and Kras:

> *If a child witnesses his parents fight violently over money after another stressful behaviour had occurred, such as serving dinner late, social learning theory suggests that the child may internalise that response as being provoked by his mother's serving dinner late.*

(2005, p. 109)

Goodness knows how Henry might react to a meal of tuna pasta bake and a pudding served with tinned custard in the future. Although Henry was not victim to savage beatings from Rob, Gross (2007) points out that merely witnessing such abuse is enough for there to be an intergenerational effect. And it must not be forgotten that Henry saw his mother stab his stepfather, his idol and role model. All of this does suppose that Henry is at risk of reproducing violent behaviour himself as an adolescent and adult: Taylor (2019) employs Rutter and Giller's 1983 assertion of the five risk factors for delinquency. These are law-breaking by the parents (Helen stabbed Rob), conflict within the family (where to start; from initial control and belittling to Rob and Helen's battle over custody), lack of consistency when dealing with unwanted behaviours (Rob was always harsh, Helen, Pat and Tony were more understanding and authorita-tive), family size and number of siblings (the Archers' very extended family), socio-economic status of the family (nicely middle class and no money worries). Three out of these five risk factors are present in Henry's life, however there are further aspects of his life which will protect Henry from living his life as an aggressive criminal. These, according to Rutter and Giller include affection from Helen, support from the wider extended family, authoritative parenting from Helen, and good life opportunities as an Archer (Taylor, 2019). Once again, the Waltons' style wholesomeness has probably terminated Henry's career as a violent offender.

The evidence for Henry becoming a serial killer is not particularly strong. His attachment to his mum was disrupted, but not at such a critical age, and his grandparents had been a major part of his life from birth, enabling a strong bond with them both. Rob did reject Henry, by arriving to kidnap Jack but not trying to take Henry. Rob and Henry's attachment was formed after the critical period; he was, by then, able to make multiple attachments. Much of the literature looks at individuals far removed from those in Ambridge, which lacks in diversity, being mainly carried out in America and in Afro-Caribbean households. Henry's background is unique, as is Ambridge and within any Archers family there are surprising and unexpected tangents on which the inhabitants are taken. Rob may reappear and upset the status quo, Henry may follow Johnny's path and become a farmer in his grandad's footsteps, his stepfather having had no influence whatsoever on his life. He may even go to university outside of Borsetshire and study media.

What should be looked for out for in Henry's future? Casual bullying (he has already been mean to Keira Grundy), a lack of remorse or guilt (kicking Johnny in the crown jewels), being superficially charming and having a short temper, intimidating smaller children and torturing small animals, to which he has access. Warning bells must start to ring if Jack begins to be bullied by his older brother and Henry is without remorse. It will be interesting to consider how adolescence will affect Henry. When Henry begins intimate relationships, it should start to become clear whether he has internalised what he saw happen when he was a toddler and become abuse to partners. Those who witnessed domestic violence early in their lives are two and a half times more liable to repeat this in their own relationships (Anderson & Kras, 2005). Should Henry do this in front of his own children, the pattern will continue. It does depend on whether Rob's need for masculine dominance in intimate relationships has been assumed by Henry. However, looking at the dynamics at Bridge Farm, it is far more likely that he will assume Tony's rather ineffectual and passive style of manhood, although it remains to be seen how Lee affects the family conventions for masculinity.

REFERENCES

Anderson, J. A., & Kras, K. (2005). Revisiting Albert Bandura's social learning theory to better understand and assist victims of intimate personal violence. *Women & Criminal Justice*, *17*(1), 99–124.

Banks, I. (2013). *The wasp factory*. London: Abacus.

Bender, P. K. D. (2015). The impact of attachment security and emotion dysregulation on anxiety in children and adolescents. *Emotional & Behavioural Difficulties*, *20*(2), 189–204.

Bowlby, J. (1944). Forty-four juvenile thieves: Their characters and home life. *The International Journal of Psychoanalysis*, *25*, 121–124.

Favero, R. (n.d.). Why is Henry wetting the bed on the Archers? Retrieved from ERIC https://www.eric.org.uk/blog/why-is-henry-wetting-the-bed-on-the-archers. Accessed on August 29, 2020.

Fox, J. A. (2018). *Extreme killing*. London: SAGE Publications.

Graves, S. A. (2006). Lessons from Erikson. *Journal of Intergenerational Relationships*, 4(2), 61–71.

Gross, R. (2007). *Key studies in psychology*. Banbury: Hodder Education Group.

Hay, C. (2003). Family strain, gender and delinquency. *Sociological Perspectives*, 46(1), 107–135.

Hoeve, M. B. (2008). Trajectories of delinquency and parenting styles. *Journal of Abnormal Child Psychology*, 36(2), 223–235.

Hoeve, M. E., Stams, G., van der Put, C., Dubas, J., van der Laan, P., & Gerris, J. (2012). A meta-analysis of attachment to parents and delinquency. *Journal of Abnormal Child Psychology*, 40(5), 771–785.

Howard, K. M. G. (2011). Early mother-child separation, parenting and child well-being in early years head start families. *Attachment & Human Development*, 13(1), 5–26.

Linsey, P. (1999). *Lifespan journey*. London: Hodder and Stoughton.

Mercer, J. (2005). *Understanding attachment: Parenting, child care, and emotional development*. Westport, CT: Praeger Publishers Inc.

Meteyer, K. P. J. (2009). Dyadic parenting and children's externalizing symptoms. *Family Relations*, 58(3), 289–302.

Mooney, C. (2013). *Theories of childhood: An introduction to Dewey, Montessori, Erikson, Piaget & Vygotsky* (second edition). St. Paul: Redleaf Press.

O'Connor, T. G. (2007). *Parenting and outcomes for children*. London: JRF.

O'Connor, S. (Ed.). (2016). *The Archers*. BBC Radio Programme.

Papagathonikou, T. (2020). The relationship between attachment and criminal psychopathy: A systematic review. *Dialogues in Clinical Neuroscience and Mental Health*, 3(1), 34–45.

Schaffer, H. R. (1964). The development of social attachments in infancy. *Monographs of the Society for Research in Child Development*, 29, 1–77.

Schaffer, M. C. (2009, October). The role of empathy and parenting style in the development of anti-social behaviours. *Crime & Delinquency*, 55(4), 586–599.

Singer, S. H. (2004). Applying social learning theory to childhood and adolescent firesetting: Can it lead to serial murder? *International Journal of Offender Therapy and Comparative Criminology*, 48(4), 461–476.

Stith, S. A. (1993). A predictive model of male spousal violence. *Journal of Family Violence*, 8, 183–201.

Taylor, S. (2019). *Forensic psychology*. Abingdon: Taylor & Francis.

WHO. (2017). Violence against women. Retrieved from https://www.who.int/: https://www.who.int/news-room/fact-sheets/detail/violence-against-women. Accessed on June 8, 2020.

Wright, J. A., & Hensley, C. (2003). From animal cruelty to serial murder: Applying the graduation hypothesis. *International Journal of Offender Therapy and Comparative Criminology*, 47(1), 71–88.

11

FEAR, FECKLESSNESS AND FLAPJACKS: IMAGINING AMBRIDGE'S OFFENDERS

Charlotte Bilby

ABSTRACT

Our perceptions of real crime, law and justice can be manipulated by fiction. This chapter addresses whether The Archers *helps us better understand today's offenders, their crimes and its policing. Some of Ambridge's known offenders are split into three categories to help explore whether usual criminal story lines and characters, seen and heard elsewhere, are perpetuated or subverted in Borsetshire. If they support usual tropes, this tells us how we view the management of crime in the twenty-first century rural idyll: outsiders are not to be trusted, the misdemeanours of the pastoral poor are tolerated, and the actions of elites brushed aside. In Ambridge, we regularly hear examples of reintegrative shaming supporting desistance from crime. Those propping up the Bull's bar might disapprove of criminal actions, but they recognise people's roles in village cohesion. Sgt. Harrison Burns preserves his identity as a dedicated police officer. Being a rural copper often means having to deal with a wide range of crimes – from attempted murder to anti-social behaviour – but on a less frequent basis than those based in Felpersham. While Harrison might not have great detective skills, he regularly supports colleagues from specialist units, and as the only officer in the village, should use his social networks and tea spots to help maintain Ambridge's mostly orderly conduct. It is questionable to what extent he does this, being at times perceptive about and dismissive of clues to significant criminal activity going on under his nose.*

INTRODUCTION

Ambridge seems be suffering from a crime wave – from the theft of farm vehicles to fraud; drug supply to cider selling; coercive control and sexual violence; the wholesale poisoning of the Am, and people being trafficked to carry out forced labour. Yet, since the mid-1990s up to a couple of years ago, crime rates in England and Wales, including serious violence, went down every year. This is not the picture that many news outlets would have you believe is the case. *The Echo* probably does not report the realities of crime and policing in Borsetshire in an even-handed manner nor give a balanced view of those who have been perpetrators of crime in the county. Less serious offences inviting fines or managed through magistrates' courts are not reported in as much gory detail as those that feed gossip in the Bull or the shop. To be fair, they need *something* more than the theatre reviews by Dylan Nells to keep circulation figures up. This chapter looks at who commits Ambridge's reported crime and considers whether we can group offenders together into one of three typologies, depending on who they are (an Archer or a

Horrobin) and what offence they have committed. It reflects on Sgt. Harrison Burns' capabilities and professionalism, especially now that the bunting has been found. It invites us to think about relationships between our own views of crime, policing, and what we think happens in the bucolic spaces of the West Midlands.

The Office for National Statistics (ONS) and Department for Environment, Food and Rural Affairs (DEFRA) show that crime in rural locations is quite different from crime in urban settings. Rural crime data (ONS, 2019) show that for a predominantly rural village of a similar size to Ambridge, there would be less than half a robbery per year, around 20 incidents of violence against the person, six domestic burglaries and six vehicle offences. Vehicle offences are of the Josh Archer type – vehicles being stolen – rather than the Matt 'splat' Crawford variety. Even if we consider significant under-reporting, Ambridge as we hear it still is not suffering from an epidemic of violent criminal activity like, say Midsomer, just down the road.

Even though crime and fear of crime are much lower in the countryside than urban areas, constabularies with large rural spaces may have a rural policing plan. These try to counteract the farming communities' lack of trust in policing capabilities (Mawby, 2015). Thus, constables who live and work in large geographic spaces, with scattered communities, have a significant job to do in managing crime and expectations (Wooff, 2017). This has not always helped if they are considered adept at lying to the village cricket team. Perhaps, Harrison, with his abilities in many specialised policing roles, is helping to raise the awareness of Borsetshire Constabulary's work. This could lead to higher trust and confidence in the police, which then might improve crime reporting and reduce fear of crime (Smith & Byrne, 2017); a positive response for any police force.

Crime dramas are incredibly popular in the United Kingdom, and they are sometimes seen as a marker of being something specifically English to other parts of the world (Bergin, 2013). They help us 'work... over and worr[y] at anxieties and exclusions of contemporary citizenship' (Brunsdon, 2000, p. 197) and what we feel about justice in the twenty-first century risk societies we live in (Garland & Bilby, 2011). While *The Archers* is not a crime drama, despite what it might have felt like in the last few years, it does still help us consider how we feel about crime and offenders, not only in our favourite village but in our own communities. Perhaps, Ambridge makes us wilfully nostalgic (Bergin, 2013) about the rural tranquillity of the past, where a little light poaching was the order of the day, and the friendly neighbourhood bobby sorted it all out with a cup of tea and a chat.

FEAR

Those committing crime in Ambridge tend to fall into three categories. These groups are not neat, there are always outliers and it is often difficult to predict how new residents will behave when they initially present as charming, with essential skills or an irrational attachment to organic farmers.

Those who are feared in Ambridge commit serious acts of violence against the person, against farm animals or 'the horses', and usually come from outside the village. From my own listening history, there was Simon Pemberton, who attacked Debbie Aldridge, Rob Titchener, and in 2017 Matt and his fraudulent cronies fleecing the irritatingly ageing of Ambridge. The unrepentant Clive Horrobin also fits within this group; his family has always been pinned as outsiders in the village (although Tracy Horrobin's cricketing triumph and job at Grey Gables might challenge this.) The only person rooted in Ambridge who caused fear in the village is Roy Tucker. In 2017, while he talked about his remorse for perpetrating hate crimes against Usha Franks over 20 years previously, Jill Archer was assaulting a celebrity chef with baked goods – the flapjacks of the title of this volume. An alternative reading is that Roy caused fear in retaliation for Usha's then perceived outsider status in the village. Generally, we see those who cause fear held at arm's length from the social cohesion of Ambridge. They arrive, disrupt and leave without waiting for healing to occur. It is the outsiders who many rural residents believe *are* committing the crime that occurs in the countryside (Smith & Byrne, 2017). Yet, it is more likely that crime in rural communities is committed by those living in them; as an officer with responsibility for rural policing said to me, 'it takes skill to round up 200 sheep and put them in a trailer, in the dark.'

Philip and Gavin Moss fit into the feared group. They have arrived and disrupted, even though at the time of writing no one seemingly knows about their involvement in modern day slavery, despite some of the warning signs being questioned by villagers. Philip could be compared to Rob; he has ingratiated himself with some solid, well-liked community members and is taking advantage of the psychological sabotage that Gavin perpetrates. The counties around Borsetshire understand that modern day slavery is a problem in rural communities, often linked to agricultural labour. It is perhaps a surprise that Adam Macy has not made comment about this, as he employs casual, seasonal labour and should be very well aware of the Gangmasters and Labour Abuse Authority (GLA). In Staffordshire, the Office of the Police, Fire and Rescue and Crime Commissioner has asked all local companies to make sure their supply chains are free from coercive practices, rather than just firms with large turnovers

(Staffordshire PFCC, n.d.). The Modern Slavery Act 2015 requires companies with a turnover greater than £36 million to ensure that their supply chains are free from slavery. This leads me to question what Borchester Land's turnover is, and whether Justin Elliott, another outsider, cares about how Philip and Gavin are going to carry out the work at Berrow Farm for the discount he demanded.

Shortly before Ambridge's delayed lockdown, Sgt. Burns (and it is still unclear which team in Borsetshire Police he is based) interviewed Philip about the Grey Gables explosion and asked about supply of materials to the kitchen job and how Blake got to the hotel, both indicators of malpractice and potential criminality. He is clearly using his interviewing training skills (College of Policing, n.d.) well, trying to unpick the detail behind the presented story. The interviews with Blake will be drawn together with this, and if there are more suspicions of modern slavery and human trafficking, escalated to the National Crime Agency for investigation. We hopefully will not have to rely on Roy, victim of Gavin's manipulation or Kirsty Miller and her concerns about waking Kenzie up with a call from Philip's phone, to realise that there is something problematic going on for everything to come to light.

FECKLESSNESS

It is difficult for some eavesdroppers to believe that fear-provoking crime would take place in the cosy confines of Ambridge. Our fuzzy thinking about rural crime and offenders as Mawby (2015) puts it might mean that we still believe only benign crimes take place in Borsetshire. These crimes, committed by those who are 'feckless' – used here as a very loaded shorthand for the 'deserving poor', always on the edges of criminal activity – are considered victimless and little more than nuisance. The families in Ambridge who flirt with crime, by poaching and small-scale tax evasion to make ends meet, are tolerated by those who rarely go without. While Yarwood (2010) suggests that in rural communities views about crime and offenders reinforce social divisions, Smith (2010, p. 374) notes it is the 'ingrained culture of silence within rural communities', rather than being blackmailed by an emeritus professor of classics, that would have stopped Joe Grundy being reported to the police for selling Tumble Tussock from the back of the cider shed. In Ambridge, it is often the case that offending by rural workers is portrayed as 'intentional pantomime' (Bergin, 2013, p. 83). Suggesting that this type of offending behaviour, brought on by poverty, is not considered important or something to be addressed within rural societies. These elements reinforce each other and are clearly demonstrated in Ambridge. The actions of each and every family group prop up the rural idyll that should not be shattered by police investigations.

The vast majority of our 80,000 prison population (Ministry of Justice, 2020) is there for short sentences of less than a year, is not a danger to the public and is in for offences linked to deprivation. In Ambridge, we can see people who have committed crimes fitting this category – think Ed Grundy, Jazzer McCreary, Alf Grundy and whoever made off with the £400 from the church charity box – but on the whole, the visible criminal community is not typical of the offenders who are in our prisons and on probation. The crimes committed recently in Ambridge seem to be of a more serious, violent and dramatic nature, which are just not typical of what is actually experienced in rural locations (ONS, 2019).

With the exposed activities of Moss Construction, we can see the interplay between the fear and feckless categories. Philip and Gavin, well placed in the feared group, are setting

Blake up to be seen as a member of the feckless group. As styled by Philip, Blake's criminal negligence is shown as a consequence of his previous life. Drug use and homelessness are often used as shorthand for offending behaviour, and Philip is aware of these vulnerabilities, having used them as markers for identifying people his organisation can exploit. It remains to be seen whether Borchester general staff have picked up on this and made a report to adult safeguarding teams, or whether Harrison's colleagues, who interviewed Blake, also remembered their interviewing training (College of Policing, n.d.) and identified causes for concern or further criminal investigation.

BUT IT IS ONLY A FLAPJACK

While Ambridge has feared the disruptive outsiders and tolerated feckless as families who are tied by strong community bonds, the crimes of the middle-classes are often swept aside, ignored, excused, manipulated out of existence. Badger killing, crop trashing, joyriding, drunk driving and public order offences involving baked goods, are simply trifles that can be walked away from relatively unscathed.

Even in the recent past, Brian Aldridge could be seen to be deploying techniques of neutralisation (Sykes & Matza, 1957) in dealing with his criminal activity. He denied responsibility, he denied injury and he condemned those who condemned his past behaviour. He thought, and probably still thinks, that money will restore his peers' and neighbours' faith in him. What we could have hoped to find was that, unlike those who are considered feckless but hold an important social position in Ambridge, Brian's social capital was easily be broken, leaving him in a difficult position after any punishment for his crimes. Despite the fear instilled by the consequences of his waterway poisoning, the Aldridges have suffered little actual social rejection within Ambridge, whatever Jennifer might imagine. Perhaps the promised, and still-awaited, contrition celebration will help remind residents what Brian did. Ruairi Donovan has shown a similar lack of remorse in joyriding with Ben Archer. Neither has formally been brought to account for this, save from a telling off by 'Disco Dave Archer', who clearly has an internal limit about what constitutes the destruction of his rural idyll. Josh Archer lacks the moral compass demonstrated by Eddie Grundy on matters of insurance fraud. I speculate Josh is buying second-hand vehicles that have been stolen, to go along with his potential fraudulent business activities.

Freddie Pargetter's offending tends to subvert this categorisation. His drug dealing meant a short stint in prison. Right up to his sentencing, I was convinced that the Ambridge Fairy (see Chapter 12) would branch out and try her luck in the criminal justice system, meaning that the good boy from a good family would be handed a suspended sentence or a community penalty rather than immediate incarceration. Even though drug dealing and consumption in rural locations are more prevalent than might be expected, the fear instilled by Noluthando Madikane's hospitalisation of could never go unpunished. However, Freddie's position in the village has now been altered by rescuing Lynda Snell from Grey Gables' explosion.

AMBRIDGE'S POSTER BOYS FOR DESISTANCE

In the rumpus about Matt being knocked down, James Bellamy said to his mother, Lilian 'a leopard never changes its spots,

Ma.' This is not the case at all. Ambridge is full of those who
have changed their lives and continue on the road from crime.
Sid Perks, Ed and Jazzer all spring to mind, not to mention Susan
Carter.

The three-stage journey of desisting from crime (see for
example, Maruna, 2001) is shown in Ambridge. Desistance is
a set of ideas that show how people grow out of crime and
stop offending (primary desistance.) They re-invent themselves
and believe in their own new identity as someone with pro-
social behaviours and responsibilities (secondary desistance),
with communities embracing the new presentations of self
(tertiary desistance.) In much literature on male offenders,
reimagining and secondary desistance are often instigated by
'the love of a good woman' – respectively Kathy Perks, Emma
Grundy or any female residents of Grange Spinney. Social
capital, having a job or institutions and groups that you
belong to, is an important element in secondary desistance. If
you are someone who people rely on to deliver milk, entertain
on Burns Night, rescue pigs, look out for older people or shear
sheep, then this helps in considering yourself as someone
needed in the community and out of prison. An example of
this is Ed's decision to not continue to work for Tim Oatey.
The position that he has worked hard at building influenced
his decision-making.

Ambridge does reintegrative shaming. This idea, linked to
restorative justice, show that communities can disapprove of
offending behaviour while at the same time supporting
offenders to form social bonds. This in turn allows new
identities to be created. Think about Leonard Berry's support
of Freddie. Leonard listened to Freddie's worries while being
taken on a hidden Lower Loxley tour. He understood Freddie
might not cope with a large Archer family gathering so soon
after his release and was appalled by Ben's questioning about
what it was like being banged up. In fact, Leonard's behaviour

led me to wonder whether he had either been in prison himself, or if he had just really paid attention during the Laurels' volunteer training covering the hidden impact of imprisonment on family members.

Yet, people sometimes zigzag on the way to being and remaining crime free. It might only take the provocation of not being able to get the business books to balance, the insulting digs of a priggish brother, the demands of a wife set on a new home or even the weight of being a celebrated rescuer to trigger re-offending. Freddie is the most recent poster boy for desistance, taking over the mantle from Ed. Freddie has been released from prison into a caring home that is *outwardly* stable. He does not have to worry about finding somewhere to sleep and has the social status to make changes in his life possible. Yet, Freddie bears the psychological scars of imprisonment, outbursts of anger and anxiety and feelings of worthlessness. The fallout from the Grey Gables explosion may not help him maintaining his crime-free life. Ambridge after the big bang is an overwhelming example of tertiary desistance, where they have accepted him back into village life. Freddie is not the drug dealer, but a hero. They have recast him in a role he is not yet able to accept. Freddie has talked candidly about how he is not able to admit to his positive actions, especially after Lynda's angst. Rather than helping him maintain non-offending, it could have entirely the opposite impact, which might mean that Harrison needs to make another arrest.

WHAT IS IT EXACTLY THAT HARRISON AND OTHER RURAL POLICE OFFICERS DO?

Despite the lower crime rates and fear of crime in the countryside, rural crime is a national concern. In 2014, the

National Rural Crime Network (NRCN) was created by
Police and Crime Commissioners (PCCs) with responsibility
for largely rural constabularies, and the National Police
Chiefs' Council (NPCC) set out a rural affairs strategy (2018)
to address the increasing concern about crime in remote areas.
They wanted to address the fact that some offences have a
disproportionate impact on rural communities and businesses
than in urban areas. Imagine how a sheep farmer would cope
with lambing if their only quad bike is stolen in February.
There is also an acknowledgement that some innocuous but
problematic offences, poaching or fly tipping for example, are
linked to organised crime groups (OCGs).

Even though the NRCN is supported by 30 PCCs, who
drive the objectives for their associated police constabularies,
tackling rural crime still relies on force operational priorities
when deciding where to put resources. While the idea of
'covering a 12 foot room with an 8 foot carpet' (Fenwick,
2015, p. 236) is not solely a rural policing issue, officers in
rural constabularies have to, for example, make decisions
about how many operational officers to deploy in geographically large, but sparsely populated areas. While at the Rural
Affairs Summit in summer 2018 (possibly one of the best days
of my academic career; I sat in the back of a police 4×4
towing a police quad bike to the venue, looked at police
branded tractors, listened to presentations about livestock
worrying, and then got to talk to the Sheep Association, who
were somewhat disinterested in my questions about rare
breeds and knitting), I asked a rural crime lead from a larger
rural constabulary just why it was that (then) Constable Burns
was both the dedicated officer for Ambridge and policing
night clubs in Felpersham. Without missing a beat, he replied
'that's perceptive of you. I think it just shows that Borsetshire
Constabulary's resources are stretched too.'

Each PCC has to publish a plan about what they expect their forces to address. It is impossible to get hold of the Borsetshire Police and Crime plan, which is something of a worry, and probably should be reported to the Home Office. We can see that in neighbouring West Mercia, the PCC believes it is important to reassure rural communities that their concerns will be met. In Gloucestershire, there are objectives about accessibility and accountability – by this they mean more visible policing, safer driving and reducing drink driving, all of which relate to rural communities' concerns. Yet, very few policing plans mention rural concerns, even constabularies with very geographically large rural populations, so it might not be a surprise that the results of the NRCN 2018 rural crime survey showed almost three quarters of victimised rural businesses feel frustrated, angry or disgusted with the way that they have been treated by the police. The survey (NRCN, 2018) attempted to identify the extent of crime and its impact in rural communities. While over 20,000 people completed the survey, older people and those in socio-economic ABC1 brackets were hugely overrepresented in the results, entirely mirroring the demographic makeup of vocal Ambridge residents. This, in turn, links to Yarwood's (2010) views of who owns policing in the countryside and whose needs are most often acknowledged. The expected management of crime reinforces the imagined rural idyll of those already privileged in country villages and estates.

The incidence of crimes specific to rural businesses, farmers, landowners and rural vets were recorded in the survey. Fly tipping had been experienced by 18% of respondents, 14% had had hare coursing on their land and 11% had had agricultural machinery stolen. Less frequent offences were sheep worrying or dog attacks (5%) and 4% being victim of vehicle fuel thefts. In Ambridge, we have heard talk of fly tipping and Josh has been 'victim' of machinery theft, but Sgt.

Burns has not mentioned any of these other crimes. This might be disappointing to eavesdroppers but is entirely consistent with adherence to the College of Policing's Code of Ethics (2014) and requirement not to discuss cases with people not in the police.

For over 20 years, parish councils in England and Wales have had to consider the impact of their work on crime and policing in their community (CDA, 1998). This means that those within positions of power, predominantly the older ABC1s with the occasional younger parent who cares about affordable housing, identifying issues for the village. It is not as simple as Susan as Central Intelligence Ambridge saying what is important, although who knows how she influences councillor Neil Carter. *Chili con carne* anyone? In Ambridge, as in Gloucestershire, there are concerns about driving safety. The parish council, as is its right and requirement, talked about crime and disorder and had the speeding initiative. However, I do not remember Harrison being involved. As the local constable, it would have been his role to take part in community policing initiatives. We have not heard of him taking part in community meetings of any kind, which leads me to wonder what the rural policing arrangements in Borsetshire actually are, and whether now Harrison is a Sergeant, he will support his neighbourhood teams to work more visibly in the villages.

Police in other constabularies involve local volunteers – game keepers, wildlife organisations, estate managers, historic monument organisations – to take part in evening operations, where they patrol sections of the countryside on the lookout for things that might be suspicious, problematic or criminal. I went along to one of these sessions, *Operation Checkpoint* (Grainge, n.d.), was briefed, shown how to contact control and was paired with an estate manager. I went out to his 4×4, moved his shepherd's crook and clambered in. He turned the engine on, and the radio blared. It was 7:02 p.m. and tuned to BBC Radio 4. The timing could not have been more deliciously perfect. We drove around the countryside, talked about crime and nuisance, and considered who might be responsible for the crimes committed. Just as Smith and Byrne's (2017) survey suggested, there was a belief that quite a lot of crimes were committed by people from outside their communities. I imagine with the wave of young people from downtown Felpersham that Kate Madikane, with her well developed and accredited youth work skills, hosted in spring 2019 there was a perception that crime rate and levels of nuisance spiked. I expect, as Kenton Archer, Roy and Jazzer speculated, Derek Fletcher had a LOT to say about this, and said it very loudly.

It is clear that much rural crime is committed by people within their communities, but there is also an understanding that some rural crime can be linked to organised crime. You start local and build a bigger picture of criminal activity. Poaching, lamping and hare coursing, fly tipping, red diesel and vehicle theft have all been linked to organised crime activity. Going on to a property to poach means that you can identify whether there are large pieces of agricultural machinery that can be stolen to order and shipped out of the country or used in the theft of money machines. Adam might rue voting to leave the European Union if his combine is stolen to order from outside the United Kingdom; there are still many questions about how European cross-border policing intelligence might be shared after the end of 2020 (Briere, 2018). Despite being a rural officer, Harrison, from what we now know about his views of Ambridge crime divulged to us during 2020's coronavirus lockdown, did not take the spate of fly tipping seriously until Tim was implicated and then arrested. If he is based in the neighbourhood team, it might be best if he re-reads the NPCC (2018) rural affairs strategy document.

During the 2019 *Academic Archers* Sheffield Conference, I gratifyingly predicted Harrison should be looking at Josh and his business in lightly used agricultural machinery. To be honest, I was convinced that Josh was part of an OCG, knowingly moving on valuable resources. His insistence that Eddie be in on an insurance scam, quick flit to Thailand, urgent request that Rex Fairbrother fraudulently backdate paperwork and his brazen disregard for keeping trading records supported my more elaborate explanations for his behaviour. Although, if he was a crime boss, he might be better at record creation. Josh thinks he is in the clear, but I wonder whether Philip's business interests will be linked back to Josh in some fashion. We still do not have a full explanation for the money machine theft. My guess is that this and the enforced labour Philip is using are part of a bigger and connected picture, and that Harrison's colleagues will be back to interview Josh. Perhaps that is what Harrison is doing – working for the West Midlands Regional Organised Crime Unit (West Midlands Police, n.d.) alongside undercover Joy Horville – in the fight against organised crime!

CONCLUSION

Buying a house on Beechwood might be a good plan if you are thinking of moving to the countryside. The burglary rate seems to be non-existent. There is little nuisance, even from the Button girls, and no low-level drug dealing since Freddie's sentence and release. Perhaps we do not hear about less *Echo*-worthy troubles because we rarely hear from the 'rural criminal underclass' (Smith, 2010, p. 382) of Borsetshire. Their voices are supressed in an 'exclusive countryside' (Yarwood, 2010, p. 61) dominated by older people from privileged socio-economic groups, whose public order offences are brushed aside as merely flapjacktivism (see Bartlett, this volume). Brian has not received a custodial sentence, and Ben and Ruairi's joyriding has gone officially undetected. The only Archer-clan member brought to justice for his offending is Freddie, who despite showing the psychological impact of imprisonment that criminologists would recognise, has swiftly moved to the third phase of desisting from crime, where he is welcomed back into the community with a hero's identity.

Police in rural areas deal with similar crimes as those in urban settings, with the likelihood of them happening less frequently, but they also need a set of social skills different from their urban counterparts. In walking a fine line by trying to manage all of the competing demands on their time and resources, often in areas where other services are being cut, rural officers must make the monthly stops and have cups of tea, as well as taking part in community meetings where policing, crime and disorder is talked about (Wooff, 2017). Harrison does not seem to be doing these things; he actively antagonises villagers and has little time to chat about crimes he considers a nuisance. He only seems to indulge his softer social skills when needing to butter older ladies up in order to buy their homes. Perhaps Harrison's fate is to deal with those who Ambridge fears, and to help uncover the OCG that will sweep up Philip and Gavin's appalling treatment of Blake, Kenzie and Jordan, while Kirsty sobs at the altar.

REFERENCES

Bergin, T. (2013). Identity and nostalgia in a globalised world: Investigating the international popularity of Midsomer Murders. *Crime, Media, Culture*, 9(1), 83–99.

Briere, C. (2018). Cooperation of Europol and Eurojust with external partners in the fight against crime: What are the

challenges ahead? Working Paper 1. Dublin City University
Brexit Institute. Retrieved from http://dcubrexitinstitute.eu/
wp-content/uploads/2018/01/WP-2018-1-Bri per centC3
per centA8re.pdf. Accessed on June 15, 2020.

Brunsdon, C. (2000). Structure of anxiety: Recent British
television crime fiction. In E. Buscombe (Ed.), *British television: A reader*. Oxford: Oxford University Press.

College of Policing. (2014). Code of ethics. Retrieved from
https://www.college.police.uk/What-we-do/Ethics/Ethics-
home/Documents/Code_of_Ethics.pdf. Accessed on March
19, 2019.

College of Policing. (n.d.). Professionalising investigation
programme (PIP1): Priority and volume crime. Retrieved
from https://www.college.police.uk/What-we-do/Learning/
Professional-Training/Professionalising-investigation-pro-
gramme/Pages/PIP1.aspx. Accessed on March 29, 2020.

Crime and Disorder Act 1998. Retrieved from http://
www.legislation.gov.uk/ukpga/1998/37/section/17.
Accessed on June 20, 2020.

Fenwick, T. (2015). Learning policing in rural spaces:
'Covering 12 foot rooms with 8 foot carpets'. *Policing: A
Journal of Policy and Practice*, 9(3), 234–241.

Gangmasters, & Labour Abuse Authority. Retrieved from
https://www.gla.gov.uk/. Accessed on June 20, 2020.

Garland, J., & Bilby, C. (2011). 'What next, Dwarves?':
Images of police culture in life on Mars. *Crime, Media,
Culture*, 7(2), 115–132.

Grainge, J. (n.d.). Operation Checkpoint- Working together
across the North of England to tackle rural crime. Retrieved

on from https://www.nationalruralcrimenetwork.net/best-practice/operationcheckpoint/. Accessed on June 19, 2020.

Maruna, S. (2001). *Making good: How ex-convicts reform and reclaim their lives*. Washington, DC: American Psychological Association.

Mawby, R. I. (2015). Exploring the relationship between crime and place in the countryside. *Journal of Rural Studies*, 39(June), 262–270.

Ministry of Justice. (2020). Official statistics: Prison population figures 2020. Retrieved from https://www.gov.uk/government/statistics/prison-population-figures-2020. Accessed on June 27, 2020.

Modern Slavery Act 2015. Retrieved from http://www.legislation.gov.uk/ukpga/2015/30/contents/enacted. Accessed on April 1, 2020.

National Police Chiefs Council. (2018). Rural affairs strategy: Strengthening safe and prosperous communities. Retrieved from https://www.npcc.police.uk/documents/crime/2018/NPCC per cent20Rural per cent20affairs per cent20 Strategy per cent202018 per cent202021.pdf. Accessed on June 20, 2020.

National Rural Crime Network. (2018). Living on the edge: Report and recommendations from the National Rural Crime Survey 2018. Retrieved from https://www.nationalruralcrimenetwork.net/content/uploads/2018/07/National-Rural-Crime-Survey-2018-Report-and-Recommendations.pdf. Accessed on August 1, 2020.

Office for National Statistics. (2019). Rural crime statistics: Crime figures in rural and urban areas. Retrieved from https://www.gov.uk/government/statistics/rural-crime#history. Accessed on April 2, 2020.

Smith, R. (2010). Policing the changing landscape of rural crime: A case study from Scotland. *International Journal of Police Science and Management*, 12(3), 373–387.

Smith, K., & Byrne, R. (2017). Farm crime in England and Wales: A preliminary scoping study examining farmer attitudes. *International Journal of Rural Criminology*, 3(2), 191–223.

Staffordshire Police Fire and Rescue and Crime Commissioner. (n.d.). Modern slavery. Retrieved from https://staffordshire-pfcc.gov.uk/initiatives/modern-slavery/. Accessed on April 1, 2020.

Sykes, G., & Matza, D. (1957). Techniques of neutralization: A theory of delinquency. *American Sociological Review*, 22(6), 664–670.

West Midlands Police. (n.d.). ROCU. Retrieved from https://west-midlands.police.uk/specialist-teams/rocu. Accessed on June 27, 2020.

Wooff, A. (2017). Soft policing in rural Scotland. *Policing: A Journal of Policy and Practice*, 11(2), 123–131.

Yarwood, R. (2010). An exclusive countryside? Crime concern, social exclusion and community policing in two English villages. *Policing and Society*, 20(1), 61–78.

Section 4

HOUSING AND THE AMBRIDGE FAIRY

HOUSING AND THE WELFARE STATE

12

RICH RELATIVES OR AMBRIDGE FAIRY? PATRONAGE AND EXPECTATION IN AMBRIDGE HOUSING PATHWAYS

Claire Astbury

ABSTRACT

Finding a suitable home can be difficult in a constrained housing market such as small rural village. Within Ambridge, only a small proportion of the homes in the village is known about, and it is rare for additional homes to be added to those where named characters live. This chapter takes a generational view of housing pathways and options, showing how Generation X, Millennial and Generation Z populations in Ambridge are housed. The chapter examines the extent to which characters rely on friends or family for solving their housing problems and considers the role of family wealth and wider dependence in determining housing pathways. The research shows that dependence on others' access to property is by far the most pronounced feature of housing options for these households. These pathways

*and housing choices are compared to the wider context
in rural England, to consider the extent to which luck, in
the form of the mythical 'Ambridge Fairy', plays a role in
helping people to find housing. The ways in which the
Ambridge Fairy manifests are also considered – showing
that financial windfalls, unexpectedly available properties and convenient patrons are more likely to be available to people with social capital and established (and
wealthy) family networks. The specific housing pathway
of Emma Grundy is reviewed to reflect on the way in
which her housing journey is typical of the rural
working-class experience of her generation, within the
wider housing policy context.*

INTRODUCTION: A PERSONAL INTEREST

I started working in housing in 1995, and I came to *The
Archers* in 2002. As a self-confessed housing nerd, I've always
noticed and been interested in the housing arrangements of the
characters in the village. I've listened as the millennial generation grew up into independent households, and as ageing
villagers made decisions about the homes they grow old in. As
a fan, I know that we refer to the 'Ambridge Fairy' when
homes, jobs or good fortune fall into the laps of characters or
provide resolutions to plots. I decided to investigate how the
Ambridge Fairy works in relation to housing and whether
good fortune in Ambridge followed similar patterns to the
benefits of family wealth and social capital that exist outside
of the village. I ask, 'Do housing outcomes provide evidence
for the Ambridge Fairy?' and this research focusses on the
generations born since 1966 to assess whether these characters

experience similar housing challenges to counterparts living in other comparable rural areas. It tests the extent to which housing pathways and outcomes reflect the realities of life outside Ambridge or provide evidence for the intervention of the infamous Ambridge Fairy, and the ways in which this fortune manifests.

AMBRIDGE AS A HOUSING MARKET

The exact number of homes and residents in Ambridge is unclear although recent estimates, collated in Chapter 17, indicate a population of around 700 people which suggests there are 300–400 homes in the village. Like many rural villages which operate as a hinterland to a market town (Borchester) and a larger cathedral city (Felpersham) as well as a wider travel to work area (West Midlands), it accommodates local people, incomers and commuters as well as supporting rural tourism and several farms. The Beechwood development of 18 homes, completed in 2020, is the latest new housing to be added to the village, with the previous significant development, Grange Spinney, built in 2003 and also providing 18 homes of which six were affordable.

We only hear from a few of the homes in the village, just as we only hear from about 10% of the population. Like many rural areas, Ambridge is a constrained housing market with limited supply and mainly reliant on occasional moves from existing residents to create availability. Based on the seasonally adjusted average transaction rate of house sales (English House Condition Survey, HMRC), it would be expected that around 27 homes would come onto the market in Ambridge each year. However, aside from the homes where named characters live, and new homes which are built, this is not included in conversation. I've never heard a character say 'Did you see that house over at Grange Spinney is for sale? I had a look at it on the internet.' Like the unknown, unvoiced characters brought to life by Bartlett's (Chapter 17) research, the unknown, unnamed homes in Ambridge remain invisible, unless the Ambridge Fairy decides to conjure them into being at an opportune time. The struggle of younger residents to secure appropriate affordable housing does reflect to an extent the wider reality of rural life in England, and the housing challenges for those generations. This paper aims to show the extent which the experiences are realistic and identify where the Ambridge Fairy becomes a necessary intervention to overcome barriers to housing.

THE NATIONAL HOUSING CONTEXT

Across the United Kingdom, a series of interconnected issues shape the housing market at local and national levels. Rural areas have some particular challenges.

Planning and Housing Supply

Reviews including the Barker Review (Barker, 2004) have highlighted an undersupply of new homes in the United Kingdom across at least the past 20 years. This is an issue which applies particularly to the wider South East but is also a consideration for rural areas, where younger generations increasingly have to leave their home villages to secure long-term housing (Grayston & Pullinger, 2018). Research indicates a need for up to 340,000 new homes per year in England and the government set a target to add 300,000 homes a year (Wilson & Barton, 2020). However, the actual level of new homes completed falls well short of this.

Financialisation

Property as an asset class has seen a significant shift since 1980. Subsequent governments have prioritised owner occupation, with the cultural impact that renting has come to be seen as a lesser form of occupation. From the mid-1990s, a long period of rising house prices, the advent of Buy To Let mortgages, and the relative poor performance of other investment options meant that housing has been valued as an asset rather than a home. For around two decades, this further advantaged those people with existing equity over new entrants to the market. One consequence of this is the increasing role for parental contributions to children's housing, with children of owner occupiers especially in higher value areas being more likely to become owners themselves. Figures from the Resolution Foundation found in 2018 that the average first-time buyer, relying on their own income alone, now needed to save for 18 years for a deposit, up from three years in the 1990s (Wood & Clarke, 2018). The government has only recently amended tax and stamp duty policy on Buy To Let to curb the trend.

Changing Role of the State

The private housing market is never able to adequately house everyone in a society. Government choices about how to manage that reality have wider consequences about what housing options exist for people at all points in the market. Changes in tenure patterns have been partly a consequence of government policy choices which encouraged home ownership, and latterly landlordism; and which shifted from a capital subsidy to personal subsidy model (Boughton, 2019). However other mechanisms include capital grant for affordable housing, tax choices and capital support for home ownership such as Homebuy. Research by Capital Economics in 2015 demonstrated that direct capital subsidy for social rent provides the best value for money in housing lower income households (Chaloner, Dreisin, & Pragnell, 2015).

Welfare and Exclusion

The provision of housing benefits to individuals is one, more visible, way of managing market failure to provide. Government attempts to reduce the costs of housing benefit, especially under austerity policies since 2010, have also accelerated the gap between the benefit available and actual rents – with high cost rural areas particularly affected.

Affordability

These various factors have combined to create a multifaced affordability crisis in housing. In truth there are a range of housing crises across the country, with some featuring more strongly in rural areas. Higher house prices and price-to-income ratios are one element of the crisis. Evidence from Action with Communities in Rural England, the Rural Coalition, suggests that low-income households in rural areas 'need nine times their income to buy the cheapest homes in the local housing market' (ACRE, 2020). Limited availability of housing to rent often means that rental costs are higher, and less than 8% of rural homes are affordable social rented housing compared to 17% nationally. The reducing security of employment also impacts on housing options as it makes it harder to pass credit checks and access mortgages. Incomes are lower in rural areas, and the gap between urban and rural wages is growing (CPRE, 2015). Meanwhile, rural housing costs are higher on average – in the West Midlands, the premium for rural living is up to 57% above urban house prices (CPRE, 2015). Finally, additional factors add to the affordability challenges in rural areas. For example, homes are more likely to be older and less energy efficient, leading to fuel poverty. Limited public transport also means that households are more burdened by transport costs.

UNDERSTANDING HOUSING PATHWAYS AND GENERATIONAL DYNAMICS

A growing body of study on life-course residential mobility, for example, the work of the Housing, Migration and Family Dynamics group within the European Network for Housing Research (ENHR, 2020) has established thinking about housing pathways. This approach, especially its use of longitudinal data, acknowledges how personal relationships interact with structural and market factors. It also provides an opportunity to evidence how *'the inequalities in housing equity and inequities in access to housing have helped to produce a particular landscape of dependence of younger generations on older ones'* (Lennarz & Ronald, 2019).

My initial thinking for this research was inspired by Rory Coulter's study of Intergenerational Housing Pathways (Coulter, 2018). In considering housing pathways for my study of Ambridge residents, I focused on household makeup and housing tenure as the main factors. As all the households under consideration live in one village, I did not take into account geographical location – which might normally be a consideration. The second aspect of my study of Ambridge was based on generational cohort, as this is increasingly a feature of how we understand housing choices and expectations in the United Kingdom and beyond. Life course stage is also a means of understanding housing pathways – with differing housing requirements as household composition changes through, for example, marriage or the establishment of a family.

For the purposes of this work, I have defined generations as follows: Silent generation, born pre-1945; Baby boomers, born 1945-65; Generation X, born 1966-80; Millenials, born 1980-94; and Generation Z, born 1995-present. By outlining the current housing situation and the pathway which each household had taken to arrive there, I wanted to explore the expectations, opportunities and dependencies which affected how and where characters live. In identifying the pivotal moments in their life and housing pathways, I hoped to reveal what if any influence the Ambridge Fairy had and how this manifested.

THE 2020 HOUSING SNAPSHOT – MAPPING INTERDEPENDENCE

Fig. 12.1 focuses on the Generation X, Millennial and Generation Z cohorts. It does not plot all the households in the village – just the main speaking characters born since 1966 and the dependencies involved. Households with family support are shown in light grey, those with support from other villagers in white and those without support in dark grey. The nature of the support is shown by a dotted line for accommodation and solid line for financial support.

Looking across the dependencies, it's clear that there is significant reliance on others for housing in Ambridge. The greater the reliance on others and lower the ability of people to secure their own housing independently, the more potential

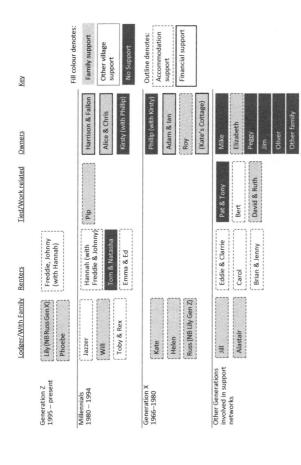

Fig. 12.1. Generational Housing Dependence in Ambridge in Early 2020.

for the Ambridge Fairy to be a factor in housing outcomes.
Most of the support provided is in the form of accommodation itself, but there is some financial support, almost exclu-
sively within the Aldridge family. The diagram evidences five
main findings which give insight into the housing options and
choices of households in the village.

1. The role of family wealth in home ownership

According to research by Legal and General in 2018,
nearly two-thirds of first-time buyers under 35 rely on
family support, 'the Bank of Mum and Dad', to access
home ownership (Legal and General, 2018). Among the
cohorts in Ambridge, the only household who didn't (to
our knowledge) have parental support was Phillip Moss
and Kirsty Miller. However, this purchase was made by
Phillip, presumably from the profits of human slavery,
without which Kirsty would still be renting a room at
Roy Tucker's house.

Every other household in the Gen X/Millennial/Gen Z
cohort required family support. Adam Macy and Ian
Craig had financial help with a deposit; Alice Carter and
Kate Aldridge own cottages on Home Farm; Harrison
Burns had financial support from his family too. Roy
didn't have financial support but was only able to own a
home in the village through Mike Tucker splitting the
Willow Farm farmhouse in two to create a home for
Roy's family. Evidence shows that reliance on parental
support increases in high-value areas (such as constrained
housing markets like rural villages) and also the greater
the parental wealth, the more likely it is that children will
receive and need support. Housing equity is very
unevenly spread throughout the country and throughout
age groups. Children of parents with no housing wealth
are 60% less likely to be homeowners at the age of 30

(Wood & Clarke, 2018). Will Grundy managed to buy an investment property at Number 1 The Green as a direct result of an unexpected financial windfall, and the convenient fact that he was living in tied accommodation at the time, so did not need to house himself. This is an example of the Ambridge Fairy – if only she had spread the good fortune to Ed Grundy as well.

One unusual feature of the 2020 diagram is the changing fortunes of Brian and Jennifer Aldridge. All their children own property, but this happened before Home Farm was sold to cover the costs of the Environment Agency fine, resulting in the heads of the Aldridge family moving into a rented home. Taken as a snapshot, the 2020 diagram implies that these children of renters have bucked the trend, which is why understanding the longer-term housing pathway is so important in contextualising the housing options of each household.

2. Where people are renting a home in Ambridge, this is often facilitated at a discount through connection or dependence

A prime example of this is the Grundy's continued residence at Grange Farm, where they are dependent on the willingness of Oliver Sterling to accept below market value income on the property. The picture at Grange Farm is indeed complicated as at March 2020, Eddie and Clarrie Grundy are providing accommodation for Will following his resignation as gamekeeper and the loss of his tied accommodation. In the adjoining land sits a mobile home where Ed, Emma, George and Kiera Grundy are living. The land is still in the ownership of Oliver Sterling, there is no planning permission for the mobile home, and the Grundys are very much in his hands. Elsewhere, Will's Buy To Let property at Number 1

The Green proved hard to let and since 2014, tenants
sourced from the village have been negotiating a discount
from market rates – firstly Emma Grundy, subsequently
Tom Archer, and now presumably Hannah Riley and
Johnny Phillips. The lack of affordable housing provided
through public provision has created a situation where,
for *Archers* characters, social capital manifested through
local relationships is more likely to yield a home at a
discounted rate than any established government
intervention.

3. Many households in Ambridge rely on sharing a home as
   their only practical housing option, although others
   actively choose to share

   Sharing as a lodger or intergenerational household is an
   established means by which *Archers* characters have
   housed themselves. Jazzer McCreary for example, as
   someone without wider family in the village has long been
   dependent on shared accommodation. Sharing a home as
   housemates is an expected part of housing pathways for
   younger people, but we have evidence for 'Boomerang'
   children in Ambridge, primarily Ed, Emma and latterly
   Will Grundy, although Kate Madikane also has a history
   of this pathway. Multigenerational sharing is also common
   across the social classes – not just the Grundys but the
   Archers too.

4. The role of farming or agricultural housing options is
   significant in Ambridge housing pathways

   Farm accommodation such as Rickyard Cottage or the
   gamekeeper's cottage has been key locations for characters.
   Bert Fry's old retainer's bungalow has also been a home for
   Rex and Toby Fairbrother. There is very little evidence about
   the prevalence and role of agricultural accommodation
   nationally, but it has a special place in Ambridge. Often in

the gift of the key farming families, it provides an opportunity to control and provide housing for key characters – more opportunity for patronage and dependence in the village.

5. The residents of Ambridge have not been well served by public housing support and provision

Although the homes at The Green were originally provided as council housing, the only home we know is still occupied as low-cost accommodation is 6 The Green, home to Tracy Horrobin, her children, father and brother. The absence of state support – even where people would have been eligible for it – is a recurring theme. Access to housing advice, welfare benefits, homelessness support (for example, immediately after the flood in 2015) and affordable housing has been notably absent. This potentially reflects the lack of awareness among either the scriptwriters or average village residents as to what support is available and how to access it.

Accommodation versus Financial-Based Interventions

As can be seen from Fig. 12.1, most of the housing dependence in the village was in the form of accommodation support. Of the 16 households in the Gen X/Millennial/Gen Z group, 11 benefitted from housing interventions (69%) and only three (19%) from financial intervention. This reflects the prevalence of co-residence, as well as personal connections and agricultural accommodation. Even among the older population which often provide the support, they themselves are benefitting from this support themselves, often across generations.

HOW THE AMBRIDGE FAIRY INFLUENCES THE
2020 PICTURE

At what point does family wealth, personal connection and
social capital take on the additional magic of the Ambridge
Fairy? The Ambridge Fairy is most noticeable in terms of
timeliness – a problem solved just at the right moment – but
there is usually underlying social capital. Within the 2020
diagram, there are several households which have benefitted
from a family or personal connection which meant that housing
became available to them unexpectedly or conveniently. For
example, Brian and Jennifer were struggling to find a suitable
place to rent as the sale of Home Farm approached. At the
eleventh hour, the Kemps at Willow Cottage were relocated to
Strasbourg for work and Brian went around to charm them
into letting the cottage to him. Also, The Grundys have been
repeatedly reliant on the timely largesse of Oliver Sterling.
Oliver offered them the occupation of Grange Farm when they
were facing homelessness following the flood and has
continued to let them stay at an undisclosed discounted rent. A
recent change at Grange Farm means that Emma and Ed now
live in a mobile home placed on the land, again reliant on
Oliver remaining tolerant because of the strong network of
relationships between him (and his late wife Caroline Sterling)
and the Grundy family. A less timely but similarly fortuitous
lucky intervention was the unexpected inheritance which
enabled Will Grundy to buy Number 1 The Green from Matt
Crawford in 2008. The comfortable housing position of the
Aldridge children, however, owes more to the traditional
privilege of family wealth than the presence of the Ambridge
Fairy. Ironically the *Archers* character who has benefitted most
from the Ambridge Fairy in recent years is not in any of the
younger cohorts. Just as Christine Barford had recovered suf-
ficiently at The Laurels to consider moving out of a care home

setting, a hitherto unknown private sheltered housing scheme emerged from the ether to provide her with an independent home at a price she could afford. It's unusual but not unheard of for sheltered housing and care schemes to share a footprint but this definitely seems to be an Ambridge Fairy intervention.

CASE STUDY: EMMA GRUNDY'S HOUSING PATHWAY

An interesting example of a housing pathway is that of Emma Grundy. Emma was a vocal campaigner for affordable housing in the village because of her own experiences of housing insecurity. Table 12.1 sets out Emma's housing career from birth, with a commentary showing how this reflects or ignores wider housing circumstances and the points at which the Ambridge Fairy could be said to intervene.

Emma repeatedly plays the role of 'home-finder' in her relationship with Ed. The only time that Ed's contacts have helped them find a place to live was his ongoing relationship with Oliver Sterling which resulted in the Grundys forming a three-generation household at Grange Farm in 2015. Ed's financial and employment insecurity has limited his ability to provide a suitable home for his growing family – a long term issue in his relationship with Emma. But their main constraint is the limited affordable accommodation in Ambridge, coupled with an unwillingness to consider living outside of the village.

The Ambridge Fairy has not blessed Emma's family with the availability of other affordable housing locally, even though some of the existing affordable housing in the village will likely have become available during the past 15 years. Her aspiration to own a home of her own, against the odds, likely means she has not been active in applying for other affordable housing

Table 12.1. Housing Pathway of Emma Grundy.

Housing/Dates	Emma's Pathway and Wider Housing Context
1984 Flat at Nightingale Farm *Agricultural tenancy* *Within household*	Born to Neil and Susan Carter. Neil has access to farm accommodation, but the owner wished to sell the property. *The role of agricultural-related housing is shown here for the newlywed couple.*
1984 1 The Green *Council tenancy* *Within household*	The Carters are allocated a 3-bedroom council house at 1 The Green. This could be considered an **Ambridge Fairy** moment in terms of timeliness and luck – this family would not usually be eligible for a 3-bedroom home, and with only a handful of council homes in the village at this point, the chances of one being available just as they needed it was fortuitous. *The Carters were among 32% of UK households in social-rented accommodation in the early 1980s which was the high point for this tenure and, therefore, the availability of council housing.*
1987? 1 The Green *Owner occupied* *Within household*	Neil and Susan take up the opportunity of *Right to Buy* to purchase their council home, benefitting from a 30% discount and beginning a process of building housing equity. This purchase meant that later they had the means to invest in their self-build home at Ambridge View, which has provided a stable base for their family – and Emma's – in the ensuing years. If they had not bought and then sold 1 The

Table 12.1. (*Continued*)

Housing/Dates	**Emma's Pathway and Wider Housing Context**
	Green, they would not have had the room to accommodate Emma later on. *The Right to Buy was a flagship policy of the Thatcher government, which provided opportunities for households to access home ownership in the hope of encouraging a 'property-owning democracy'. In rural areas, only one in eight council homes sold has been replaced (Lavis, CPRE, 2019), which has limited the affordable housing options for future generations. In Ambridge, however, the Grange Spinney development included six affordable homes, as did the Beechwood site, meaning that the village may have bucked this trend – sadly not to Emma's advantage.*
June 2004 Caravan *Owner occupied Within household*	Just before her wedding to Will, Emma's parents sell their home to Matt Crawford as an investment property and move into a caravan while self-building their new home. Emma chooses to spend more time at Will's flat than with her family in the cramped caravan. *The sale of 1 The Green as a Buy to Let investment was typical of the time – property investment was a more attractive investment class compared to other options. An outcome of this was that emerging first time buyer households struggled to compete (in this case Roy and Hayley Tucker).*

Table 12.1. *(Continued)*

Housing/Dates	**Emma's Pathway and Wider Housing Context**
August 2004 Dower House Flat *Dependent* *accommodation* *Own household*	Emma married Will Grundy who was lucky enough to have an annexed flat provided by his godmother Caroline Sterling. *The trend over the past 20 years has been for young adults to stay longer in the family home before leaving to set up their own household. However, the age for moving in with a partner has been fairly stable at around 26 years, making Emma and Will comparatively young to be making this move (ONS, 2018).*
October 2004 Gamekeepers cottage (Casa Nueva) *Agricultural tied* *accommodation* *Own household*	Will becomes Home Farm gamekeeper following Greg's death, and Emma and Will move into the gamekeeper's cottage, renaming it Casa Nueva to commemorate their Mexican honeymoon. This tied accommodation is a key aspect of Will's subsequent financial security in comparison to his less fortunate brother.
October 2005 Ambridge View *Owner occupied* *Within household*	After the birth of her son, George, Emma leaves Will to be with Ed Grundy. Her first stop is back to her parents' house.
October 2005 Caravan, Ambridge View *Dependent* *accommodation* *Own household*	Unable to afford a place of their own, Ed and Emma move into the caravan which is now in the garden of the Carter's completed self-build home, Ambridge View. However, there is no evidence that Emma and Ed made any application for affordable housing at this time, despite being technically homeless. Perhaps this reluctance to seek

Table 12.1. (*Continued*)

Housing/Dates	Emma's Pathway and Wider Housing Context
	formal support reflects the recent experience of the Grundys who were rehoused at Meadow Rise after being evicted from Grange Farm. *With a lack of affordable housing available, informal arrangements and dependence on family is heightened.*
May 2006 Ambridge View *Owner occupied* *Within household*	Under the pressure of living in an unsuitable caravan, Ed and Emma split up. Ed is unable to provide a home for the family, but there was no suggestion of seeking social housing, or of moving to a more affordable location. *Housing stress is a contributory factor to relationship breakdown. Research by Rory Coulter shows that 'growing difficulties obtaining secure and affordable housing could have negative consequences for partnership stability' (Coulter & Thomas, 2019).*
October 2008 Rickyard Cottage *Rented* *Own household*	Reunited with Ed, Emma negotiates a long term let at Rickyard Cottage which had been used as a holiday cottage at Brookfield Farm. Ruth Archer is convinced to accept a lower income from the property because it will be less work for her than managing a holiday home. *Competition between long-term and short-term accommodation is a real challenge in areas popular with tourists. Recent findings show that up to 10% of landlords are considering switching from long-term to short-term lets, further restricting the supply*

Table 12.1. *(Continued)*

Housing/Dates	Emma's Pathway and Wider Housing Context
	of private-rented housing and driving prices up (Evans & Osuna, 2020). Property owners have more potential to offer homes for short term rather than long term let, although this comes with less security of income and more requirement to service the property.
December 2012 Ambridge View *Owner occupied* *Within household*	In financial difficulty, Emma, Ed, George, and baby Kiera leave Rickyard Cottage rather than default on the rent – hard to do when personal relationships and work connections are at play with their landlords. If they had accessed housing advice at this point, they could have applied for housing benefit to help cover the rent at Rickyard or made an application as homeless to their local council, which would likely have resulted in temporary accommodation and support with finding long-term housing. They are able to move as a family to stay with Neil and Susan Carter, whose large home has sufficient space for their growing family. *Inability to engage with the welfare system was a key consideration at this point in their housing career. Housing benefit, child tax credits and other income support are designed to fill the gap between low incomes and real-life housing and other costs. However, the absence of this financial support may accurately reflect the inability of the system to support families in remote rural areas and those with irregular or business income – Ed's main income at this*

Table 12.1. (*Continued*)

Housing/Dates	Emma's Pathway and Wider Housing Context
	point was from his self-employed management of a herd of cows.
December 2014 1 The Green *Rented* *Own household*	After another two years at her parents' house, Emma convinces Will to let 1 The Green to her and Ed at a discount. This housing – and its affordability – is in the hands of a personal contact. Emma has now lived in her childhood home as part of a social-rented household, an owner-occupied household and a private-rented household. *Estimates show that 40% of former council homes are now owned and let by private landlords (The Guardian, 2017). 2014 was also the year that statistics showed that private renting took over from social renting as the second most prevalent tenure. 18% of the population were now private tenants (Channel 4, 2014), with limited security of tenure – the ending of a private tenancy has now become the most common reason for homelessness in the United Kingdom.*
March 2015 Ambridge View *Owner occupied* *Within household*	Their home flooded out, Emma and her family are back with Neil and Susan at Ambridge View. Once again, they could seek homelessness support from their local council but do not, nor do they seek alternative accommodation outside of the village. This is the fourth time that Neil and Susan Carter have accommodated Emma and her family since she left their home to get married. Households made homeless through natural disaster are eligible for emergency temporary

Table 12.1. *(Continued)*

Housing/Dates	Emma's Pathway and Wider Housing Context
	housing from their local authority – especially where they have dependent children. A homelessness application at this point would have set the family up well for access to any affordable housing becoming available in the village, although it may have led to Emma being forced to leave Ambridge. *The impact of Boomerang children has been observed to have a negative impact on parents, especially if they return after having left the family home (Tosi & Grundy, 2018; LSE).*
December 2015 Grange Farm *Dependent/Rented* *Within household*	Oliver Sterling, personifying the **Ambridge Fairy**, allows the Grundys to move into Grange Farm and Emma, Ed and the children form part of the extended household.
August 2019 Ambridge View *Owner occupied* *Within household*	Unable to secure their affordable home at Beechwood, Emma and Ed separate, and Emma returns with the children to Ambridge View. This is the fifth time she has returned to her parents' home during her adult life. George has now moved 10 times in his 15 years, the kind of housing insecurity which lies behind poor educational outcomes. *The impact of poor housing, homelessness and repeated moves on child health and educational outcomes is well documented. The evidence suggests that the academic under-achievement of homeless children can be related to their housing status, as opposed to other factors, and that*

Table 12.1. (*Continued*)

Housing/Dates	Emma's Pathway and Wider Housing Context
	developmental delay is still a factor a year after rehousing of homeless families (Harker, 2006). *However, a significant factor is the disruption to schooling caused by changing schools – not a factor for George Grundy.*
April 2020 Mobile Home at Grange Farm *Mobile home is owned, land is rented* *Own household*	Emma's solution to their housing shortage is to purchase a mobile home. Without the required planning permission, the mobile home is situated on land in Oliver Sterling's ownership, possibly without his permission. *The division of an existing property and creation of additional dwelling (even if that is in the form of a mobile home) requires planning permission and the creation of an addition Council Tax account. This is a permanent change which the property owner should be aware of. The current legal position of Emma's new 'forever home' is vulnerable indeed.*

until the new homes at Beechwood were proposed. Her dream of owning a home is typical of older renters (McKee, Mihaela, & Munro, 2019) but bucks the housing market trend observed over the course of her adult life, which means that people of her generation are less likely to become homeowners at a similar time to previous generations – less than half as likely if they are among the bottom 40% of incomes (Cribb, Hood, & Hoyle, 2018). This homeownership dream was not sufficient to encourage a move out of the village, which is the more likely real-life choice that a family like Emma's would have made, which is a key factor in the ageing trend of rural areas (DEFRA, 2018).

THE AMBRIDGE FAIRY: LUCK, WEALTH OR SOCIAL CAPITAL?

What does a look at a long-term housing pathways, alongside the wider snapshot of the current living arrangements, reveal about the Ambridge Fairy? For those households whose housing dilemmas have been solved, the help has tended to come in the following forms: farm accommodation; a room in a friend's home – or extended family; a property which is in the gift of a friend or family member; family money; and the presence of a hitherto unknown property. One important note is that there has not been an expectation on property businesses in the village to take a benevolent approach to the housing needs of local residents. Lillian Bellamy's Amside property business is not a first port of call for people looking for a discount on accommodation, despite what appears to be a substantial local portfolio of homes. Neither Bridge Farm's sale of the land nor Justin Elliot's development of the properties for the Beechwood development made an attempt to go over and above the minimum planning requirements for affordable housing. Neither has there been an expectation of public sector support from characters experiencing housing stress. Opportunities to seek assistance from national or local government have been repeatedly missed, even while Ambridge families had the right to access this support.

Despite the occasional presence of the Ambridge Fairy, which usually manifests in a timely vacancy at an appropriate property, property problems do tend to reflect real life. Mitigations against housing insecurity are primarily in the form of social capital and relationships across the village. These connections are more common than financial solutions. In theory, this opens up the potential to build social capital to all characters. However, Headlam's work on Ambridge networks (Headlam, 2017; Chapter 2) demonstrates that some individuals are better placed to build and leverage social capital; and these advantages tend to reflect class status in the village, helping to 'transmit cultural capital and assets through the generations' (Headlam, 2017). So, whether it comes to financial interventions or social capital; just as in the outside world, it helps to have a rich relative in order to generate the Ambridge Fairy.

ACKNOWLEDGEMENTS

I would like to acknowledge my thanks to the excellent Think-House resource (www.thinkhouse.org.uk) which collates key pieces of housing research in one place and made my background research much easier.

REFERENCES

ACRE. (2020). Retrieved from https://acre.org.uk/rural-issues/housing. Accessed on August 30, 2020.

Barker, K. (2004). *Delivering stability: Securing our future housing needs.* London: HM Treasury.

Boughton, J. (2019). *Municipal Dreams the rise and fall of council housing.* London: Verso.

Challoner, J., Dreisin, A., & Pragnell, M. (2015). Building new social rented homes; an economic appraisal. Capital Economics for SHOUT and the National Federation of ALMOs.

Channel 4. (2014). Retrieved from https://www.channel4.com/
news/social-housing-rent-private-landlord-tenant-benefits-
reforms-broken-ladder. Accessed on August 30, 2020.

Coulter, R. (2018). Parental background and housing outcomes
in young adulthood. *Housing Studies, 33*(2), 201–223.

Coulter, R. & Thomas, M. (2019). A new look at housing
antecedents of separation. *Demographic Research, 40,*
725–760. Article 26.

Cribb, J., Hood, A., & Hoyle, J. (2018). *The decline of
homeownership among young adults.* London: Institute of
Fiscal Studies.

DEFRA. (2018). *Statistical digest of rural England.* London:
Government Statistical Service.

European Network for Housing Research. (2020). *English
house condition Survey.* Retrieved from https://www.enhr.
net/housingandfamilydynamics.php. Accessed on August
30, 2020.

Evans, A., & Osuna, R. (2020). The Impact of Short-Term
Lets; Analysing the scale of Great Britain's short-term lets
sector and the wider implications for the private rented
sector. *Capital Economics,* Commissioned and published
by ARLA Propertymark, 2020.

Grayston, R., & Pullinger, R. (2018). Viable villages. CPRE &
Shelter.

Harker, L. (2006). *The Chance of a Lifetime: The impacts of
bad housing on children's lives.* London: Shelter.

Headlam, N. (2017). Kinship networks in Ambridge. In C.
Courage & N. Headlam (Eds.), *Custard, culverts and cake:
Academic Archers on life in Ambridge.* Bingley: Emerald
Publishing Limited.

HM RevenueCustoms. (2020, May). Property transactions statistics. Retrieved from. https://www.gov.uk/government/statistics/monthly-property-transactions-completed-in-the-uk-with-value-40000-or-above

Legal & General. (2018). Bank of Mum & Dad. Retrieved from https://www.legalgeneralgroup.com/media/2483/bomad-report-2018-v15.pdf. Accessed on August 30, 2020.

Lennarz, C., & Ronald, R. (2019). *Housing careers, inter-generational support and family relations*. Abingdon: Routledge.

London School of Economics. (2018). Retrieved from http://www.lse.ac.uk/News/Latest-news-from-LSE/2018/03-March-2018/Boomerang-generation. Accessed on August 30, 2020.

McKee, K., Soaita, M., & Munro, M. (2019). Beyond Generation Rent: Understanding the aspirations for private renters aged 35-54. *UK Collaborative Centre for Housing Evidence*.

Office for National Statistics. (2018). Retrieved from https://www.ons.gov.uk/peoplepopulationandcommunity/populationandmigration/populationestimates/articles/milestonesjourneyingintoadulthood/2019-02-18.   Accessed on April 30, 2020.

The Campaign for the Protection of Rural England. (2015). *A living countryside*.

The Campaign for the Protection of Rural England. (2019). Response to the affordable housing Review. *CPRE*. Retrieved from.   https://www.cpre.org.uk/resources/cpre-s-response-to-the-affordable-housing-commission-call-for-evidence/

The Guardian. (2017). Retrieved from https://www.theguardian.com/society/2017/dec/08/right-to-buy-homes-owned-private-landlords. Accessed on August 30, 2020.

Tosi, M., & Grundy, E. (2018). Returns home by children and changes in parents' well-being in Europe. *Social Science & Medicine*, *200*, 99–106.

Wilson, W. & Barton, C. (2020). Tackling the under-supply of housing in England. House of Commons library briefing paper n. 07671.

Wood, J., & Clarke, S. (2018). *Land of the Rising Son (or Daughter); the impact of parental wealth on their children's homeownership*. London: Resolution Foundation.

13

STAYING IN THE SPARE ROOM: SOCIAL CONNECTEDNESS AND HOUSEHOLD CO-RESIDENCE IN *THE ARCHERS*

Paula Fomby

ABSTRACT

Ambridge residents live with extended kin and non-family members much more often than the population of the United Kingdom as a whole. This chapter explores cultural norms, economic need, and family and health care to explain patterns of coresidence in the village of Ambridge. In landed families, filial obligation and inheritance norms bind multigenerational families to a common dwelling, while scarcity of affordable rural housing inhibits residential independence and forces reliance on access to social networks and chance to find a home among the landless. Across the socioeconomic spectrum, coresidence wards off loneliness among unpartnered adults. Finally, for Archers *listeners, extended kin and non-kin coresidence creates a private space where dialogue gives added dimensionality and*

*depth to characters who would otherwise be known only
through their interactions in public spaces.*

Daybreak, Ambridge. At The Lodge, Kate Madikane stirs to
the sound of her grandmother's light step in the hallway, then
returns to sleep beneath her organic heathered cashmere
duvet. Hannah Riley shuffles into the kitchen at Number 1
The Green and reproaches housemate Johnny Phillips for his
failure to add enough water to the kettle for her tea and sits
down to review a running list of her colleagues' professional
missteps. And at Greenacres, Jim Lloyd pauses on his way to
collect *The Borchester Echo* from the front step to cast a
rueful glance at lodger Jazzer McCreary, asleep on the settee
after a long night at The Bull.

These imagined tender moments remind us that the living
arrangements of Ambridge residents are varied. They are also
largely distinct from national trends. In this chapter, I document
the remarkable prevalence of extended family and non-kin
coresidence in Ambridge and apply and build upon theoretical
perspectives from the field of household demography to understand the social patterning of these arrangements in the context
of contemporary village life. I also highlight how the social
intimacy of coresidence is deployed in *Archers* story lines to add
dimensionality and nuance to characters who would otherwise
be known only through their public interactions with others.

TERMINOLOGY AND BACKGROUND

The field of household demography considers the prevalence,
patterns, determinants and consequences of household living

arrangements. In this field, coresidence refers to an arrangement where two or more individuals occupy a shared dwelling
as their common primary residence. Extended family coresidence occurs in households where at least one adult is
related to but is not married or romantically connected to the
householder. Vertically extended families include two or more
generations of adults, including a householder's adult children
who are no longer enrolled in school. The Brookfield Archers
offer a current example of a vertically extended three-
generation household in Ambridge (with fourth-generation
Rosie in shouting distance from Rickyard Cottage.) Laterally
extended families included related members of the householder's own generation such as siblings or cousins. Peggy
Woolley and Christine Barford, sisters-in-law through Peggy's
first marriage to Jack Archer, provided an example of this
arrangement until cat Hilda Ogden successfully got underfoot
to usurp Christine's position in the household. Non-family
coresidence occurs when two or more unrelated individuals
with no romantic attachment share a dwelling, such as the
houseshare between Roy Tucker and Kirsty Miller at Willow
Farm in the interlude between Kirsty's ill-fated engagements.
I contrast these arrangements with solo residence (e.g., Carol
Tregorran at Glebe Cottage) and simple family coresidence,
which includes married or cohabiting couples with or without
minor children and lone parents with their minor children
(Robert and Lynda Snell at Ambridge Hall; Adam Macy, Ian
Craig, and Alexander Macy-Craig at Honeysuckle Cottage.)

The prevalence of extended family and non-family coresidence in Ambridge is exceptional. In 2019, the most recent
year for which data are available, 2.8% of UK households
were composed of non-related individuals and 1.1% of
households included extended or multiple coresident families
(Office for National Statistics, 2019). In contrast, of the 31
households with known occupancy in Ambridge (Table 13.1),

12 (38.7%) were characterised by extended family or non-family coresidence in April 2020. Half of these households had also experienced turnover in their extended kin or non-family composition sometime since 2018. An additional four households with simple family coresidence in April 2020 had included extended family or a non-relative at some point during the preceding two years. This churning is consistent with evidence that extended family and non-family coresidence is often a short-term strategy to respond to immediate need, although some arrangements endure for many years (Perkins, 2019; Pilkauskas & Martinson, 2014; Raley, Weiss, Reynolds, & Cavanagh, 2019).

EXPLANATIONS FOR EXTENDED FAMILY AND NON-FAMILY CORESIDENCE

Household demography identifies three prevailing causes for extended family and non-family coresidence: cultural norms, economic need, and health and family care. These reasons are conceptually distinct but may overlap empirically; that is, people may have more than one reason for living together. I review each of these explanations below and find that their application to the context of Ambridge generates new insights about the circumstances that bring villagers into shared residence. In turn, using a rural, highly interconnected village as a site of inquiry adds important contextual nuance to existing theory.

Cultural Norms

Cultural norms are the attitudes and behaviours that are considered normal or typical in a group whose members share

Table 13.1. Household Composition in Ambridge. Extended Family Coresidence Shown in Bold and Non-family Coresidence in *Italics*. Current as of April 2020.

Dwelling	Occupants	Prior Shared Occupancy since January 2018
Ambridge Hall	Robert and Lynda Snell	
Ambridge View	Susan and Neil Carter	**Emma and Keira Grundy**
April Cottage	**Kathy and Jamie Perks**	
Beechwood Estate	Philip Moss, Kirsty Miller	**Gavin Moss**
Beechwood Estate	Joy Horville	
Blossom Hill	Jakob Hakansson	Previously occupied by Anisha Jayakody
Brookfield Bungalow	*Bert Fry, Rex Fairbrother*	*Toby Fairbrother*
Brookfield Farm	**David, Ruth, Jill, Josh and Ben Archer**	
Rickyard Cottage	*Pip Archer, Rosie Archer, Toby Fairbrother*	
Bridge Farm	**Tony, Pat, Helen, Henry and Jack Archer**	**Tom Archer; Johnny Phillips**

Table 13.1. (Continued)

Dwelling	Occupants	Prior Shared Occupancy since January 2018
The Bull (pub)	Kenton and Jolene Archer	
Dower House	Justin Elliott, Lillian Bellamy	
Glebe Cottage	Carol Tregorran	
Grange Farm	**Eddie, Clarrie, Will, George and Poppy Grundy**	**Joe, Ed, Emma, George and Keira Grundy**
Modular home on Grange Farm land	Ed, Emma and Keira Grundy	
1 The Green	*Johnny Phillips, Hannah Riley*	*Tom Archer; Freddie Pargetter*
6 The Green	**Tracy, Brad, Chelsea Horrobin; Bert Horrobin**	
Greenacres	**Jim and Alistair Lloyd;** *Jazzer McCreary*	
Greenwood Cottage		Will, Nic and Poppy Grundy; Jake and Mia
Grey Gables (hotel/restaurant)	Oliver Sterling	
Home Farm	The Gills	**Brian and Jennifer Aldridge; Kate Madikane; Phoebe Tucker; Noluthando Madikane; Lillian Bellamy**

The Nest at Home Farm — Chris and Alice Carter

Honeysuckle Cottage — Adam Macy, Ian Craig, Zander

The Lodge — **Peggy Woolley, Kate Madikane** — **Christine Barford**

Lower Loxley — *Elizabeth, Freddie and Lily Pargetter; Russ Jones*

The Stables — Shula Hebden-Lloyd — Alistair Lloyd, **Freddie Pargetter**

The Vicarage — Alan and Usha Franks

The flat above the Village Shop — Tom and Natasha Archer

Willow Farm — **Roy and Phoebe Tucker** — *Kirsty Miller*

Willow Cottage — Brian and Jennifer Aldridge; Ruairi Donovan

Woodbine Cottage — Harrison Burns, Fallon Rogers

a common identity. Often, these norms are hard to recognise among the people who live by them; they are simply the way things are, even if local norms do not hold universally. In the context of a small community built around a local agricultural economy, norms of late home-leaving by adult children and coresidence with elderly parents may be a tradition held over from earlier generations, even if the practical function of such coresidence is no longer apparent (Schürer, Garrett, Jaadla, & Reid, 2018).

In Ambridge, cultural norms associated with land owner-ship create distinctive opportunities and enforce obligations among individuals who have some tie to the land. The legal and economic framework that supported a system of primo-geniture and reliance on family members to work landhold-ings in rural England is no longer in force, but echoes of this system remain in place at Brookfield, Bridge Farm and, until recently, Home Farm. These are places adult children can remain or return to, giving them some measure of security in the world. Yet their own sense of agency is constrained by a shared sense of filial obligation.

At Brookfield, Pip Archer offers a poignant if not entirely sympathetic example of this predicament. While other unmarried women like Brenda Tucker and Amy Franks have left Ambridge to pursue professional careers, Pip soldiers on at Brookfield, seeking some measure of independence in her residential choices only to be lured back by her anxious par-ents and the assurance that there will always be a flapjack in the tin with her name on it. Since the birth of daughter Rosie, Pip has moved out of the family dining room and into Rickyard Cottage, a liminal space that provides some measure of privacy and separation while allowing her to remain on the threshold of Brookfield as the anticipated heir and to rely upon her parents and grandmother for child care in the course of

Toby Fairbrother's frequent lapses as a (sometimes coresident) co-parent.

At Bridge Farm, Helen and Tom Archer have each returned to the parental home repeatedly after experiencing personal crises while living elsewhere. This arrangement has allowed them easy proximity to their family-funded enterprises (the farm shop, dairy and Montbeliard pastures for Helen, the pigs and polytunnels for Tom), and for Helen, her parents have provided a source of abundant, often spontaneous, and uncharacteristically patient child care. But living and working together exacerbates an enduring power struggle about the current and future business model at Bridge Farm. Filial obligation and expectations about inheritance feature heavily in this conflict, particularly between father and surviving son. For father Tony Archer, securing the legacy of Bridge Farm as a successful organic producer would offer a definitive rejoinder to his flinty mother's harsh judgement and his sisters' significantly greater upward economic mobility. For Tom, the drive to expand and transform the Bridge Farm brand is the compromise between a tragic sense of obligation to live up to his deceased favoured brother's potential and his own entrepreneurial ambition. Alternating between stints of coresidence with his parents and a peripatetic march around the village's rental properties with a succession of ill-matched *fiancées*, Tom engages in and retreats from a ceaseless duel with his father over their competing, blinkered visions for Bridge Farm's direction.

Lastly, the sale of Home Farm and Brian and Jennifer Aldridge's move to Willow Cottage highlights extended kin's access to coresidence in the presence or absence of landed home tenure in the family network. In the five years prior to the sale, Home Farm offered a revolving door to kin claiming access to tenured family property. At various times, daughter Kate Madikane, granddaughters Noluthando Madikane and

Phoebe Tucker and sister Lillian Bellamy turned up on the Home Farm doorstep with an unstated expectation of lasting welcome, which Jennifer willingly provided. When Home Farm reached its densest occupancy, Brian retreated to The Bull in the evenings for breathing room. Jennifer clearly valued the opportunity to display and share the abundance of Home Farm. For that reason, it was revealing of her genuine loyalty to family that she insisted that she and Brian sell their home to cover the costs of cleaning the River Am rather than to put their children in conflict over a family land sale. Yet once the tie between manse and landholding was severed, access to extended family coresidence in the Aldridge home was also foreclosed, and Jennifer balked at Kate's expectation that Willow Cottage would contain a bedroom for her use.

Economic Need

Economic need describes circumstances where at least one household member cannot afford to live independently. Lodger Jazzer McCreary is an example of someone who coresided initially out of economic need, but housemate and homeowner Jim Lloyd is not. In contrast, the Grundys at Grange Farm represent a case where no one in the extended family household has ever been able to afford to live separately for long.

Ambridge offers an opportunity to consider how rural housing scarcity and unaffordability creates economic need for homeseekers outside of the landholding class. Those who lack a land connection rely instead on patronage from a less well-endowed, mostly unmarried tier of homeowners to secure a property rental, sublet or temporary lodging. Often these arrangements are precipitated by an unpropertied village resi-dent's decision to leave Ambridge in pursuit of affordable housing elsewhere only to be won back as the beneficiary of another villager's largesse or misfortune. For the landless in Ambridge, then, housing is a precarious business, with shared living arrangements emerging from an unpredictable combination of social connectedness and happenstance rather than from a rationalised market offering attendant legal and financial protection.

Examples of such serendipity from the last five years include the four-generation Grundy family household, which was granted a return to Grange Farm when the Tuscan sun beckoned Oliver and Caroline Sterling. Their below-market rate rental agreement brought the Grundys back to the land from which they had been evicted many years earlier. It has endured even beyond Caroline Sterling's death and allowed Eddie and Clarrie Grundy to support their sons through a succession of hardships, including daughter-in-law Nic Grundy's untimely death and the near dissolution of Ed and Emma's marriage. Eventually, access to the land at Grange Farm also enabled Emma to install a modular home for herself, Ed, George and Keira Grundy in an apparent socially classed rightsizing of her home ownership ambitions. Each person involved in the exchange draws practical and emotional satisfaction from the arrangement, but it is built on a long history of loyalty, forbearance, mercy and compromise that more closely resembles a relationship between lord and vassal than between landlord and tenant. Only class-conscious Emma, who has married into the Grundy family, chafes at the arrangement.

Elsewhere, renters Harrison Burns and Fallon Rogers were prepared to give up the shabby charm and convenience of Woodbine Cottage in order to become homeowners in a more affordable district when Harrison's parents silently stepped into the breach with a private loan that gave Christine Barford the opportunity to sell her cottage to the young couple and convert the proceeds into a cash windfall for Hugo Melling. In the absence of a bank-backed mortgage, it remains unclear whether the property underwent a valuation and inspection to determine that the buyers paid a fair price. Given that the home's disrepair was what prompted Harrison and Fallon to begin looking elsewhere in the first place, it is not inconceivable that the young couple overpaid. Having done so, they would have contributed to inflated home values in an Ambridge housing bubble, putting village properties further beyond the reach of prospective buyers lacking access to private wealth.

Health and Family Care

Health and family care offer a third reason for extended family and non-family coresidence. This describes circumstances where household members provide nursing care to an infirm adult or where relatives other than a parent provide care to young children. As noted above, Helen Archer depends on these arrangements for care to sons Jack and Henry at Bridge Farm, as Pip Archer does for Rosie at Brookfield. And Kate Madikane has relied upon the illusion that her grandmother needs her help both to give purpose to her lack of residential independence and as an ill-conceived strategy to woo partner Jakob Hakansson.

Beyond these examples, *The Archers* opens a new window on this topic. I suggest that in Ambridge, coresidence by older adults in non-family or extended family households is less about seeking physical health care and more a strategy to protect against isolation and loneliness. In a country that brought the plight of Eleanor Rigby to public attention and appointed a Minister of Loneliness in 2018, it is fitting that Ambridge's older residents would accept or seek out coresidence as a means of social connection and companionship. Recent examples have included the frequently fraught and occasionally charming shared living arrangements between

Peggy Woolley and (in turn) Christine Barford and Kate at The Lodge, the unlikely grouping of Bert Fry and Rex and Toby Fairbrother at Brookfield Bungalow, and the surprisingly deep connection established between Jim and Lloyd Alistair and Jazzer McCreary at Greenacres.

PRIVATE HOMES, PRIVATE VOICES

Finally, the living arrangements described here give *The Archers* listeners the pleasure of hearing the private voices of Ambridge residents. With no companion at home (and with the exception of monologues produced during the 2020 pandemic), listeners would know some individuals only as public figures in the village shop or at The Bull. Hearing these private voices add dimensionality and richness to these individual personalities. We hear tenderness in how Lynda Snell speaks to husband Robert at home and feel more patient with her imperious command of the Christmas panto. That history also makes the couple's shared adjustment to Lynda's injuries after the Grey Gables explosion more difficult to bear. We cringe through chilli night at Ambridge View but find the good behind Susan Carter's social striving because husband Neil sees through it.

Similarly, extended family coresidence exposed listeners more than once to Lillian's broken heart laid bare to Jennifer at Home Farm during her separation from Justin Elliott, and we understood the context of Pip's pregnancy decision better than her parents did after her conversations with Aunt Elizabeth Pargetter while living at Lower Loxley. And only listeners and Peggy knew the true extent of Christine's penury after her *naïve* investment in racehorses. But the most significant recent illustration of this point is among the men at Greenacres. Alistair

Lloyd and Jazzer McCreary have the most complete account of Jim Lloyd's experience of childhood sexual abuse at the hands of Harold Jayston and its lasting impact on his emotional health and relationships. Each initially responded to this knowledge in his own imperfect way, but ultimately provided Jim with the combination of emotional intimacy and space that he required to move forward. While perhaps not producing an advisable mental health policy recommendation, the story line deepened listeners' appreciation for the characters as individuals and as a quasi-family unit.

SUMMARY

The context of Ambridge reveals fresh insights about how extended family and non-family coresidence arises and persists in rural contexts. First, land ownership creates and constrains residential opportunity and stability for the adult children of a privileged few (see Headlam, this volume). Second, a scarcity of affordable rural housing exacerbates economic need and presents unique challenges to nuclear family and solo residence for people lacking access to a landed estate. This need forces reliance on access to social networks and chance to locate shared housing or to gain a toehold on the property ownership ladder. Third, coresidence may serve as a balm against loneliness and improve mental health, particularly for older village residents. Finally, for *The Archers* listeners, extended family and non-family coresidence creates a private space where dialogue gives added dimensionality and depth to characters who would otherwise be known only through their interactions in public spaces. This last point may explain why Ambridge residents are far more likely than the general population to contrive excuses to live together – while listeners crave 13 minutes alone each day to imagine ourselves transported to Ambridge, we would find ourselves bereft upon arrival without the villagers' private grumblings, squabbles and occasional endearments to eavesdrop upon.

REFERENCES

Office for National Statistics. (2019). Families and households in the UK: 2019. Retrieved from https://www.ons.gov.uk/peoplepopulationandcommunity/birthsdeathsandmarriages/families/bulletins/familiesandhouseholds/2019. Accessed on August 30, 2020.

Perkins, K. L. (2019). Changes in household composition and children's educational attainment. *Demography*, *56*(2), 525–548.

Pilkauskas, N. V., & Martinson, M. L. (2014). Three-generation family households in early childhood: Comparisons between the United States, the United Kingdom, and Australia. *Demographic Research*, *30*, 1639–1652.

Raley, R. K., Weiss, I., Reynolds, R., & Cavanagh, S. E. (2019). Estimating children's household instability between birth and age 18 using longitudinal household roster data. *Demography*, *56*(5), 1957–1973.

Schürer, K., Garrett, E. M., Jaadla, H., & Reid, A. (2018). Household and family structure in England and Wales (1851–1911): Continuities and change. *Continuity and Change*, *33*(3), 365–411.

14

CAN'T AFFORD THE LAURELS?: CARE PROVISION IN AMBRIDGE IN 2045

Ruth Heilbronn and Rosalind Janssen

ABSTRACT

Care options for older people are important to individuals and to society, and currently, there is a crisis in this care. The chapter presents a research base projection onto the situation in England in 2045, using Office for National Statistics (ONS) modelling based on current population reaching the age of 85-years plus. We take three The Archers *characters and fantasise about their lives in 2045, Shula and Kenton Archer and Hazel Woolley. Through them, we illustrate three options for care, namely, cared for by family members, buying in care in own home and moving into a care home. The financial aspects of these choices are explored.*

INTRODUCTION

The Laurels care home is a feature of Ambridge – the late Marjorie Antrobus and Jack Woolley lived there, and now Christine Barford is a resident. The Laurels residents have featured in a recent episode when they took a minibus outing to Lower Loxley for Jim Lloyd's ghost stories event. There is even a dark fantasy called *Life at The Laurels*, involving dastardly deeds to secure a place there when there was no vacancy (BBC, 2014a). Thinking about The Laurels was our starting point to consider options for care in older life, through the lens of some *The Archers* characters. We thought about the characters ageing into the future and looked at projections which the Office for National Statistics (ONS) (2019) has published to inform government about what provision will be required in the future, based on modelling of population growth into 2045. This led us to think about the age of *The Archers* residents.

The cohort born before the Second World War was evidently not suitable for a fantasy scenario 25 years hence. This older generation included Peggy Archer (1924), Jill Archer (1930), Christine Barford (1931) and Bert Fry (1936). Our target generation needed to be around 60 years of age in 2020 in order to work with our projections onto 2045. The generation from the early 1950s baby boomer cohort was a possibility, and included Eddie Grundy and Tony Archer, both born in 1951, and Pat Archer and Clarrie Grundy who were born in 1952. The next generation from the late 1950s included Hazel Woolley (1956), Neil Carter (1957), twins Shula Hebden-Lloyd and Kenton Archer (1958) and David Archer (1959). These were all possible for our scenario. We choose the twins, Kenton and Shula, and Hazel Woolley from the baby boomer cohort of the later 1950s to be indicative of those who will be 85-years-plus in 2045, 25 years from now, and we have produced a fantasy projection of what their older years might look like if they need care.

The projections are based on what we know about them, at the time of writing, through what they say and how they behave, and what the options for care are currently (BBC, 2019). These options are to stay in one's own home or to go into a care home. The first option, home care, relies on family members willing and able to help or on buying in care, with or without financial support from the local authority. The second option, a care home, has a variety of possibilities which vary in quality, facilities and price. The Laurels is a private care home and while it may not be in the league of some (e.g. one in London with sunroom, library, cinema, restaurant, hydrotherapy treatment, salon with baby grand piano), it does offer good facilities and nursing at a price. Costs can vary hugely and will depend upon several factors including the type of care needed, which can change over time; the care home's annual fee increase, and how long care is received. A care home of the standard of The Laurels could cost £50,000 a year at current prices.

A good care home will provide opportunities for classes and social events among other facilities. A bad care home may lack stimulation for older people, but what may be worse than lack of stimulation might be poor or even abusive levels of care. Abuse in care homes has been given a high profile in the media (Age UK, 2015; Beach, Carpenter, Rosen, Sharps, & Gelles, 2016; Pedley & McDonald, 2019). There have been programmes made by undercover reporters in residential homes, one of which showed shocking sights of the abuse of residents (BBC, 2014b; Holt, 2014). A *Channel 4 Dispatches* (2016) programme also exposed abuse in people's homes as well as in care homes. These abuses went on despite the Care Act 2015 which lays down the statutory safeguarding regulations regarding vulnerable adults. How did we get to the current way in which care is organised and funded?

THE HISTORICAL PERSPECTIVE

The so-called 'New Poor Law', initiated by the Poor Law Amendment Act of 1834, saw local authorities and voluntary organisations making small cash payments to older people in a community setting. As a result, older people attached a far greater stigma to having to enter the workhouse, an institution increasingly perceived by the poor of all ages as pitiless 'bastilles' (Thane, 2009, p. 166). From then on, there was a key policy shift away from the workhouse, to the aspiration of the welfare state to provide cradle to grave care, which necessarily included for its older and disabled people (Rivett, 1998).

With the National Assistance Act of 1948 and the final abolition of the Poor Law, the onus was on local authorities to provide residential care and to register and inspect voluntary and private care homes (National Archives, 2020). In the same year, the inception of the National Health Service (NHS) as part of the post war welfare state made all health services 'free at the point of delivery'. There were obvious advantages but on the downside the end result was an increased separation of health and social care provision. Further, from the 1950s, it became policy to increasingly shift from institutional to community care (Thane, 2009, pp. 7–8). The policy rationale was underpinned with the idea of improving quality of life for older and disabled people. While this rationale was based on advances in medical knowledge and treatments, there was also an inherent belief that community care presented a cheaper option, at a time when the demand for and the costs of services were rapidly rising. However, there was continuous concern at the inadequacy of community services, and the difficulty of defining and co-ordinating health and social care. A move to private sector provision accelerated during the 1980s (Kindred, 2013, p. 13), largely driven by the free market politics of Britain's Thatcherite government. Increasing financial demands on social care were made due to private sector charges and reduced public expenditure. These well-publicised factors – the different providers, the role of the private sector and austerity – take us rapidly to the present day.

In his first speech as Prime Minister, delivered on the steps of 10 Downing Street, Boris Johnson pledged: 'We will fix the crisis in social care once and for all, and with a clear plan we have prepared to give every older person the dignity and security they deserve' (Global News, 2019). It was quickly evident, however, that no plan existed and the Queen's speech that December merely promised to try and reach what was termed 'a cross-party consensus' on proposals for long-term reform of social care (GOV.UK, 2019). In January 2020, columnist Polly Toynbee estimated that the projected cost of restoring care provision to 2010 standards would be £14 billion, whereas Johnston was simply offering what she dismissively referred to as 'a £1b emergency bung to keep the collapsing system afloat a little longer' (Toynbee, 2020). Since then we must factor in the impact of Brexit on migrant care workers, and coming close on its heels COVID-19, which have again reinvented the social care landscape. At the time of writing, politicians and health bodies are lobbying the government to scrap the £624 NHS surcharge for all migrant healthcare staff coming from outside the European Economic Area, rather than simply for medics (Proctor & Marsh, 2020). In his first budget in March 2020, Chancellor Rishi Sunak allocated £2.9 billion for the most vulnerable during the coronavirus; just two months later, he was forced to come up with an additional £600 million in order to support care home providers in preventing and controlling the infection (GOV.UK, 2020). How much more will he need to find to deal with what are likely to be much higher staff burnout levels in UK care homes than those attested in a recent longitudinal study (Costello, Cooper, Marston, & Livingston, 2020)?

Writing this in June 2020, when Britain is very tentatively emerging from three months of enforced lockdown, the final impact of COVID-19 on its care sector is far from clear. We can fantasise that, as is already the case in Wales and Northern Ireland, Boris Johnston's government will be forced to appoint a dedicated Commissioner for Older People to ensure the future safety of care home residents. Rather less speculatively, we can surmise that projecting forwards to 2045, the residents of Ambridge will recall the 2020 pandemic and its aftermath as a devastating period.

THREE CHARACTERS IN SEARCH OF CARE

Turning now to Kenton, Shula and Hazel as indicative of their generation and to our projections of where they may be on the care options choice – they will be in the cohort of older people projected to number three million by 2043 as compared with 1.6 million in 2018, taken from a large-scale study (Kingston, Comas-Herrera, & Jagger, 2018), together with ONS (2019) statistics. The reason for this is that the 1950s baby boomers (Bristow, 2015) are reaching 85-years-plus in the 2040s, and general life expectancy is rising.

Kenton Archer

Kenton Archer is first of our three examples of care options in older life. He has had a checkered history of financial mismanagement and personal failings. In 1994, Kenton married a woman in New Zealand, had a daughter, then left the country due to debts. Kenton now runs the village pub with his wife, Jolene Archer, a talented singer-musician. In our projected future, Kenton has severely compromised mobility and gets about in a wheelchair. We have assumed that Jolene needs help and for her story have given her a bad back, on account of her falling over an amplifier lead on her tour of the West Country in 2022 after taking up music again in 2018. This is a plausible situation as many older people are not physically fit enough to care for their partner due to their own compromised health.

Kenton's daughter lives in New Zealand with her mother, so it falls to his stepdaughter, Fallon Rogers, to care for him and to help her mother out. Knowing what we know about Fallon's husband, Sergeant Harrison Burns, we surmise that in 2045 he has done well in his police career but it is not a far stretch to imagine that living costs are rising and Fallon is working flat out in her various ventures. Fallon is creative, judging by her early career, juggling music, still running a tearoom business, upcycling and helping out at various events. Fallon does not do things by halves and in her responsibilities she is stretched, being a mother of a teenage boy and a grandmother to her daughter's baby. In this, she is not alone. Research provided by Carers UK (2019b) attests that one-in-four female workers and one-in-eight male workers have caring responsibilities and the research states that the care provided unpaid by UK carers could be costed out at around £132 billion per year, which is actually more than total spending on the NHS in England. The number of those juggling work and care in a survey carried out in 2019 is around 4.87 million (compared with 3 million in the 2011 Census). The number giving up work to care has increased from 2.3 million in 2013 to 2.6 million in 2019, a rise of 300,000 people; an almost 2% increase. We also know from the same research that the majority of carers are below state pension age and that the peak age for caring is 50–64 years of age. Over two million people in this age bracket are carers. However, people of pension age also make up a fair proportion with almost 1.3 million people in England and Wales aged 65 years or older having some caring responsibilities. Moreover, the number of carers over the age of 65 years is increasing more rapidly than the general carer population with suggestions that there could now be over two million people aged 65 years or older who are carers (Carers UK, 2019a).

Fallon is then one of the 'sandwich carers', also known as the 'pivot generation' (Železná, 2018, p. 974) who provide intergenerational help and care. Such family members belong to the most important dimensions of contemporary welfare regimes (Železná, 2018). Intergenerational caring impacts on the carer's ability to take on much paid work. Combining paid employment with caregiving was not an option for a signifi-cant minority of women with caring responsibilities in mid-life. One-in-five mid-life women who have ever had caring responsibilities reported that, upon starting caring, they stopped work altogether, and another one-in-five reported that they worked fewer hours, earned less money or could only work restricted hours (Železná, 2018, p. 974). There are also implications for later life as fewer men and women who stopped work as a result of caring were members of an occupational pension scheme than other groups; and they had accumulated fewer years of contributions than their counter-parts who continued working, with direct implications for their level of pension income in later life (Evandrou & Glaser, 2003, p. 583). Fallon, sandwiched between helping her grandchild and parents, is not alone in her situation. Indeed, the highest tendency to care for grandchildren has been found for people regularly helping their parents. This effect holds after controlling for grandparents' characteristics and country effects (Železná, 2018, p. 974). Železná points out from the research that caring responsibilities tend to accumulate rather than compete with one another, and this points to a danger which could impact on Fallon, namely a potential risk of overburden for those who have a general tendency to care.

However, Fallon is fortunately not in this position. We are imagining Jolene, physically suffering from a bad back but with her vitality still in evidence, enjoying her great granddaughter and a source of emotional and moral support for Fallon herself.

Shula Hebden-Lloyd

Shula Hebden-Lloyd has made wiser financial decisions than her twin brother. Shula bought the stables from her aunt, Christine Barford, and has run it as a successful business, and she married professional men who were able to provide a share of their income, first Mark Hebden, a solicitor, and then Alistair Lloyd, a vet. We imagine her at the age of 85 still healthy but with moderate care needs. She is fortunate in having equity to release in her properties, the stables and her home. Her son, Daniel (Dan) Hebden-Lloyd, is overseas with his regiment, having made a good career in the army, so he is glad that his mother can stay in her own home, at least for the time being, but he watches his inheritance drain away. Shula is fairly independent and only needs four hours of support a day when she first releases the equity. The current costs of care average at around £15.00 per hour, although that is not what the workers, most of whom work for agencies, get. Shula's four hours a day amounts to around £420.00 per week or over £38,000.00 per year at 2020 prices. Dan is resigned for costs to shoot up if Shula needs more care, for example at night. Calculating the costs at £15.00 per hour, at 12 hours a day, the cost is £180.00 day or £5,400 per month. What if Shula is severely disabled and continues to be cared for in her own home? In this situation, the cost would rise exponentially, and Shula's capital might reduce down to a level where she could expect some funding from the local authority. The amount of support that can be expected in 2020 ranges from someone with over £23,250 having to pay the full fees, from someone with an annual income of less than £14,250 having these met by the local council, less deductions from income. In between, people pay proportionally according to their financial status. Whatever happens, Dan is going to see his inheritance reduced. There is also the question of who takes the role of primary carer in this situation. In the case of Shula's needs becoming severe, she and Dan would have a responsibility to the primary carer, as they need support for their needs in these work settings (Marino, Badana, & Haley, 2020; Rajnovich, Keefe, & Fast, 2005).

Does Shula have other options? As a vicar, she may have retirement housing options provided by the Church of England (C of E) for people who have served or worked for the church. It provides a variety of retirement houses, shared ownership, rental and supported housing rental, to people who qualify – retired clergy, deaconesses, licenced lay and church workers, spouses/civil partners, widows and widowers of beneficiaries, those with non-stipendiary ministry service, clergy from other denominations, and even non-clergy who receive a pension from the C of E. Maybe when Shula becomes a vicar she will sell up, move to a new parish and live in a tied house as her vicarage – the BBC has an example in the television character of *The Vicar of Dibley*. Or possibly when she is 85 and has run out of money, the C of E has not been able to keep its housing stock nor its care homes. There is an example of the C of E being forced to close Manormead Nursing Home in Surrey in 2017, a residential home that served clergy and their spouses, and included two dementia wings (Church Times, 2016). It had become increasingly difficult to recruit nursing and care staff. There may be further closures, as there is a problem of staffing in the social care sector (Razavi & Staab, 2010; Costello et al., 2020).

The impact of COVID-19 in 2020 further exacerbated already prevalent and significant weaknesses in the social care system, notably its alienation from healthcare provision in the NHS as highlighted in our historical perspective above. The Health Foundation (2020) published sobering statistics based on ONS reporting regarding the pandemic and social care and reminded us that 'high death rates during the pandemic demonstrated the stark impact of the virus on care home residents and social care workers.' Taking a snapshot in mid-April 2020, the Foundation analysed data which showed that while deaths in hospitals declined from a peak in the week ending 17 April 2020, COVID-19 continued to spread in care homes. In the week ending 1 May 2020, the number of deaths in care homes from all causes (6,409) exceeded the number of deaths in hospital (6,397) for the first time since the outbreak started in the United Kingdom. In addition, the pandemic took a heavy toll on people working in social care; when adjusted for age and sex, social care workers had twice the rate of death due to COVID-19 compared to the general population. Between 10 April 2020 and 8 May 2020, the number of people receiving home care in the community who died (3,161) was more than twice the number expected at this time of year. The Foundation expressed the opinion that 'action to tackle the coronavirus pandemic in social care has been late and inadequate.' It recognised that the government had at that point announced a package of £600 million to be used for infection control in care homes and stressed at the time of writing the urgent need to protect frontline providers. It further expressed the hope that 'the huge practical challenges of personal and protective equipment (PPE) and testing logistics are resolved' (Health Foundation, 2020). However, at the point in the future at which we speculate on Shula's fortune, she only needs moderate care in 2045 and is fortunate to have equity which enables her to stay in her familiar environment.

Hazel Woolley

Hazel Woolley illustrates the third case option for care in our imagined future world of Ambridge. Hazel's father, Jack Woolley, was a wealthy businessman, married to Peggy Archer. In his later years, Jack declined in health and in 2009 went to live in The Laurels, where he died in 2014. Hazel has a large portion of his wealth and property but unfortunately in our scenario cannot enjoy it – except to be able to buy the comfortable surroundings and care of The Laurels. She too, like her father Jack, has advanced dementia. It is lucky for her that she does have wealth because her care costs are high. The general guide to care costs for people who need this intensive dementia care is £1,000 a week which comes to £52,000 a year. There are projected to be serious impacts on healthcare and social care services when Hazel reaches the age of 86, according to a report published in 2019 by the Care Policy and Evaluation Centre (CPEC) at the London School of Economics for the Alzheimer's Society (Wittenberg, Barraza Araiza, & Rehill, 2019). The key findings of this report are: the total cost of care for people with dementia in the United Kingdom is £34.7 billion; this is set to rise sharply over the next two decades to £94.1 billion in 2040; these costs are made up of healthcare costs (costs to the NHS), social care costs (costs of home care and residential care) and costs of unpaid care (provided by family members); the largest proportion of this cost, 45%, is social care, which totals £15.7 billion; and social care costs are set to nearly triple over the next two decades, to £45.4 billion by 2040. Hazel is lucky that she can afford to pay for good quality care. The needs of people with dementia can be demanding, and this can impact on the quality of their care (Hoe, Hancock, Livingston, & Orrell, 2006; Lawrence, Fossey, Ballard,

Moniz-Cook, & Murray, 2012; Spector & Orrell, 2006). Staff need to be well trained and supported (see review of evaluated programmes in Kuske et al., 2007).

CONCLUSION

Ambridge still remembers the 2020 COVID-19 outbreak when thousands died in care, care homes went under, and thousands of residents had to find alternative accommodation. But Ambridge is a place where people can age with dignity, as seen by the example of Joe Grundy, Peggy, Jill, Jim Lloyd, all taking a central role in their communities and families. All in all, we conclude that whatever the options for care in later life, Ambridge seems a good place to age.

REFERENCES

Age UK. (2015). *Agenda for later life 2015: A great place to grow older*. Retrieved from https://www.ageuk.org.uk/Documents/EN-GB/For-professionals/Policy/agenda_for_later_life_2015_full_report.pdf?dtrk=true. Accessed on June 5, 2020.

BBC. (2014a). *Life at the Laurels*. Retrieved from https://www.bbc.co.uk/radio4/archers/listeners/fantasies/laurels.shtml. Accessed on August 20, 2020.

BBC. (2014b). *Panorama - Behind closed doors: Elderly care exposed*. Retrieved from https://www.youtube.com/watch?v=W-hyQjS6M50. Accessed on June 5, 2020.

BBC. (2019). *The Archers characters*. Retrieved from https://www.bbc.co.uk/programmes/profiles/3VLG6MxxfQpKXF2Chky4Fmh/characters. Accessed on June 5, 2020.

Beach, S., Carpenter, C., Rosen, T., Sharps, P., & Gelles, R. (2016). Screening and detection of elder abuse: Research opportunities and lessons learned from emergency geriatric care, intimate partner violence, and child abuse. *Journal of Elder Abuse & Neglect*, 28(4–5), 185–216.

Bristow, J. (2015). *Baby boomers and generational conflict*. Basingstoke: Palgrave Macmillan.

Carers UK. (2019a). Facts about carers. Retrieved from https://www.carersuk.org/images/Facts_about_Carers_2019. pdf. Accessed on August 30, 2020.

Carers UK. (2019b). *Juggling work and unpaid care: A growing issue*. Report. Retrieved from http://www.carersuk.org/images/News_and_campaigns/Juggling_work_and_unpaid_care_report_final_0119_WEB.pdf. Accessed on June 5, 2020.

Channel 4. (2016). *Dispatches Britain's Pensioner Care Scandal*. Retrieved from https://www.channel4.com/press/news/britains-pensioner-care-scandal-channel-4-dispatches. Accessed on June 5, 2020.

Church Times. (2016). C of E nursing home to close owing to staffing shortage. Retrieved from https://www.churchtimes.co.uk/articles/2016/25-november/news/uk/c-of-e-nursing-home-to-close-owing-to-staffing-shortage. Accessed on June 5, 2020.

Costello, H., Cooper, C., Marston, L., & Livingston, G. (2020). Burnout in UK care home staff and its effect on staff turnover: MARQUE English national care home longitudinal survey. *Age and Ageing*, 49(1), 74–81.

Evandrou, M., & Glaser, K. (2003). Combining work and family life: The pension penalty of caring. *Ageing and Society*, 23(5), 583–601.

Global News. (2019). Boris Johnson: We will fix the crisis in social care once and for all: July 24th 2019. Retrieved from https://globalnews.ca/video/5677005/boris-johnson-we-will-fix-the-crisis-in-social-care-once-and-for-all. Accessed on June 5, 2020.

GOV.UK. (2019). Queen's speech December 2019. Retrieved from https://www.gov.uk/government/speeches/queens-speech-december-2019. Accessed on June 5, 2020.

GOV.UK. (2020, May). Guidance- Coronavirus (COVID-19): Support for care homes. Retrieved from https://www.gov.uk/government/publications/coronavirus-covid-19-support-for-care-homes. Accessed on June 5, 2020.

Health Foundation. (2020). What has been the impact of COVID-19 on care homes and the social care workforce? COVID-19 Chart Series, 15 May 2020. Retrieved from https://www.health.org.uk/news-and-comment/charts-and-infographics/what-has-been-the-impact-of-covid-19-on-care-homes-and-social-care-workforce. Accessed on October 21, 2020.

Hoe, J., Hancock, G., Livingston, G., & Orrell, M. (2006). Quality of life of people with dementia in residential care homes. *British Journal of Psychiatry*, *188*(5), 460–464.

Holt, A. (2014). Staff sacking and suspensions over poor elderly care. Retrieved from https://www.bbc.co.uk/news/uk-27128011. Accessed on June 5, 2020.

Kindred, M. (2013). *Training and supporting the care force: … that's nearly all of us*. Dartford: Pneuma Springs.

Kingston, A., Comas-Herrera, A. & Carol Jagger, C. (2018). Forecasting the care needs of the older population in England over the next 20 years. Estimates from the Population Ageing and Care Simulation (PACSim) modelling study. *Lancet Public Health 3*(9), e447–e455.

Kuske, B., Hanns, S., Luck, T., Angermeyer, M., Behrens, J., & Riedel-Heller, S. (2007). Nursing home staff training in dementia care: A systematic review of evaluated programs. *International Psychogeriatrics*, *19*(5), 818–841.

Lawrence, V., Fossey, J., Ballard, C., Moniz-Cook, E., & Murray, J. (2012). Improving quality of life for people with dementia in care homes: Making psychosocial interventions work. *British Journal of Psychiatry*, *201*(5), 344–351.

Marino, V., Badana, A., & Haley, W. (2020). Care demands and well-being of primary and secondary non-spousal caregivers of aging adults. *Clinical Gerontologist*. doi: 10.1080/07317115.2020.1759748

National Archives. (2020). National Assistance Act 1948. Retrieved from http://www.legislation.gov.uk/ukpga/Geo6/11-12/29/enacted. Accessed on June 5, 2020.

ONS. (2019). Ageing: Number of over-65s continues to increase faster than the rest of the population. Retrieved from https://www.ons.gov.uk/peoplepopulationandcommunity/populationandmigration/populationestimates/bulletins/annualmidyearpopulationestimates/mid2018#ageing-number-of-over-65s-continues-to-increase-faster-than-the-rest-of-the-population. Accessed on June 5, 2020.

Pedley, Y., & McDonald, P. (2019). Media reports of abuse in adult residential care: Implications for staff and practice. *Working with Older People*, *23*(3), 177–184.

Proctor, K., & Marsh, S. (2020, May 19). UK government urged to scrap £624 NHS charge for migrant workers. *The Guardian*. Retrieved from https://www.theguardian.com/

society/2020/may/19/uk-government-urged-to-scrap-624-nhs-charge-for-migrant-care-workers-helping-combat-coronavirus. Accessed on June 5, 2020.

Rajnovich, B., Keefe, J., & Fast, J. (2005). Supporting care-givers of dependent adults in the 21st century. Healthy balance research programme report. Retrieved from https://cdn.dal.ca/content/dam/dalhousie/pdf/diff/ace-women-health/Healthy%20Balance/ACEWH_hbrp_supporting_caregivers_of_dependent_adults_21st_century.pdf. Accessed on June 5, 2020.

Razavi, S., & Staab, S. (2010). Underpaid and overworked: A cross-national perspective on care workers. *International Labour Review*, *149*(4), 407–422.

Rivett, G. (1998). *From cradle to grave: Fifty years of the NHS*. London: King's Fund.

Spector, A., & Orrell, M. (2006). Quality of life in dementia: A comparison of the perceptions of people with dementia and care staff in residential homes. *Alzheimer Disease and Associated Disorders*, *20*(3), 160–165.

Thane, P. (2009, May). Memorandum submitted to the house of commons health committee inquiry: Social care. Retrieved from http://www.historyandpolicy.org/docs/thane_social_care.pdf. Accessed on June 5, 2020.

Toynbee, P. (2020, January 9). It'll cost Johnson 14bn to keep his promises on social care. Will Javid pay up? *The Guardian*. Retrieved from https://www.theguardian.com/commentisfree/2020/jan/09/boris-johnson-tories-social-care-sajid-javid. Accessed on June 5, 2020.

Wittenberg, R., Hu, B., Barraza Araiza, L., & Rehill, A. (2019). Projections of older people with dementia and costs of dementia care in the United Kingdom, 2019-2040.

CPEC Working Paper 5. Retrieved from https://www.alz-heimers.org.uk/about-us/policy-and-influencing/dementia-scale-impact-numbers. Accessed on June 5, 2020.

Železná, L. (2018). Care-giving to grandchildren and elderly parents: Role conflict or family solidarity? *Ageing and Society*, *38*(5), 974–994.

Section 5

IT TAKES A VILLAGE...

15

PARENTS, SIBLINGS AND THE PURSUIT OF POWER: PREDICTING THE FUTURE LEADERS OF AMBRIDGE

Timothy Vercellotti

ABSTRACT

Who will lead Ambridge in the years to come? Theories rooted in psychology and political science, when applied to family dynamics in The Archers, *allow for some educated guesses. Social learning theory suggests that children who see their parents vote, run for office and participate in other civic activities are more likely to do the same in adulthood. Emma Grundy did just that when she followed in the footsteps of her father, Neil Carter, in winning a seat on the parish council. Previous research has found that birth order also can shape future leaders, with the eldest child more likely to benefit developmentally from parents' undivided attention in the early years, and also more likely to establish a hierarchy of power over younger siblings. With these factors in mind, who are the most probable contenders to lead Ambridge in the spheres of politics, business and civic affairs? The extant research points to Pip Archer, Lily Pargetter, Phoebe Aldridge and George Grundy. The unique circumstances of Ruairi Donovan's childhood suggest he may also be a formidable candidate. And, as is the case in so many contexts, one would be wise not to overlook Molly Button.*

INTRODUCTION – PAST, PRESENT AND FUTURE LEADERS

One of the many pleasures of listening to *The Archers* over the years is witnessing the characters as they pass through the stages of life. Few other dramas offer fans the opportunity to observe individuals as they move from childhood (in many cases, a silent childhood) to adolescence and then adulthood. As may be true with people we know personally, some of the characters' lives take unexpected turns, while others end up pretty much as we expected. Consider, for example, the trajectory of Jennifer Aldridge, who shocked polite Ambridge society by giving birth as a single mother at the age of 21 in 1967. Many years and two tumultuous marriages later, Jennifer has gained upper middle-class respectability as wife of a landowner, editor of the village website, a local historian, and celebrated competitor at the Flower and Produce Show. Roy Tucker also has undergone a significant transformation from his teenage involvement with white nationalists plotting an attack on Usha Gupta to middle-aged stability as a staff member at Grey Gables, doting father and reliable participant on the village cricket team.

One could argue that David Archer, on the other hand, has followed a fairly predictable path. Growing up on Brookfield

Farm, he worked alongside his father, Phil Archer. After completing a two-year course at the Royal Agricultural College, David worked on a farm in the Netherlands for a few years before returning to Brookfield in 1983 (Toye & Flynn, 2001). Listeners may recall clashes between father and son over how to run Brookfield, but it came as no surprise when Phil indicated in 2001 that David would take over managing the farm as Phil neared retirement. David also has emerged as a leader in the village on farm issues, from his involvement in the local chapter of the National Farmers' Union to his organising activities as a member of the Hassett Hills lamb cooperative. He also has dabbled in local politics, winning a seat on the parish council in 2006 (Coleman, 2008). While there have been some twists and turns in David's trajectory (Ruth Archer's bout with breast cancer in 2000, the near sale of Brookfield in 2015), his current role as a leading citizen of Ambridge seems almost pre-ordained.

What makes for a successful leader? Some of the qualities might include having the respect of the community. Successfully managing a business could serve as another metric. A record of getting things done would also be a reasonable indicator of leadership qualities. When it comes to commanding the respect of the community, one might argue that Neil Carter, in his position as chair of the parish council, qualifies as a leader. When Helen Archer needed a character witness to testify on her behalf during her trial for attempted murder of her husband, Rob Titchener, Neil's unimpeachable reputation for honesty made him a sound choice for the task. David Archer also appears to have the respect of the community as a result of his leadership in farming, on the parish council, and in his role as flood warden after the great flood of the River Am in 2015.

In the realm of business leadership, one could argue that Justin Elliott commands perhaps not the respect, but certainly the wariness, of villagers when he proposes developments in the community. Justin may not be liked, but he is feared, which some might argue is an indicator of success in the business world. Lilian Bellamy, with her management of Amside Property Holdings, has achieved a more conventional type of recognition of her business acumen, winning the title of Borsetshire Businesswoman of the Year. Shula Hebden-Lloyd has emerged as a community leader through her management of the stables and her role as Master of the South Borsetshire Hunt, and Elizabeth Pargetter's stewardship of Lower Loxley also places her among the business leaders in the village. Brian Aldridge had been perceived as a savvy businessman over the years, but his reputation deteriorated after the discovery that he had permitted the dumping of toxic chemicals on his land at Low Mead (see Chapters 5 and 6). His years of experience in farming and business negotiations, however, still attract others seeking his advice. Alice Carter relies on her father for career guidance, and David turned to Brian for negotiating strategies when it came to striking a deal with Vince Casey for abattoir services. If we measure leadership by getting things done, Lynda Snell stands out. From Speed Watch to the village fête to the Christmas pantomime, Lynda has amassed a record of achievement without parallel in Ambridge. Whether through flattery, threats or simply sheer persistence, Lynda manages to coax or wear down many a reluctant participant into getting involved in the community.

The leaders of Ambridge in governance, business and civic activities come from a variety of backgrounds, with some growing up in the village (David, Shula, Elizabeth, Lilian), and others arriving from other places (Neil, Justin, Brian, Lynda). One common element currently is stage of life, with all of them well into middle age and beyond. How much longer can they keep the village humming? While residents of Ambridge typically live full and vital lives well into old age, perhaps to a greater extent than people who live elsewhere, this still begs the question of how to fill the power vacuum when the current stalwarts inevitably step back from their leadership roles. With regard to the future leaders of Ambridge, the programme's scriptwriters do not let on, but it is clear that they think of the long game as they craft storylines. Scriptwriter Keri Davies, in a post on the BBC blog *BBC Writersroom* in 2013, wrote,

> The Archers *writing and production team have two meetings a year where we concentrate on long-term planning. And I mean long-term. It's not unusual for us to be thinking of the potential consequences of a birth 15 or 20 years ahead.*

(Davies, 2013)

Lacking access to the writers' long-range plans, fans are left to speculate about future plot and character developments. What clues could we use to inform our speculation? Research on childhood socialisation from political science and psychology can help us to identify potential markers of leadership qualities. Social learning theory holds that children will imitate their parents' behaviour, suggesting that the children of some of the current leaders may themselves occupy those positions someday. Research on the impact of birth order on the development of leadership qualities can also provide guidance in identifying which of the young villagers may go on to lead Ambridge in the future.

SOCIAL LEARNING THEORY

Research on political socialisation finds that children tend to imitate their parents' habits when it comes to civic engagement and political involvement. Pancer (2015) argues that a specific style of parenting is more likely to foster imitation from children. Adults who approach parenting with a combination of warmth and structure are more likely to see their children imitate their behaviour in areas like community involvement. This, combined with young people's feelings of warmth toward their family, leads to greater civic engagement in the next generation. Family discussion can also play an important part in fostering participation in public affairs. McIntosh, Hart and Youniss (2007) found that young people who reported having regular discussions about politics with their parents were also more likely to monitor the news, know more about politics, engage in community service and contact government officials. Andolina, Jenkins, Zukin and Keeter (2003) also found a positive relationship between political discussion among young people and their parents and volunteering, following politics, voting and engaging in political activism.

Young people, however, also have agency in deciding whether to follow their parents' cues when it comes to involvement in civic affairs. They actively work to construct their own understanding of what it takes to be an active and engaged citizen, using information from their parents, peers, teachers and religious leaders (Pancer, 2015). Because political participation is often a social act, witnessed by others, approval from members of one's social network can often be a motivating factor as well, particularly if the sources of approval are important to the individual (Sinclair, 2012). The political socialisation process that Pip and Josh Archer experience illustrates how coming from the same family background does not guarantee the same outcome when it comes to involvement in politics and public life. As the time came for each to participate in their first election, they responded differently to the civic engagement messages coming from their father.

The Archers marked the 2015 general election with a brief story line on Pip Archer's first opportunity to vote in a national election. The story began in the episode that aired on 6 May 2015, the day before the election. Pip accompanies David to the annual Hunt Landowners Dinner at Grey Gables. Pip heads to the bar to retrieve drinks for herself and David. On the way back, she gets into an argument with the father of a university friend about gay marriage and her cousin, Adam Macy, and his partner Ian Craig. David observes the argument from a distance and asks Pip what happened. He uses the ensuing exchange to remind Pip about the value of voting:

> *Pip*: Well, it was Lawrence's dad from my course, making nasty remarks about Adam.
>
> *David*: Adam?
>
> *Pip*: Yes, telling everyone exactly what he thought about gay marriage. Oh, I couldn't help myself.
>
> *David*: Well, good for you. That is one of the points of politics, you know.
>
> *Pip*: What?
>
> *David*: What your Mum was saying the other day. The stuff you feel strongly about. That's what voting's for.
>
> *Pip*: Well...
>
> *David*: You see?
>
> *Pip*: Yeah, OK, I suppose so (chuckles).
>
> *David*: You know where the polling station is, don't you? That hut in the village hall car park?
>
> *Pip:* Yeah, OK Dad, I get it.

(BBC Radio 4, 2015a)

In the episode on polling day the next day, 7 May 2015, Pip heeds her father's advice and casts her first vote, taking Jazzer McCreary with her as well, giving Jazzer an opportunity to vote for the first time (BBC Radio 4, 2015b).

In contrast, Josh Archer is not nearly as receptive to his father's guidance when Josh has his first chance to vote in 2016. In the episode on June 23, the day of the Brexit referendum, David and Josh have a brief conversation as Josh heads out the door to sit for his last college exam. Then, he plans to go out with his friends to celebrate:

> *David*: Good luck. And, hey, you won't forget to vote, will you?
>
> *Josh*: Huh?
>
> *David*: Your first ever chance to exercise your democratic rights, wherever you decide to put your cross.
>
> *Josh*: Yeah, yeah.
>
> *David*: (Frustrated) It's a very important decision. It's one of the biggest we'll ever have to make.
>
> *Josh*: (Annoyed) I know!.
>
> (BBC Radio 4, 2016)

Josh's mobile phone rings, he takes the call, then heads out the door. While listeners never hear whether Josh voted, it seems unlikely that a stop at the polling station was part of his post-exam plans. The difference between Pip and Josh in their reactions to their father's encouragement may circle back to approval, and whether David's approval matters to them. Pip appears to crave her father's affirmation to a greater degree than does Josh, at least when it comes to civic participation.

Parental expectations play out in a different way in the Carter family. Emma Grundy and Chris Carter also observe their parents' involvement in the community, but their parents do not appear to expect them to follow suit in terms of civic participation. Neil Carter is chair of the parish council, church warden at St. Stephen's, and 'tower captain' for the bell ringers at the church. Susan Carter works in the village shop and is game to participate in the annual village Christmas panto. Emma, busy with a young family and juggling multiple jobs, does not have much time for civic participation. Her brother Chris plays on the village cricket team, but that appears to be the extent of his involvement in village life. In recent years, however, Emma has undergone a political awakening. In the 19 April 2017 episode, the day after a general election was called in the United Kingdom, Emma and Ed discussed the upcoming election. Emma expressed satisfaction about having an opportunity to vote, saying, 'any chance to get our voices heard by politicians is all right by me' (BBC Radio 4, 2017a). A few months later, in October, Emma learns of an opening on the parish council and expresses interest to her father, who seems surprised. Oliver Sterling, owner of Grey Gables, is leaving the council and Robert Snell is also interested in filling the position:

> *Emma*: What's this about a vacancy on the parish council?
>
> *Neil*: How did you hear about that?
>
> *Emma*: Fallon's party last night. The Snells were talking about it.
>
> *Neil*: Oh, well, that's right. Robert has kindly offered to take Oliver Sterling's place.
>
> *Emma*: What, just like that?

Neil: Well, it's normally more a case of having to twist someone's arm. People aren't usually that interested.

Emma: I would have been.

Neil: You?

Emma: Yeah. I still am, actually. Unless it's a done deal now.

Neil: No.

Emma: All stitched up between you and Robert.

Neil: No, not really. I've still got to get approval from the other members before he gets co-opted. Are you really serious about applying, Emma?

Emma: Yeah. Why not?

Neil: Well, uh, no reason. I'm just a bit surprised, that's all.

Emma: I don't see why.

Neil: You never showed much interest in council business before.

Emma: Well I can start, can't I?

Neil: Yeah, yeah, of course.

Emma: So, how do I apply then?

Neil: Well, ok um. Well, what you'd have to do is write a letter saying why you'd be a good candidate, and I would ask Robert to do the same, assuming he wants to be considered against you.

Emma: OK, fine, that's what I will do then.

Neil: Well, good for you love. Can you make it fairly quick, though? I don't want to keep Robert hanging on because at the moment he thinks he's the only one in the frame.

Emma: OK.

After Neil leaves, Ed also expresses surprise over Emma's political ambitions.

Ed: Em...

Emma: Yeah?

Ed: This parish council thing.

Emma: What about it?

Ed: You ain't serious, are you?

Emma: I am, actually.

Ed: But...

Emma: You don't think I could do it.

Ed: I, I don't know where you'd find the time. You've got three jobs as it is.

Emma: I'd have to work around them.

Ed: And, I mean, it's dead boring, innit.

Emma: Maybe.

Ed: And weren't you saying the other week that you felt like an outsider in Ambridge?

Emma That's why I'm doing it. It's about time people in this village took me and my family seriously

(BBC Radio 4, 2017b).

The contrast between David's encouragement of Pip and Neil's surprise at Emma's ambition is telling. The difference may lie in the expectations that each family has. The middle-class Archers have a history of community involvement going back generations, while the working-class Carters do not. David's grandfather Dan Archer served on the parish council, as did David's mother, Jill Archer. Phil Archer was a justice of the peace, as well as chairman of the local chapter of the National Farmers' Union (Toye & Flynn, 2001). While both David and Neil hold leadership roles in the community, the expectations for their daughters are different. Both daughters appear to have learned from their fathers' examples, despite these varying expectations. Gender also intersects with class, in that Emma is expected to juggle jobs and domestic responsibilities with involvement in civic affairs, while Pip does not face those expectations. When Pip joins the rewilding project to compete for £500,000 from the Ambridge Conservation Trust in 2019, her parents react negatively, but only because she is involved in a project that competes with the family's proposal. There are no concerns about whether the re-wilding initiative would take Pip away from her farm duties or from caring for her daughter, Rosie Archer.

Despite the different circumstances, Pip and Emma appear to be following the examples set by their fathers regarding community involvement and civic leadership (although Emma, as a parish council member, is further along than Pip). Their trajectories are consistent with what we would expect from social learning theory. Will the same hold true for their children? Will Rosie carry on the family tradition of civic engagement? Will Emma's children, George and Keira Grundy, emulate the examples of their mother and grandfather? Social learning theory suggests that they might, but other factors could come into play as well. Having parents who are active in the community is not completely predictive of future involvement, as is evident with Josh and Chris. Social science gives us another theoretical framework to use, that of birth order. Eldest children hold an advantaged position in the family power dynamic, and those early experiences can play a role in leadership development. Perhaps Pip and Emma had an edge over their younger brothers, and the same may be true of other young people in Ambridge. Before extending the speculative net to others, though, it is useful to summarise the previous research on the effects of birth order on future leadership success.

BIRTH ORDER AND LEADERSHIP POTENTIAL

Scholars have found that first-born children tend to be overrepresented among national government leaders compared to general populations cross-nationally (Hudson, 1990; Steinberg, 2001) and across levels of government (Andeweg & Van Den Berg, 2003). While first-born men and women occupy a higher proportion of leadership positions compared to their prevalence in the population, the effect is stronger for women than men (Steinberg, 2001). What are the characteristics of first-born children that might give them an advantage in pursuing leadership positions? Steinberg (2001) argues that first-born children tend to be more highly educated than those falling later in the birth order of their families, more dominant and aggressive, more focused on achievement and may face higher expectations from parents than later children.

Andeweg and Van Den Berg (2003) offer two theoretical models that might explain why first-born children might have an advantage over those who fall later in the birth order. The parental resources model predicts that first-born children receive a larger share of parental resources than the later born. That would include material resources, but also parental attention and engagement, possibly leading to more rapid verbal and intellectual development, and a greater sense of ambition in the child. The second model is the sibling interaction model, which suggests that first-born children are better prepared for power struggles later in life, having experience as both followers (with parents) and leaders (with siblings), and having the experience of being displaced by the next-born child. In a study of nearly 1,200 leaders at all levels of government in the Netherlands, Andeweg and Van Den Berg found a disproportionate number of first-born children among the leaders compared to the population. They concluded that their findings provided more evidence to support the parental resources model, in part because they found not only a disproportionate number of first-born among the leaders in the study but also a disproportionate number of only children. In an earlier study of world leaders, Hudson (1990) also found an over-representation of first-born children and only children. But Hudson provides a broad definition of only child – not only a child without siblings, but also children whose nearest sibling is more than five years older or younger.

The effect of birth order on leadership prospects appears to be more pronounced for women than for men, and this gender difference is stronger for women who came to power prior to 1990 than after 1990 (Steinberg, 2001). The time variant suggests that as norms about women's roles in society change over time and women leaders become more widely accepted, the effect of birth order will vary less in terms of gender. Steinberg suggests that eldest daughters also may be more confident and may achieve more as a result of strong mentoring by their fathers, but she speculates that this type of mentorship may give way to meaningful guidance from both mothers and fathers as larger numbers of women achieve leadership roles in society. A more recent review of the literature by Nielsen (2014) suggests that the mentoring relationships between fathers and daughters continue to be important, particularly in the areas of academic and career development.

How might birth order and mentorship shape the future leaders of Ambridge? At Brookfield Farm, it would appear that Pip holds an advantage as first-born, and David attempts to provide mentoring from time to time (particularly when Pip left Brookfield to work for a corporate agribusiness, Webster Agri International, and then quit after only a week). The pair do clash from time to time over new farming techniques, reminiscent of David's disagreements with Phil.

The family dynamic at Home Farm is more complicated because Brian and Jennifer have had multiple families over the years. Jennifer had Adam as a single mother in 1967, then married Roger Travers-Macy the following year. They had Debbie in 1970, later divorced, and Jennifer married Brian in 1976. They had Kate in 1977 and Alice in 1988. Brian also has a son, Ruairi Donovan, born in 2002 during Brian's affair with Siobhan Hathaway. Focussing on the younger members of the family, Alice Carter and Ruairi may have leadership potential based on the literature on birth order and mentoring. Alice's nearest older sibling, Kate, precedes her by 11 years, giving Alice the status of an eldest child in the later configuration of the Aldridge family. Alice also benefits from a strong mentoring relationship with Brian, with whom she regularly consults about career decisions and advancement (demonstrated during her ill-fated tenure as a field representative for the farming technology company Pryce Baumann). Ruairi, while only four years younger than Alice, also might be considered an only or

eldest child by virtue of having lived with his late mother for
the first few years of his life, and then attending boarding
school for part of his time while living at Home Farm after
his mother's death. One constant at Home Farm has been
loving attention from Jennifer and Brian, and the start of a
mentoring relationship with Brian as Ruairi has advanced
through his teen years.

Looking to the next generation of Aldridges, Kate's
daughter, Phoebe Aldridge, appears to have leadership
potential based on the birth-order paradigm. Phoebe also is
part of a blended family and is the eldest with half-siblings
Abbie Tucker and Noluthando and Sipho Madikane. Phoebe
has already demonstrated the ambition associated with an
eldest child, having successfully read for a Philosophy, Politics
and Economics undergraduate degree at University of Oxford.
She has a close relationship with her father, Roy Tucker,
although mentoring between this particular father and
daughter sometimes travels in both directions. Phoebe is more
likely to receive useful business advice from her grandfather,
Brian. An early sign of Phoebe's leadership potential was her
skill at assembling a successful bid, with Rex Fairbrother and
Pip, for £500,000 from the Ambridge Conservation Trust for
Rewilding Ambridge.

Other potential leaders of Ambridge include Lily Pargetter,
first-born child (by a few minutes over her twin Freddie) of
Elizabeth and Nigel Pargetter (Toye & Flynn, 2001). The
death of Nigel when Lily was 11 years old may have contributed to her self-sufficient nature and growing up watching her
mother manage Lower Loxley may have provided a template
for how to operate a successful business. Lily showed her
leadership capability when she stepped in to run Lower
Loxley while Elizabeth dealt with depression in 2019.

Some of the younger residents of Ambridge may have
leadership qualities, but it is early days. George Grundy

benefits from being the eldest child, and he has a role model in his mother Emma, who has shown that it is possible for a Grundy to win elected office in Ambridge. Alexander (Xander) Macy-Craig, as an only child and son of Adam Macy and Ian Craig, two working parents in their 50s and far along in their careers, may benefit from access to more resources than would a child of younger parents. The oldest in the next generation of Archers at Bridge Farm, Henry Archer, obviously has had a difficult start in life, and he will need a strong mentor as he grows up.

If we apply criteria drawn from social learning theory and research on birth-order effects and mentoring, we can make predictions about probable future leaders of Ambridge (Table 15.1).

Table 15.1. Future Leaders of Ambridge.

Name	First-born? (In the Broadest Sense of the term)	Parent Mentor?	Parent as Civic Leader?	Prospects for Leadership?
Phoebe Aldridge	X	X		Likely
Pip Archer	X	X	X	Very Likely
Alice Carter	X	X	X	Very Likely
Ruairi Donovan	X	X	X	Very Likely
George Grundy	X		X	Likely
Lily Pargetter	X		X	Likely

Pip, Alice and Ruairi all benefit from either being the eldest child or by not having a sibling in close proximate age to them. They also profit from having a parent as a mentor and a parent who is considered a leader in the community. They seem to have the best prospects for moving into leadership positions either in the realm of politics (parish council), business, civic affairs or a combination of areas. Phoebe, George and Lily each have two of the three elements that might help them to attain leadership roles, making them possible contenders.

As with most academic studies, however, this one comes with caveats. Personal factors, either present or unforeseen, may intervene to prevent these individuals from moving into leadership positions in the future. For example, Alice struggles with alcohol, which could get in the way of her reaching her full potential. They also may face competition from outsiders who arrive in the village bringing similar advantages and ambitions. Also, familiar characters who have left Ambridge might return. For example, if Dan Hebden-Lloyd tires of military service and moves back to the village, he would be a formidable leadership candidate as an only child, with a strong parent mentor (Alistair Lloyd), and a parent who manages a successful business (Shula Hebden-Lloyd). Also, from within the village, some of the younger silent characters might someday find their voices and might make a play for leadership roles. Molly Button, for example, is the older of the Button sisters and has already plunged into village life in many ways (amateur theatrics and cricket) that suggest burgeoning leadership qualities. As others have found, most notably Rob Titchener, one would be wise not to underestimate Molly Button. Time will tell.

REFERENCES

Andeweg, R. B., & Van Den Berg, S. B. (2003). Linking birth order to political leadership: The impact of parents or sibling interaction? *Political Psychology, 24*(3), 605–623.

Andolina, M., Jenkins, K., Zukin, C., & Keeter, S. (2003). Habits from the home, lessons from school: Influences on youth civic engagement. *PS: Political Science and Politics, 36*(2), 275–280.

BBC Radio 4. (2015a, May 6). *The Archers*. Retrieved from https://www.bbc.co.uk/programmes/b05stt42. Accessed on June 25, 2020.

BBC Radio 4. (2015b, May 7). *The Archers*. Retrieved from https://www.bbc.co.uk/programmes/b05sy25y.   Accessed on June 25, 2020.

BBC Radio 4. (2016, June 23). *The Archers*. Retrieved from https://www.bbc.co.uk/programmes/b07gh581.   Accessed on June 25, 2020.

BBC Radio 4. (2017a, April 19). *The Archers*. Retrieved from https://www.bbc.co.uk/programmes/b08mbjqk.   Accessed on June 25.

BBC Radio 4. (2017b, October 6). *The Archers*. Retrieved from https://www.bbc.co.uk/programmes/b096jkg8. Accessed on June 25, 2020.

Coleman, S. (2008). The depiction of politicians and politics in British soaps. *Television & New Media, 9*(3), 197–219.

Davies, K. (2013, October 21). Writing The Archers: From idea to airwaves. BBC Writersroom. Retrieved from https://www.bbc.co.uk/blogs/writersroom/entries/989184e1-10a1-3c2d-916e-cfbf67c7a334. Accessed on June 25, 2020.

Hudson, V. M. (1990). Birth order of world leaders: An exploratory analysis of effects on personality and behavior. *Political Psychology, 11*(3), 583–601.

McIntosh, H., Hart, D., & Youniss, J. (2007). The influence of family political discussion on youth civic development: Which parent qualities matter? *PS: Political Science and Politics, 40*(3), 495–499.

Nielsen, L. (2014). Young adult daughters' relationships with their fathers: Review of recent research. *Marriage & Family Review, 50*(4), 360–372.

Pancer, S. M. (2015). *The psychology of citizenship and civic engagement.* Oxford: Oxford University Press.

Sinclair, B. (2012). *The social citizen: Peer networks and political behavior.* Chicago, IL: The University of Chicago Press.

Steinberg, B. S. (2001). The making of female presidents and prime ministers: The impact of birth order, sex of siblings, and father-daughter dynamics. *Political Psychology, 22*(1), 89–110.

Toye, J., & Flynn, A. (2001). *The Archers encyclopaedia.* London: BBC Worldwide Limited.

16

'FROM THE MOMENT THOSE TWO JOINED THE COMMITTEE IT'S BEEN GRUNGE BANDS, SUMO WRESTLERS AND SOUFFLE COMPETITIONS': WHAT AMBRIDGE'S CIVIL SOCIETY SAYS ABOUT UK POLITICS IN 2019

Amy Sanders

ABSTRACT

This study examines the discursive accounts of civil society in a rural English village to understand what these reveal about contemporary political discourses. It employs a critical discourse analysis of the conversational interactions of Ambridge residents. The sample comprised all recorded conversations referencing charities, volunteering and civic action drawn from the two-week period corresponding with the change in UK Prime Minister (July 2019). Using three analytical tools derived from extant theory, it considers the salient political ideology underpinning these social interactions. These tools are illustrated with earlier examples of individual civil activities such as the oat-based civil disobedience of a respected older resident. This analysis scrutinises the philanthropic nature of Peggy Woolley's Ambridge Conservation Trust. The fraught process of village fete planning is cited as exemplifying conventional decision-making mechanisms. Problems of staffing a community shop are considered in the light of an increasing political reliance on community volunteers replacing paid staff. Thus, the relative impact of Thatcher, Blair, Cameron and May are considered in exchanges between Ambridge residents from Lynda and Robert Snell to Jazzer McCreery and Jill Archer. The aim is to explore what Ambridge's civil society tells us about Boris Johnson's Britain.

This study is concerned with the ways civil society is addressed in the 'everyday story of country folk' examining what this reveals about political discourses at a pivotal point in UK politics. The political ideas of British Prime Ministers have shaped our understanding of civil society, and their historical discourses continue to compete in our everyday communication; thus, the conversations in a rural English village can inform of the contemporary nature of civil society. This illuminates the political discourses that currently prevail, at a point when the next Prime Minister steps into power. The research question addressed in this chapter is 'how do civil society discourses in Ambridge reflect historical and contemporary political discourses?' This chapter begins by outlining the association between civil society and political discourse. An explanation of methods is then offered including a brief focus

on the ethics of using recorded conversations and an introduction to the three analytical tools. The results are presented in
three corresponding sections to explore dimensions of firstly,
social stability and change, secondly, underpinning principles
and finally, differing roles. This entails a detailed examination
of Ambridge's Village Fete Committee, the Ambridge Conservation Trust and the Village Community Shop. Reflections are
made throughout this about the civil society that Johnson
inherits as Prime Minister.

POLITICAL AND CIVIC CONTEXT

Civil society is a contested term. It is sometimes used inter-
changeably with the third sector (Alcock, 2016) or voluntary
sector (Day, 2009). Their meanings are also contested but
usually refer to organisations that are both non-governmental
and non-profit making (Alcock, 2012). For example, they
might include 'voluntary and community organisations,
charities and social enterprises' (2016, p. 96). However, civil
society is also considered to have a broader meaning than
third sector (Buckingham, 2012; Milbourne & Murray,
2017). Thus, one interpretation is to view civil society as all
associations in which membership and activities are voluntary
(Edwards, 2014). Understanding civil society to mean associations stems back to De Tocqueville (1835). This broader
definition adds to the organisations listed above by including,
for example, religious groups, social movements and business
associations (Edwards, 2014, p. 20). It should also be noted
that a different understanding of civil society is to view it as
'an arena for societal deliberation' (Edwards, 2014, p. 4). This
can be traced back to Athenian notions of democracy, and this
arena is frequently referred to as the 'public sphere', due to
Habermas' work (1987). Thus non-profit, non-governmental,

voluntary associations and the public sphere are all facets of civil society.

Political discourse has shaped the way in which civil society is perceived and operates. Other studies have detailed the relationship between UK political discourse and civil society extensively (Aiken & Taylor, 2019; Alcock, 2016). The purpose of the following overview is to briefly illustrate some key links between civil society discourse and UK politics in the last four decades in order to lay this study's foundations. Ambridge-hungry readers less concerned with UK politics may choose to skip ahead.

Margaret Thatcher brought notions of the market to public services which led to privatisation (Aiken & Taylor, 2019). The corollary in civil society was a move towards New Public Management and a corresponding professionalisation of the sector (Chapman, Brown, Ford, & Baxter, 2010). Additionally, Thatcher promoted individualism through active citizenship and civil duty (Aiken & Taylor, 2019). In contrast, Tony Blair introduced the Third Way whereby he gave specific roles to the third sector (Alcock, 2012, 2016; Buckingham, 2012; Chapman et al., 2010; Davies, 2011; Fyfe, Timbrell, & Smith, 2006; Zimmer & Pahl, 2018). Third sector roles included being contracted to deliver public services as well as engaging in decision-making partnerships to develop state policy (Milbourne & Cushman, 2013; Newman, 2001). The term 'third sector' became associated with New Labour (Alcock, 2016). When David Cameron formed his coalition government, he dropped 'third sector' in favour of 'civil society' (Alcock, 2012). Cameron also introduced the Big Society (Chapman et al., 2010). This concept shared some underlying trends with Blair's Third Way, but in the context of austerity after the banking crisis of 2008, the fundamental difference was there was less financial support for the sector (Alcock, 2012, 2016; Milbourne & Cushman, 2013). Big

Society was envisaged to subsidise public services with community volunteers playing a role in local amenities such as libraries, parks and surgeries (Aiken & Taylor, 2019; Alcock, 2016; Milbourne & Cushman, 2013). Similar models were adopted for rural pubs and shops to ensure their long-term sustainability. In contrast, May's government had an absence of civil society discourse, given the dominating issue of negotiating leaving the European Union. Hence, May's 'Civil Society Strategy' (HM Government, 2018), was non-committal and characterised by vagueness, which is unsurprising, given the ongoing austerity agenda (Bennett et al., 2019). Notably, May did emphasise young people's civic participation linked to the National Citizen Service to promote youth volunteering (Bennett et al., 2019). These youth volunteering policies excited controversy given the introduction of compulsory volunteering as a condition of certain welfare benefits (Aiken & Taylor, 2019; Bennett et al., 2019). Thus, we have traced the impact of political discourse on how civil society is constructed in public discourse through four prime ministers.

Political ideas continue to compete in public discourses. It is possible to show how some ideas from political elites succeed and others fail in being conveyed and adopted (Schmidt, 2008). Discourse analysis provides a scientific basis for understanding social life in moral and political terms, whereby implicit assumptions in language reflect the hegemony of its society (Fairclough, 2003). One example of how discourses can be analysed to explore civil society is seen in the work of Wiley (2019). Wiley undertook an analysis of voluntary action in US television programmes. Her research assistants watched many hours of TV programmes such as *The Big Bang Theory* (Lorre et al., 2014) and *Parks and Recreation* (Daniels et al., 2015) identifying references to volunteering. These were analysed to explore the portrayal of voluntary action. The methodological similarity between this study and

Wiley's is the use of discourse analysis to explore civil society. However, our study shares its ontological position with the *Archers Anarchists* (2020), recognising Ambridge is real, and rejecting 'castism', which refers to the misguided belief that there is a cast acting out the roles of Ambridge residents. So, where Wiley's (2019) study was concerned with fictional characters from television, this study's discourse is taken from actual conversations of real Ambridge residents.

This paper focusses on the different ways civil society is addressed in one rural village in Borsetshire. Ambridge's civil society has already been the subject of an analysis when Headlam (2019) examined women's role in the village's civil society. Headlam argued that civil society can be a mechanism for social stability or social change. The aim of the current paper is to build on Headlam's work in analysing Ambridge inhabitants' discourses to ascertain what this tells us about civil society in the United Kingdom in the summer of 2019.

METHOD

The study design was ethnographic observation as it comprised apparently natural conversations between village members who knew each other. Critical discourse analysis was used as a tool to understand the interconnectedness of social life and discourses (Fairclough, 2003).

Ethical Considerations

Fully informed consent was assumed as these conversations took place in such a manner as to enable any interested parties to listen to the discussions. Moreover, recordings of these conversations were subsequently made available to the general public irrespective of this research. These natural conversations between individuals have been launched in the public domain for some years now, for example BBC Radio 4's own *Listening Project*. Criterion for 'implied consent' was discussed by Sanders (2010, p. 153), drawing on the British Psychological Society's guidelines on ethical practice, which maintain observation of public behaviour can only take place 'where people would reasonable expect to be observed by strangers'. Individuals who permit their conversations to be recorded and made publicly available can be assumed to be granting permission for analysis and research.

Sampling

This sample frame comprised all available conversations recorded over a two-week period, from 14 to 28 July 2019, the two weeks before and after Boris Johnson becoming Prime Minister of the United Kingdom (24 July). All conversations that pertained to Civil Society Organisations were transcribed, coded (using NVivo) and analysed.

Analysis

Three analytical tools were deployed for this study building on the work of previous research on civil society. Each of these allowed any given activity to be mapped on to one or more dimensions; the dimensions selected reflect differing theoretical approaches to understanding this field.

First Analytical Tool: The primary analytical tool was designed by Evers and Von Essen (2019). Similar to Headlam's (2019) distinction between 'social stability' and 'social change',

Evers and Von Essen scrutinised the distinction between 'volunteering' and 'civic action'. They recognised 'volunteering' is often viewed as a 'private, morally motivated and individual' form of volunteering that does not aim to change society whereas 'civic action' is often conceived as 'public, political and collective' aiming for societal change (Evers & Von Essen, 2019, p. 3). They argued the distinction is context dependent and developed a framework for a more nuanced analysis. They proposed popular engagement in civil society fits on to two axes, one of which ranges from the *Social Sphere*, characterised by associational activities, to the *Political Sphere* where deliberation and decision-making take place. Intersecting this, the second axis reflects the potential pressure for change ranging from the *Consensual* activities where convention maintains the status quo to *Contested Political* activities which are more conflictual. Thus, activity in the Social and Political Spheres can be either Consensual or Contested (Fig. 16.1). As this analytical tool is more complex than the other two, it is illustrated below with Ambridge examples.

Applied to Ambridge: Aiken and Taylor (2019) applied this framework to homelessness strategies to illustrate the different dimensions. Their example is adapted to select Ambridge equivalents. Consider Pat Archer's volunteering at The Elms, the homeless shelter in Borchester. This is an example of Social and Consensual in that she was part of a service provision, which constituted a conventional form of voluntary activity (lower right.) However, Pat then acted beyond the remit of her volunteering role, by taking Olwen home to Bridge Farm. This could be considered to be a form of peer-to-peer buddying, which she might argue is an innovative solution to a problem. Her example could then be categorised as Social and Contested (lower left.) How wise or effective that innovative solution may have been is a matter of judgement. In both sectors, Pat is firmly in the Social Sphere, providing services for homeless people.

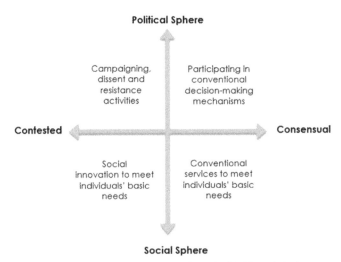

Source: Adapted from Evers and Von Essen's (2019) analytical framework.

Fig. 16.1. Civic Action and Volunteering.

Compare these examples with the case of Emma Grundy whose first concern when she secured a position on Ambridge Parish Council was to campaign for affordable housing. Emma's activity is an example of Consensual Political activity, in that she was operating at decision-making level, but local parish councils are a conventional political mechanisms (upper right). In contrast, Jill Archer provides an example of civil society that is Contested and Political when, on 25 July 2017, she threw a piece of oat-based confectionary (the flapjack of the title of this volume) in anger at a public meeting. This act of civil disobedience, for which she was subsequently arrested and charged, was a protest at the imminent closure of Happy Friends Café due to the opening of the Duxford sisters' fine dining restaurant. The project had tackled both food waste and hunger. Jill's act of dissent was intended, however spontaneously, to effect change, thereby exemplifying contested activity in a decision-making sphere (upper left). These historical events are presented to illustrate how the tool can be understood.

Second Analytical Tool: This tool comes from a distinction made by Aiken and Taylor (2019) between mutualism and philanthropy. They described philanthropy as giving to others (Us to Them) and contrasted this with mutualism founded on a community's shared interests (Us to Us). According to Aiken and Taylor, Philanthropy is characterised by altruism and is associated with giving alms to the poor, whereas Mutualism is a community-based pooling of resources defined by solidarity and cooperative working.

Third Analytical Tool: This final tool for analysing civil society comes from the professionalism-volunteerism binary found in extant voluntary sector research (e.g. Aiken & Taylor, 2019; Buckingham, 2012; Fyfe et al., 2006). Volunteer-run grassroots organisations are frequently contrasted to organisations with hierarchical, bureaucratic structures involving managers, professionals, and volunteers. The literature has highlighted the rise in professionalisation in response to New Public Management (Aiken & Taylor, 2019; Newman, 2001) stemming from Thatcher's influence. Such professionalised organisations are often accused of losing touch with their volunteers or community members (Buckingham, 2012). Contrastingly, Cameron's Big Society resulted in volunteers replacing paid members of staff.

FINDINGS

In total, the recordings from the sampling period comprised 148 minutes of dialogue. Of this, the time when the dialogue was relevant to an analysis of civil society was 55 minutes 42 seconds of conversation.

Conventional or Contested Activities in the Political or Social Spheres

In the first instance, selected activities were mapped on to the framework analysis of Evers and Von Essen (2019).

Social Sphere, Conventional

There were three examples of civil society activity located in this quadrant that were discussed in the recorded conversations. Firstly, Kirsty Miller secured a new job working as a volunteer coordinator at the Wildlife Trust, which is a charity. Kirsty described her job as: 'I'll be recruiting volunteers to assist the conservation professionals on a project the wildlife trust are running on the river Am.' Secondly, Alistair Lloyd telephoned a charity-provided helpline for advice about how to support his father to deal with abuse in his own childhood. Thirdly, the community shop featured as a result of some tensions concerning volunteering responsibilities. All three are examples of conventional services provided either by charities and/or volunteers. This quadrant representing conventional forms of activity undertaken in a social sphere had the greatest number of Ambridge examples during the sample time frame. This may reflect how contemporary civil society is most likely to be understood in Johnson's era.

Social Sphere, Contested

A singularly significant event which dominated the discourse over these two weeks was Peggy Woolley's Ambridge Conservation Trust, forming 68% of the civil society transcribed conversations. This initiative was intended to be of benefit to the village, so sits well in the social sphere, but it was certainly an innovative initiative designed to create lasting change. The nature of this innovation holds some important insights into the new direction of civil society in Ambridge, which are explored through the other two tools below.

Political Sphere, Contested

Throughout this particular fortnight, there was no mention of activity that could be categorised as Political and Contested. The absence of any acts of resistance to fill the upper right quadrant of the framework could be viewed as a worrying indicator. Researchers have expressed concern that there is current trend for civil society to be self-muting its critical voice (Hemmings, 2017), and a growing political discourse constraining civil society's ability to hold authority to account (Aiken & Taylor, 2019). However, a limitation of this study was the short time frame. Thus, further research to examine future rebellious acts in Ambridge is required to establish whether they are on a par with their historical predecessors: burning GM crops, the SAVE campaign that fought Route B link road from destroying Ambridge countryside and the infamous flapjack incident. Frequent visitors to Ambridge are encouraged to look out for such acts of dissent.

Political Sphere, Conventional

The Village Fête Planning Committee featured in the dialogue during the time sample. A village fête epitomises conventional activity in rural Britain, given that fetes derive from the early twentieth century and village fairs date from medieval times. These conversations concerned the decision-making of the planning committee, and, therefore, this example is located firmly in the political sphere.

Further scrutiny of the discussions about the Village Fête Planning Committee reveal a new tension in the political sphere. The committee featured in the context of whether Jim Lloyd (70-plus years) would be attending as an older committee member to support Lynda Snell (72 years) in her struggles to agree plans with the new youth members, Ben Archer (17 years) and Ruairi Donovan (16 years). The boys inclusion in decision-making signals a shift in notions of young people's roles in civil society. Giving young people a say can be traced back to the United Nations Convention of the Rights of Children (1989) (UNCRC). Article 12 refers to children's right 'to express their views on all matters affecting them, and to have their views considered and taken seriously'. However, these youth committee members' engagement in civil society could signal May's renewed focus on youth citizenship. Of course, those who know these boys well will realise their motives were less concerned with children's rights or May's plans for their personal improvement. They were more interested in attracting young women to Ambridge with Tiggy's grunge band headlining the fête.

However, the way that Lynda responds to the young people's views is perhaps the most significant feature of this analysis. Amongst their more extreme suggestions for novel inclusions in the festivities were 'grunge bands, sumo wrestlers and souffle competitions'. Lynda, whose preeminent role on the committee over decades cannot be overstated, struggled to come to terms with their ideas, as seen here:

Lynda: *I simply don't know what to do anymore… Clearly, I must be an old stick in the mud.*

Robert: *What on earth's happened?*

Lynda: *All I'm trying to do is protect the fete from the vagaries of the modern world … <sigh>…Augmented* *reality... That's Ben and Ruairi's latest fad. An augmented reality treasure hunt, but instead of there being physical clues, you have to find them, using an app on your phone... What the matter with keeping things the way they were?*

Lynda's account encapsulates some key shifts in the future direction of civil society. It recognises that new technology will take civil society in new innovative directions (Aiken & Taylor, 2019). It is also understood that a substantial proportion of older, retired people do volunteer (Lie & Baines, 2007). The tension between the older and younger committee members is representative of a growing conflict between the generations. There is a developing literature on intergenerational conflict in civil society, in which the older generation is frequently perceived to have 'stolen the futures' of their children, associated in the United Kingdom with differing opinions on the European Union (Fox, Hampton, Muddiman, & Taylor, 2019). As ever, Lynda's patient husband Robert comes to her side to ease her through this turmoil and reconcile her to change:

Robert: *I know change is difficult, but... what would you prefer; that this swarm of millennials about to descend on the village weren't interested in the fete at all? ...You don't like not being in control. Sometimes, if you want something to have a future, you have to let it go.*

Lynda: *You know, you really can be quite infuriating Robert...*

Robert: *I can?*

Lynda: *the way you're right, all the time, especially about me.*

<Robert chuckles>

Robert's argument captures two opposing responses to young people's active voice in decision-making. On the one side, his words represent the fear of young people, portraying them as a form of pestilence, with the 'swarm of millennials' descending on Ambridge. However, Robert counters this by recognising the value of their engagement and equating them with the village's future. This latter point is a crucial argument to resolving this conflict. It has been recognised that strength of relationships between the generations are key to both easing intergenerational conflict (Fox et al., 2019) and encouraging youth civic participation (Muddiman, Taylor, Power, & Moles, 2019). This was described in the context of family relationships, but our analysis suggests further exploration of the impact of the extended 'family' that is offered by the village community. If Lynda can get this right, she will be reinforcing future village participation of young people. If she gets it wrong, she might expect Ruairi to respond with the contemporary phrase which signifies young people's frustration of their views being denigrated by the older generation: 'Okay Boomer'.

The fact that the Village Planning Committee is the only civil society example in the Political Sphere rather than the Social Sphere lends support to the argument that there is a push towards the decoupling of civil society from the state (Macmillan, 2013). This suggests a reversal of Blair's Third Way is taking place in civil society.

Mutualism and Philanthropy

The second analytical tool was used to map Ambridge's civil society against the mutualism – philanthropy dimension. Both the examples of the village fete and the community shop represent acts of mutualism in Ambridge's civil society. In each case, village residents worked together for the common good in which themselves, their families and friends formed part of the beneficiaries. In contrast, philanthropy would presumably be more in line with the motivations of Kirsty's river-wading volunteers. To volunteer in the Wildlife Trust is an act of altruism, whereby the environment is the principle beneficiary. However, it is Peggy Woolley's launch of the Ambridge Conservation Trust which provides a notable philanthropic example. This is evident in Peggy's explanation to Lilian:

> *I have thought about it and I'm certain it's the right thing to do. I want to invest in our future. This money could make a real difference for all of Ambridge.*

Certainly, these words convey a strong foundation on philanthropy, but its nature is distinct from notions of her donating her time. Peggy's contribution is a significant financial sum, namely quarter of a million pounds. Thus, Peggy's philanthropy actually signals a shift in funding for civil society in Ambridge, whose history has hitherto lacked philanthropic trusts (Rich, 2019). Some predict such philanthropic funding becoming the backbone of the sector (Enjolras, 2018). Such a change in the United Kingdom towards a North American model of financing the third sector has been recognised by Phillips and Hebb (2010). They cited wealthy individuals using their fortunes to fund enterprises as an example. Edwards (2014, p. 27) described this as 'philanthropicapitalism'. This could suggest that Peggy is Ambridge's answer to Microsoft's founder, Bill Gates.

However, further scrutiny of the Ambridge Conservation Trust provides additional insights into the underpinning philosophy of the village's civil society. The diversity of proposals submitted to the Trust each represented a potential civil society association from Adam Macy's Soil Academy to Tom and Natasha Archer's Orchard Village or from Eddie Grundy's wildflower meadow to David and Ruth Archer's Low Carbon Brookfield. None of these were easily amenable to the philanthropy-mutualism distinction. Analysis of the discourses concerning people's motivations underpinning their proposals required mutualism to be regarded as a midpoint on a continuum from altruistic philanthropy at one end and 'self-interest' occupying the other end point. For example, Eddie was heard to say to Edward when discussing the Trust: 'It's how we're going to get our hands on Peggy's £500 grand'. This is a clear demonstration of self-interest. Similarly, when Tom and Natasha had decided to exclude Eddie from their project, Natasha explained this to Eddie in the following way: 'But the thing is Eddie. The thing that's really important to Tom and I... is that it's a family project. That we work on it together, as a team'. Here we see an instance of family interests being presented as a motivation. When the family is framed as a 'self-interested entity', it accords with conservative, neo-liberal discourses on family values (Muddiman et al., 2019). Another example of self-interest can be seen in what turned out to be the winning pitch, Rewilding Ambridge. Phoebe Aldridge had appeared to embrace the philanthropic principle of the trust when she was speaking to her aunt, Alice: 'This is a brilliant chance for someone to really make a difference'. However, when she spoke to Kirsty Miller, her personal ambition also became apparent: 'It just feels so flat being back here...I want to make something happen.' Phoebe is both a high-flying, Oxford graduate and Brian Aldridge's granddaughter. Perhaps we should expect to see more of her drive and ambition fuelled by self-interest, in keeping with the Aldridge *modus operandi*. Viewed collectively, it is clear the Ambridge Conservation Trust has introduced a self-interested principle to Ambridge's Civil Society. This can be traced back to Thatcherism with the primacy of the individual self-interest, the family and the market driven by competition. This return towards Thatcher's individualism suggests a shift away from ideas associated with the Big Society, be they fuelled by either philanthropy or mutualism. Certainly, it seems there are some older conservative values underpinning the capital C of the Ambridge Conservation Trust.

Professionalism and Volunteering

The final dimension for consideration is that of professionalism-volunteering. Once more, the Ambridge Conservation Trust in the dialogue provides a case for consideration. Peggy is not to be underestimated. As she said to Lillian Bellamy (her daughter and, therefore, one of her potential heirs who has been awarded the title of the Trust's Chief Operating Officer): 'I had to make sure the Trust was set up properly. With all this money at stake it needs to be watertight'. To expect anything less would be to overlook the fact that Peggy was a professional businesswoman throughout her career and although now in her nineties, she retains a sharp mind and her business acumen. It was this professional approach of his grandmother which had inspired Tom's approach to his application leading Tom to exclude Eddie. As he told Natasha:

> *The bottom line is… it's crucial we don't have a dead weight on our side… Honestly, if Gran sees Eddie Grundy's name on our proposal, she won't touch it with a barge pole.*

Ever focussed on the financial bottom line and his profit margin, Tom here is seen applying a hard-nosed, business approach to his proposal. This proves the apple does not fall far from the Bridge Farm Orchard Tree. As we can see, Peggy's impact on Ambridge's civil society is the promotion of professionalization, reminiscent of the New Public Management of the 80s. It is possible, therefore, that a more appropriate analogy is to consider Peggy as Ambridge's answer to business magnate and media personality, Alan Sugar.

The polar opposite of this business-based approach to civil society is the village shop. Formerly part of Jack Woolley's business portfolio, it was leased with a peppercorn rent to the community by Peggy Archer in the same year that Cameron became Prime Minister. Archetypal of the Big Society principles, Susan Carter is now the only paid member of staff, and the community shop is manned (mostly womanned) by volunteers. During the time period of interest to this study, the village shop epitomised volunteering in all its complexities. This was illustrated when one volunteer was unable to fulfil their voluntary role due to a personal crisis. An organisation dependent on volunteers to function is put under strain when volunteers experience life events that may interfere with their scheduled role. Such an incident occurred when Jim Lloyd was having difficulty sleeping following an event that triggered a childhood trauma. His (unlikely) housemate counselled him in the middle of the night against feeling obliged to fulfil his village shop role:

Jim: *I'm meant to be opening the village shop this morning. Even with another hour or two in bed, I doubt I'll feel much better...*

Jazzer: *Skip it then.*

Jim: *I can't.*

Jazzer: *Is there not other people that can do your shift for you?*

Jim: *Well yes but then I'd have to let Susan know and she'll start asking all sorts of questions...*

Jazzer: *I'll phone her then.*

Whilst this exchange reflects Jazzer McCreary's genuine concern for his friend, it also reveals a personnel systems failure that would have protected confidentiality about absences if it had concerned a paid staff member. As it transpired, not everyone was as understanding as Jazzer, particularly his volunteer shift replacement, Jill Archer. Jill's bull-headed judgement of Jim came to light when she and her gentleman friend had an acrimonious encounter with Jazzer in the aptly named local pub, The Bull. Here, Jazzer endeavours to protect Jim's privacy:

Jill: *He seems to be doing this a lot at the moment.*

Jazzer: *Doing what?...*

Jill: *Not turning up when he said he would. Letting people down...*

Jazzer: *He's just double booked himself, that's all.*

Leonard: *There. There you see.*

Jill: *Well then, in that case, he's just being rude.*

Jazzer: *Rude?...*

Jill: *It isn't only the shop. He hasn't been to parish council meetings, he hasn't been attending the fete committee.*

Jazzer: *Hey now, hold your horses...*

Jill: *That might wash with some, but it sounds pretty hollow when he carries on treating everyone in the same thoughtless way.*

Jazzer: *What would you know about it?... There's people in this world who have done far worse things than not turning up for the shift at the village shop, for crying out loud.*

In this exchange we see Jill, whose past record was one of unstinting kindness and generosity. Here, she is harshly judgemental, demonstrating a recent shift in her temperament. Jazzer, on the other hand, does not hesitate to loyally defend his friend. On a side note, this lack of tolerance and censorious approach that Jill shows suggests that, perhaps, she is increasingly becoming Ambridge's answer to controversial outspoken columnist, Katie Hopkins.

However, this exchange is also significant for our analysis of volunteering. It is evident that the cracks are starting to show in this community-run project. The overreliance on volunteers to deliver services in the place of paid staff places a strain on the community. This concern was raised at the introduction of the Big Society when it was suggested communities would be put under strain at taking on new responsibilities (Alcock, 2016). Now, it is a well-established criticism levelled at the Big Society that it is 'instrumentalising volunteer roles as a form of necessary (or even compulsory) unpaid work' (Aiken & Taylor, 2019, p. 22). Here then, this argument is representative of a discourse that criticises the principle of Cameron's Big Society.

CONCLUSION

The discourse in Ambridge at the point that Johnson became Prime Minister provides insight into how contemporary civil society is constructed in rural England. The positioning of Ambridge's civil society overwhelmingly in the Social Sphere rather than the Political Sphere suggests a reversal of Blair's Third Way. The tensions between generations in the decision-making of the Fête Planning Committee expose a growth in intergenerational conflict in political discourse. The lack of contested, political activity may suggest a self-muting of civil society but could also be explained by the narrow time sample. Therefore, further study is needed to explore the acts of resistance and protest in Ambridge. Elements of both philanthropy and mutualism can be seen in Ambridge's civil society. However, the Ambridge Conservation Trust signals a growth in self-interested individualism underpinning the village's civil society. Its emergence as a philanthropic funding model is akin to the funding of civil society in America. These factors, combined with how the Trust drives professionalism, suggests Thatcher's ideology either still has resonance, or perhaps is having a resurgence within Ambridge's civil society. In contrast, the rising tensions between community volunteers in the shop can be seen to reflect the flaws in Cameron's Big Society. Overall, this analysis indicates the nature of the civil society that Johnson has inherited, which inevitably poses the question: how will Johnson's time in government shape Ambridge's civil society?

REFERENCES

Aiken, M., & Taylor, M. (2019). Civic action and volunteering: The changing space for popular engagement in England. *Voluntas: International Journal of Voluntary and Nonprofit Organizations*, *30*(1), 15–28.

Alcock, P. (2012). New policy spaces: The impact of devolution on third sector policy in the UK. *Social Policy and Administration*, *46*(2), 219–238.

Alcock, P. (2016). From partnership to the big society: The third sector policy Regime in the UK. *Nonprofit Policy Forum*, *7*(2), 95–116.

Anarchists, A. (2020). @rchers @narchists - The Archers are real – there is no cast. Retrived from https://www.archersanarchists.com/. Accessed on June 14, 2020.

Bennett, E., Coule, T., Damm, C., Dayson, C., Dean, J., & Macmillan, R. (2019). Civil society strategy: A policy review. *Voluntary Sector Review : An International Journal of Third Sector Research, Policy and Practice*, *10*(2), 213–224.

Buckingham, H. (2012). Capturing diversity: A typology of third sector organisations' responses to contracting based on empirical evidence from homelessness services. *Journal of Social Policy*, *41*(3), 569–589.

Chapman, T., Brown, J., Ford, C., & Baxter, B. (2010). Trouble with champions: Local public sector–third sector partnerships and the future prospects for collaborative governance in the UK. *Policy Studies*, *31*(6), 613–630.

Daniels, G., Schur, M., Poehler, A., Sackett, M., Blitz, J., Gordon, S., … Universal Studios Home Entertainment (Firm). (2015). *Parks and recreation: Season one.*

Davies, S. (2011). Outsourcing, public sector reform and the changed character of the UK state-voluntary sector relationship. *International Journal of Public Sector Management*, *24*(7), 641–649.

Day, G. (2009). The independence of the voluntary sector in Wales. In M. Smerdon (Ed.), *The first principle of voluntary action: Essays on the independence of the voluntary sector from government in Canada, England, Germany, Northern Ireland, Scotland, United States of America and Wales*. London: Baring Foundation.

De Tocqueville, A. (1835). *Democracy in America*. London: Saunders and Otley.

Edwards, M. (2014). *Civil society*. (3rd ed.). Cambridge: Polity.

Enjolras, B. (2018). The road ahead: A policy agenda for the third sector in Europe. In B. Enjolras, L. M. Salamon, K. Henrik Sivesind, & A. Zimmer (Eds.), *The third sector as a renewable resource for Europe: Concepts, impacts, challenges and opportunities*. Cham; London: Palgrave Macmillan.

Evers, A., & Von Essen, J. (2019). Volunteering and civic action: Boundaries blurring, boundaries redrawn. *Voluntas: International Journal of Voluntary and Nonprofit Organizations*, *30*(1), 1–14.

Fairclough, N. (2003). *Analysing discourse: Textual analysis for social research*. London, New York, NY: Routledge.

Fox, S., Hampton, J. M., Muddiman, E., & Taylor, C. (2019). Intergenerational transmission and support for EU membership in the United Kingdom: The case of Brexit. *European Sociological Review*, 35(3), 380–393.

Fyfe, N., Timbrell, H., & Smith, F. M. (2006). The third sector in a devolved Scotland: From policy to evidence. *Critical Social Policy*, 26(3), 630–641.

Habermas, J. R. (1987). *The theory of communicative action* (Vol. 2). Lifeworld and system: A critique of functionalist reason. Cambridge: Polity.

Headlam, N. (2019). Women's work?: Civil society networks for social stability or social change in Ambridge. In C. Courage & N. Headlam (Eds.), *Gender, sex and gossip in Ambridge: Women in the Archers*. Bingley: Emerald Publishing Limited.

Hemmings, M. (2017). The constraints on voluntary sector voice in a period of continued austerity. *Voluntary Sector Review*, 8(1), 41–66.

HM Government. (2018). *Civil society strategy: Building a future that works for everyone*. London: Cabinet Office.

Lie, M., & Baines, S. (2007). Making sense of organizational change: Voices of older volunteers. *Voluntas: International Journal of Voluntary and Nonprofit Organizations*, 18(3), 225–240.

Lorre, C., Prady, B., Molaro, S., Galecki, J., Parsons, J., Cuoco, K., … Warner Home Video (Firm) (2014). *The big bang theory: The complete seventh season*.

Macmillan, R. (2013). Decoupling the state and the third sector? The 'Big society' as a spontaneous order. *Voluntary Sector Review*, 4(2), 185–203.

Milbourne, L., & Cushman, M. (2013). From the third sector to the Big society: How changing UK government policies have eroded third sector trust. *Voluntas: International Journal of Voluntary and Nonprofit Organizations*, 24(2), 485–508.

Milbourne, L., & Murray, U. (2017). *Civil society organizations in turbulent times: A gilded web?*. Stoke-on-Trent: Trentham Books.

Muddiman, E., Taylor, C., Power, S., & Moles, K. (2019). Young people, family relationships and civic participation. *Journal of Civil Society*, 15(1), 82–98.

Newman, J. (2001). *Modernising governance New Labour, policy and society*. London: SAGE Publications.

Phillips, S., & Hebb, T. (2010). Financing the third sector: Introduction. *Policy and Society*, 29(3), 181–187.

Rich, B. (2019). The Ambridge Conservation Trust. Retrieved from https://abarbararich.medium.com/the-ambridge-conservation-trust-c7f44f7a79c8. Accessed on June 14, 2020.

Sanders, L. D. (2010). *Discovering research methods in psychology: A student's guide*. Chichester: BPS Blackwell.

Schmidt, V. (2008). Discursive institutionalism: The explanatory power of ideas and discourse. *Annual Review of Political Science*. 11, 303–326.

Wiley, K. (2019). What can volunteer managers learn from TV binge watching? An analysis of voluntary action on U.S. television. Voluntary Sector and Volunteering

Research Conference 2019, Aston University, Birmingham, 10th-11th Sept 2019, Voluntary Sector Studies Network (VSSN).

Zimmer, A., & Pahl, B. (2018). Barriers to third sector development. In B. Enjolras, L. M. Salamon, K. Henrik Sivesind, & A. Zimmer (Eds.), *The third sector as a renewable resource for Europe: Concepts, impacts, challenges and opportunities*. London: Palgrave Macmillan.

17

A DIVIDED VILLAGE: A NARRATIVE STUDY USING A THEORETICAL LENS OF SPECULATIVE ONTOLOGY

Maggie Bartlett

ABSTRACT

Ambridge has a population of around 700. Of these around 60 have voices heard by around 5 million people per week, a few are named but have no direct voice, and the rest are anonymous and unvoiced. This study explores the perceptions of this anonymous group and their ontological status. Purposive sampling recruited 16 representatives from a variety of demographic groups. Focus groups were used to gather data. A phenomenological approach within an interpretative paradigm was used, with an analytical lens of speculative ontology. Three main themes were identified from the data: the participants perceived an existential co-dependence with the voiced group; most resented their repression and aspired to having a voice, though they perceived this to involve a serious risk of adverse life events and concomitant psychological trauma;

all expressed empathy towards the named but unvoiced
group, perceiving that group to have an unfairly high risk of
adverse life events without the opportunity to vocalise
for themselves. The participants appeared to see three
distinct classes within the society of the village (based on
namedness and voicedness) which transcended the more
generally accepted class divisions in UK society which are
based on occupation. The unnamed population of
Ambridge exists in a state of ontological tension, which is
likely to have a negative impact on their psychological
wellbeing. This study raises a question about the creator's
moral responsibility for this group.

INTRODUCTION

Ambridge is a village somewhere in the middle of England. In
2011 the population was 700 (Stepney, 2011); this is likely to
have fluctuated a little due to births and deaths, and the
recently completed Beechwood development has brought in at
least one new resident. Though Ambridge does not have its
own primary school or doctor's surgery, it does have a community shop, a pub, a farm shop and café, a livery stables and
riding school, a veterinary practice and a thriving church,
though we know that this is part of a shared benefice with
other parishes. As a rural community, many local people are
employed in agriculture, tourism and related services, but
being within commuting distance of Borchester, Felpersham
and even Birmingham, many residents have other kinds of
occupation and it is these residents who are the customers and
patrons of local services.

As listeners, we are familiar with around 60 of Ambridge's
inhabitants (BBC Blogs, 2011; Stepney, 2011) and we know
quite a lot about what happens in their lives. We know

something of their place in the community, both how they perceive and experience it and how they are perceived and experienced by others. We know the names and some of the relationships of a number of others, but we do not hear them speak. There is some controversy about how many of these there are; Stepney (2011) estimated this to be around 55 in 2011, but *The Archers* website does not include as many as this in its 'Who's Who' section (BBC Radio 4, 2020) and notably does not include Mr Pullen, Nathan Booth, Sabrina Thwaite and the Button children. There are some residents whose voices we heard extensively in the past but no longer do so, for example Kathy Perks who still has an important role at Grey Gables and is mentioned quite often, but we know nothing more about her current life. In a personal count of these known but unvoiced characters in the late summer of 2019 when I was planning this work, I reached a total of around ten, but this figure was vigorously challenged and disputed at the *Academic Archers* conference in February 2020 (Academic Archers, 2020) as being too conservative an estimate. This leaves a total of some 600 people whom we know to exist as the customers in the village shop and Bridge Farm, the patrons of the pub, the owners of the horses at the stables, the commuters from Glebelands and Beechwood, and the families of the children who use the school bus, but of whom we know nothing else. We neither know their names nor hear their individual or collective voices.

It seems possible that there are existential inequities between the named and voiced, the named and unvoiced, and the un-named and unvoiced groups and these could give rise to some complex and interesting sociological and psychological phenomena related to perceptions of categorisation (a parallel of class), importance (a parallel of power) and ontological position (the understanding of, or nature of, being) within this very

small and specific population. This study explores the ontological position of the un-named and unvoiced group.

METHODOLOGY

This is a qualitative study (Crotty, 1998, pp. 14–16) within an
interpretative paradigm (Crotty, 1998, pp. 66–72) using a
phenomenological approach (Crotty, 1998, pp. 78–86). This
means that I was interested in the participants' lived experiences in a specific socially constructed system and the data
I collected were their narratives shared in group discussions. I
did not set out to test defined ideas or themes; my intention
was that these would be identified from within the data
collected, and I was not seeking universal or generalisable
truths. The theoretical lens I used for the analysis of the data
was that of Speculative Ontology – a metaphysical approach
which is justified because the data relate to participants who
could not be directly observed ethnographically or investigated using experimental methods based in scientific realism.
The use of Speculative Ontology here is entirely consistent
with the interpretative paradigm as it makes use of intuitions
and cognitive extrapolations (Humphreys, 2013) as part of
the evidence which underpins any conclusions drawn. This is
legitimate as long as they can be explained satisfactorily and
where universal truths are not being sought.

Sampling Strategy

A purposive strategy was used to ensure that participants from
a variety of demographic groups (over the age of 16 years)
were included which were representative of the community as
a whole. A particular challenge in reaching potential participants was the risk of a biased sample should one particularly
dominant Ambridge resident (Lynda Snell) have become

involved in recruitment. This led to a degree of subterfuge which could be considered to be reprehensible in research, but which I considered to be justified in these extreme circumstances in order to avoid the very real possibility of this bias.

Data Collection

Focus groups were used to collect data, with a broad topic guide designed to promote sharing of experiences by means of conversation. The meetings were recorded and transcribed and field notes were kept to record perceptions of emotional responses and interpretations of body language.

Ethical Review

Ethical approval was not obtained; formal review panels would not recognise any ethical responsibility for the participants, perceiving them not only to be fictitious, but unidentifiable within the relevant fictional entity.

RESULTS

Two focus groups were held, each with eight participants and lasting one hour. Demographic details are given in Table 17.1. It is clear that in Ambridge the range of occupations is broad and transcends traditional gender and geographical stereotypes.

The Themes

Three main themes were identified from the transcribed data: (1) an existential co-dependence; (2) resentment and the aspiration to have a voice, but fear of having one and (3) empathy for the named and voiced, and named but unvoiced groups.

Table 17.1. Participants' Demographic Data (All Self-defined) and Shows Which Focus Group the Individual Attended.

ID/Self-identified Gender	Self-identified Occupation	Age	Focus Group
PO/f	Granny Providing Childcare	75	1
RD/f	Midwife	55	2
AW/f	Bus Driver	50	2
DP/f	Refuse Collection Operative	38	1
GY/f	Self-employed Spinner, Dyer and Weaver	35	1
TR/f	Airline Pilot (on maternity leave)	34	2
AM/f	Junior Hospital Doctor (Borchester General)	25	2
QZ/f	Apprentice Narrow Boat Builder	17	1
GH/m	Retired Jelly Baby Maker	80	2
LY/m	Primary School Teacher	55	1
TS/m	Electrical Engineer	48	2
NV/m	Llama Farmer	41	1
GA/m	Synchronised Swimmer	35	1
IM/m	District Nurse	29	2
UL/m	Artificial Inseminator	25	1
XZ/m	Giblet Processor (chicken factory)	18	2

Theme 1 – an Existential Co-dependence

The un-named and unvoiced group perceived an existential co-dependence with the named and voiced group. Within the discussion there were clear expressions of uncertainty about the nature of the existence of all of the inhabitants of Ambridge. There were a number of ambiguities about who might be responsible for and directing their existence and who might be influencing the courses of their lives. As well as the uncertainty about the nature of their existence, the groups were also unclear about the direction of the dependence between themselves and the other groups, particularly the named and voiced group, and the implication was that the dependence was mutual; no group would exist without the others.

The following extract of a discussion in Focus Group 2 demonstrates these points:

> *'They need us – how could there be a shop with no customers?' GH/m*

> *'And we need them – would we be here without them? I'm not sure we would- but it's not like it's the Truman Show[1] – is it?' UL/m*

> *'More like the chicken and the egg really[2]...' NV/m*

> *'Bridge Farm – they need us – think of all the things that wouldn't have happened if there wasn't the tearoom- and a tearoom needs customers too- bit pricey in the farm shop though' PO/f*

> *'Both too pricey for me – I go to Aldi[3] on the bypass- means I miss out on a lot, but at least I don't get caught in the crossfire...' GY/f*

Theme 2 – Resentment and the Aspiration to Have a Voice, but Fear of Having one

In both focus groups, a considerable amount of time was spent sharing examples of perceived unfairness which clearly led to resentment. Participants spoke fervently about this topic and some expressed anger about the injustice they had experienced. The discussion in Focus Group 1 was centred around some resentment expressed by one participant that triumphs and successes amongst the un-named and unvoiced went uncelebrated by the named and voiced. In the following exchange, one participant (GA/m) identified that if 'they' became aware of an individual resident of Ambridge the consequence would be some kind of trouble. In the final comment GY/f makes a clear and rather wistful statement that she feels in the lowest category in terms of importance in the village and that her needs are secondary or even tertiary to those of the other groups. Unquestionably, both GY/f and GA/m see a direct causal relationship between the nature and context of the exposure and the likelihood of adverse life events occurring:

> *'When good things happen, they don't come up in the gossip…when our Lyra won that medal…they could've talked about that – things to be proud of in the village, and just a mention wouldn't do any harm…'* PO/f

> *'Yeah – and when I got that contract for Borsetshire Land…'* NV/m

> *'You wanna be careful what you wish for there, mate – there'll be trouble sooner or later with that lot – I'd say you'd be in for something really bad once they knew who you were – then you'd be really screwed'* GA/m

> *'It would be nice, just now and then, to be a little bit known. Not enough for bad things to happen – them not knowing anything about you when they know so much about the others – and it's hard having to wait so long to get served in the shop or the Bull cos that Jim Lloyd's having a rant or Kenton and Jolene are*

having some kind of drama, when all you want is a
quick loaf or a G&T – I feel like a second class
citizen, no actually a third class citizen, sometimes'
GY/f

In Focus Group 2, a parallel discussion clearly describes the resentment of one participant relating to how the community differentiated between the named and voiced and the un-named and unvoiced groups on the occasion of a bereavement. This description was swiftly followed by a strongly expressed caution from another participant about the consequences of even a small appearance as a named and voiced individual, while one expressed contentment with contributing vocally but anonymously in order to avoid the risk of the negative consequences of being named and heard:

'When anything happens to one of them, there's a big
hoo-ha, lots of sympathy and casserole – when my
Pearl died it would have been nice to have had a
mention – she was a friend of Jill Archer – and there
was nothing – she could've brought me a casserole –
and I could've said how hard it was – just one little
sentence…' GH/m

'…Yeah, but if you did, nothing would be simple
then. You'd have had to be depressed, or your Jerry
would've gone off the rails, or you'd be burgled
during the funeral – or fall in love with someone
really awful' TR/f

'Probably not worth it, really, the risk, just for a
moment of being. I like a quiet life, safely off their
radar…I'm happy just to roar in the Bull once in a
while' TS/m

Theme 3 – Empathy for the Named and Voiced, and Named but Unvoiced Groups

In Focus Group 1, there was a rapid-fire exchange which followed on from the discussion reported under Theme 2 above. There is a clearly expressed empathy particularly for individuals in the named but unvoiced group. In the final part of this exchange one participant raises the question of the risk to two young named but unvoiced characters which is taken up by two other participants who express uncertainty about the extent of their parents' knowledge about the riskiness of their situation, and start to explore the responsibility of the group to protect them. This is met with a shocked response by another participant who vehemently expresses her view that it is not the place of the group to intervene. There is a short silence – the group does not return to the subject:

> 'The thing is – the minute they know who you are, you're in for something – that's the price you pay...' UL/m
>
> 'Yes, or you get taken the mickey of...' GY/f
>
> 'Yeah, like poor old Mr Pullen...' LY/m
>
> 'Yeah, or that woman Alistair Lloyd bonked a while back – she must have been really traumatised by the gossip...' GY/f
>
> 'And you don't get to say anything about it at all...' GA/m
>
> 'What about the Button girls – they're at risk, I'd say' LY/m
>
> 'Do you think their parents know?' GY/f
>
> 'Should we make sure they do? We should do something' QZ/f

> *'No, no, no – we can't do that – that's not right at all. It's not for us to do that, we really can't' DP/f*

In Focus Group 2, a discussion about the named but unvoiced group centres on a particular Ambridge resident who died a number of years before in notably traumatic and emotional circumstances, which is unusual for a named but unvoiced character. They speak very fondly of this character as they speculate about how she might have felt about her named and very much voiced husband's poems:

> *'It was Freda Fry I felt sorry for – she had to put up with Bert's poems all those years and never got a chance to let off steam about it' TR/f*

> *'Yeah, then she had to die – so nobody'll ever know how she felt about them [the poems] – or anything really' TR/f*

> *'Do you think she knew she was going to die – would anyone have told her? That would be hard, but they must have known – so they should have' AM/f*

> *'Yes, then if it was me, I would've insisted, one little speech is what I would've demanded, just before the end – I'd want everyone to know I was proud of his poems – if I was, that is – which I suspect she wasn't actually' PO/f*

> *'That's probably why they didn't tell her – and why she wasn't allowed to speak' TR/f*

> *'But we, and they, don't know if she was or not; no-one can ever know now – and that's really sad' AM/f*

> *'Yes – and really, really unfair – I don't want that to happen to me – what can we do about it?' TR/f*

> 'You wanna leave it alone – it'll just mean trouble for
> you and your little one – and just think about your
> what you do for a living[4] – plenty of drama possible
> there' TS/m

DISCUSSION

What we see from the discussions reported above is that the
un-named and unvoiced residents who participated in the
study exist in a state of ontological tension. They do not
understand the nature of their existence, being uncertain if
they exist because of the needs of the named and voiced who
may or may not be dependent on them in their turn for their
own existence (the 'chicken and egg') situation mentioned by
one of the participants. They are not certain about the nature
of the ambiguous 'they' whom they perceive to direct their
lives and grant them any power that they have. If we accept
that Ambridge is fictitious, 'they' could be the single entity of
the British Broadcasting Corporation (BBC Radio 4, 2020) or
could be the listeners, or even a conflation of the two into a
single mysterious theistic force (Armstrong, 1993). A further
study using Speculative Ontology could explore the nature of
this theistic force more fully.

In more than one of the reported conversations, participants' perceptions of the powerlessness of all three groups is
evident, but towards the named and unvoiced group there is a
strongly expressed empathy for the risks perceived as inherent
to this status. The focus of their empathy is the perceived
powerlessness of this group who are more likely than themselves to suffer adverse or dramatic events without the miti-
gation of having a voice; things happen to them and they have
to endure them and the consequences in terms of gossip or

defamation, with no opportunity to comment, explain their actions and feelings or to retaliate, unlike the named and voiced group. They express some aspirations to become named and voiced though with an awareness of the risks of this. They have some ideas about a correlation between the extent and context of any named exposure and the extent of concomitant risk. They also express resentment both about their own status and, empathically, that of the named and unvoiced group. This resentment is clearly directed not at the named and voiced group but at 'they' – the possible theistic force.

In Focus Group 1 under the heading Theme 2, one participant says she feels like a 'third class citizen' because of her status as an un-named and unvoiced inhabitant. From the perspectives of the participants, during these discussions they are seeing three distinct classes within the village which transcend the more generally accepted class divisions in society which are based on occupation (UK Government, 2016). However, it is possible to draw some conclusions about the participants' perceptions of power linked to their social class and the expectations of power and influence inherent in certain types of occupation that are now perhaps beginning to transcend issues of gender. An example of this is in the exchange that took place in Focus Group 2, reported under Theme 3, where we see an idea broached by an older woman (PO/f) who had described herself as a 'granny providing childcare' but whose career had in fact been as a veterinary surgeon, taken up by two younger women both with careers in traditionally male-dominated fields (TR/f, an airline pilot and AM/f, a hospital doctor). We see some seeds of rebellion against the powerless status of the unvoiced groups, perhaps based on perceptions of the possibility of influencing the creator, that align with those of the male primary school teacher (LY/m) and the young female apprentice narrow boat builder (QZ/f)

but contrast with the position of the male electrical engineer
(TS/m), who gives a very strong and specific statement against
it related to potential adverse effects for TR/f, and the female
Refuse Collection Operative (DP/f) in Focus Group 1, who
clearly saw any challenge to the situation as impossible or
unwise in a much more general sense. This is perhaps a
statement of her perceived powerlessness linked to her
ontological position as an un-named and unvoiced character
and possibly her social standing in the village as a refuse
collection operative.

There is a risk here – that this group, who had previously
been united in that they are all un-named and unvoiced
inhabitants of a small community, could lose their solidarity
because of the divergence in their beliefs about the possibility
or desirability of challenging the status quo, perhaps based
on another social categorisation (UK Government, 2016).
This small research project, by making explicit the three
categories of inhabitants, has also made explicit the powerlessness of this group, and as a result could inadvertently
cause an upheaval in Ambridge which might lead to some of
the participants becoming named and voiced regardless of
the intentions of their creator. As a result of their ontological
uncertainties, their perceptions of powerlessness in directing
their own lives and their fear of what would happen to them
if they became named and voiced, or even named and
unvoiced, those in this group exist in state of tension. They
are not comfortable or confident about themselves, their
families or their futures – an ontological state which is likely
to lead to anxiety and stress. In the long term, stress has a
negative effect on the health of individuals because it leads to
unhelpful behaviours and has wide-ranging physiological
consequences such as raising blood pressure, affecting hor-
monal balance and reducing the effectiveness of the immune
system (McEwan, 2017).

This study has raised a question about the moral responsibility for this group – though it is difficult to know how they understand or perceive the theistic force that caused and drives their existence, we know that Ambridge was created in the fairly recent past (before the first broadcast in 1951) by a known force and therefore it should be easy to identify where this responsibility lies.

Notes

1. *The Truman Show* (BBFC, 2020) is a film released in 1998 by Paramount Pictures1. In it, the main character lives his life in a town which is actually a film set; all the other people in the town are actors and everything he does or that happens to him is being filmed. He is the only one who is unaware of the situation and that his life is being dictated by the show's creators for the entertainment of viewers.
2. This is a metaphorical device commonly used in the English language and refers to a sequencing dilemma. A chicken, being a bird, comes out of an egg, but an egg must come from an existing chicken. It is not possible to be certain, therefore, whether a chicken or an egg existed first.
3. Aldi (Aldi Supermarkets, 2020) is a chain of supermarkets known for their low prices.
4. note: TR/f is an airline pilot.

REFERENCES

Academic Archers, conference, University of Reading. (2020). Retrieved from http://academicarchers.net/. Accessed on May 24, 2020.

Armstrong, K. (1993). *A History of God*. London: Vintage Books.

BBC Blogs. (2011). The Archers. Retrieved from https://www.bbc.co.uk/blogs/thearchers/entries/3e4df109-6162-3a26-87d1-efb0bd5d3f91. Accessed on August 22, 2019.

BBC Radio 4. (2020). The Archers revisited-characters. Retrieved from https://www.bbc.co.uk/programmes/profiles/3VLG6MxxfQpKXF2Chky4Fmh/characters. Accessed on August 30, 2020.

British Board of Film Classification. (2020). The Truman Show (1998). Retrieved from https://www.bbfc.co.uk/releases/truman-show-1998. Accessed on February 15, 2020.

Crotty, M. (1998). *The foundations of social research: Meaning and perspective in the research process*. London: SAGE Publications.

Humphreys, P. (2013). Scientific ontology and speculative ontology. In D. Ross, J. Ladyman, & H. Kincaid (Eds.), *Scientific metaphysics*. Oxford: Oxford University Press.

McEwan, B. S. (2017). Neurobiological and systemic effects of chronic stress. *Chronic Stress*, *1*, 2470547017692328. doi: 10.1177/2470547017692328.

Stepney, R. (2011). A series of unfortunate events? Morbidity and mortality in a Borsetshire village. *British Medical Journal*, *343*, d7518. doi:10.1136/bmj.d7518.

UK Government. (2016). The national statistics socio-economic classification. Retrieved from https://www.ons.gov.uk/methodology/classificationsandstandards/otherclassifications/thenationalstatisticssocioeconomicclassificationnssecrebasedonsoc2010. Accessed on May 20, 2020.

INDEX

Index

345